THE SILVER DONS

THE

Volume Three of a Series
on the Historic Birthplace of California

THE HISTORY OF SAN DIEGO

SILVER DONS

Written By
RICHARD F. POURADE

EDITOR EMERITUS, THE SAN DIEGO UNION

Commissioned By
JAMES S. COPLEY

CHAIRMAN OF THE CORPORATION, THE COPLEY PRESS, INC.

Published By The Union-Tribune Publishing Company

BOOKS IN THE SERIES
The Explorers, published 1960
Time of the Bells, published 1961
The Silver Dons, published 1963
The Glory Years, published 1964
Gold in the Sun, published 1965

THE SILVER DONS
First Printing 1963
Second Printing 1965
Third Printing 1966

CONTENTS

LIST OF ILLUSTRATIONS

DEDICATION

The years of change and turmoil . . . like the years of hardship and toil for mankind . . . can be the fashioning blocks to the greatness of a geographical area. And so it was that the years from 1830 to 1865 were the building blocks upon which California came into statehood and began its rise to leadership among the commonwealths of the nation.

JAMES S. COPLEY

THE BACKGROUND

Before the war with Mexico, the people of the United States knew very little about California. Crude maps indicated it embraced the present states of California, Nevada, Utah, Arizona, and parts of New Mexico, Wyoming and Colorado.

Presidents Jackson and Tyler had wanted to buy California from Mexico. Others thought it should become independent. Sam Houston in Texas had a dream of a new and mighty nation that would encompass all of the vast area from Texas to Oregon, as well as Chihuahua and Sonora in Mexico.

Orators demanded to know what anybody would want with such a vast and worthless area of savages and wild beasts, of deserts of shifting sands and whirlwinds of dust, of cactus and prairie dogs, of endless and impenetrable mountain ranges covered to their bases with eternal snow, and of thousands of miles of rockbound and cheerless coast.

Sen. Daniel Webster of Massachusetts, for one, in opposing the acquisition of any new territory, saw only San Francisco Bay as having any possible value to the United States. As for the rest of California, it was "not worth a dollar."

President Polk, however, was determined to acquire California. If war developed with Mexico over the annexation of Texas, might not California seek the protection of England, or even France or Russia? The manifest destiny of California was

THE MEXICAN FLAG COMES DOWN and the American flag goes up over San Diego as 300 years of neglect by Spain and Mexico come to an end.

to run with the destiny of the United States. "The Silver Dons" tells how this destiny unfolded within California, as seen through the experiences of its birthplace, the pueblo of San Diego.

"The Silver Dons" is the third volume in a series on the history of California and the Southwest as centered on San Diego. The two previous books were "The Explorers," on the discovery and settlement of California, and "Time of the Bells," on the mission period. "The Silver Dons" deals with a period of thirty-five years that began with the secularization of the missions and ended with the close of the Civil War.

Diaries, journals, state papers, official and personal correspondence, and documents, many from the archives of Mexico and Old California, have been examined for the story of how California became a part of the United States, and the effect it had on the lives and fortunes of the old Spanish and Mexican families, who claimed so much of its vast lands, and on the early adventurers, settlers and traders, who had arrived from across the Plains and the Rockies or by ship from distant Atlantic seaports.

The records are to be found in the depositories of the nation, our great libraries and institutions, the Bancroft Library of the University of California at Berkeley, the University of California at Los Angeles, the California State Library at Sacramento, the Henry E. Huntington Library and Art Gallery at San Marino, and in the Archives of the United States.

The files and publications of the California Historical Society, the Historical Society of Southern California, and the San Diego Historical Society and those of other institutions from New York to New Orleans to San Diego also hold the flesh of the personal experiences of those who came by land and which must go on the bare ribs of historical record.

The stories of the men who came by sea, to stay or to trade or to chase the whale, and of the ships they sailed, must be followed from Johnnycake Hill in New Bedford to the Silver Gate at San Diego. They lie in the museums or libraries of Boston, of Mystic Seaport, of Salem, of Nantucket, and of Sag Harbor.

There is, in addition, a vast field of literature on California, and thousands of individual researchers have added their bits to a story that never grows old, that of old struggles and old defeats, and of new lands and new hopes, of the passing of one generation and the temporary triumph of another. For change is the essence of history, and the Silver Dons of California tasted of the rewards as well as the bitterness of momentous movements.

Richard F. Pourade

CHAPTER ONE

"I and my hammock are swinging,
Down by the side of the sea.
My little cabin is clinging
Where the bananas grow free."

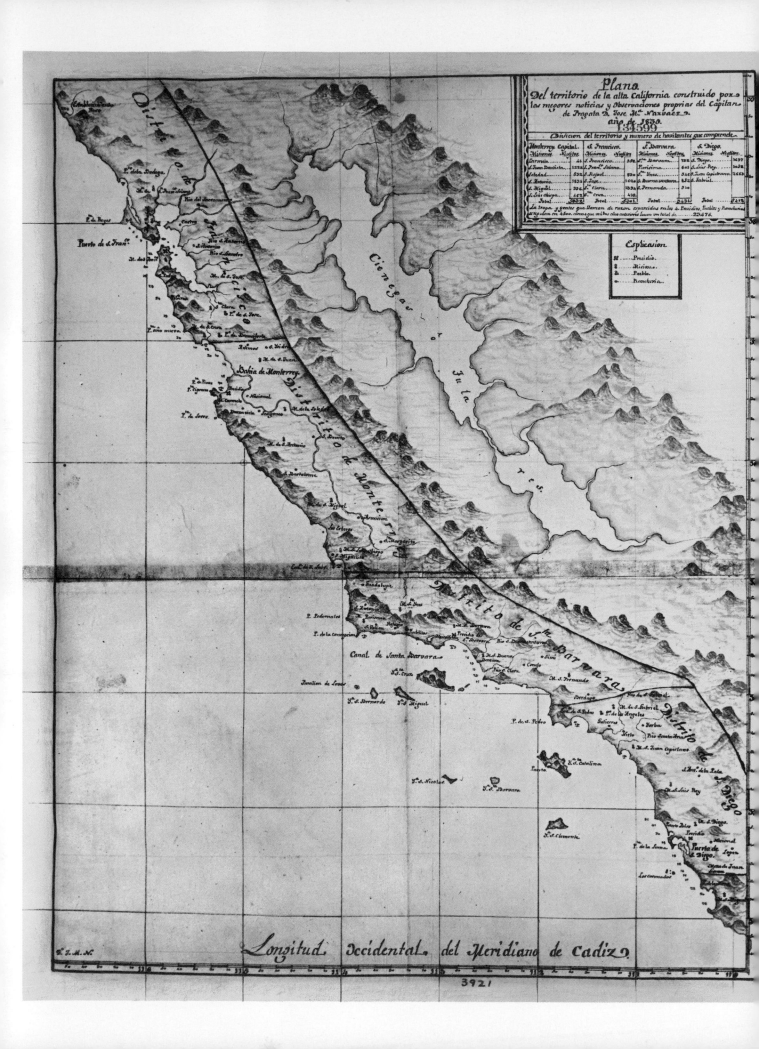

CALIFORNIA IN 1830

Three American ships lay at anchor off La Playa, the beach, the old Spanish anchorage in the Bay of San Diego, in the lee of Point Loma, their crews preparing, storing or loading cattle hides from California missions for far-off Boston. On one of them, the bark *Louisa*, was a ten-year-old boy, William Heath Davis. Obtaining a horse on the beach, he rode around the north shore of the bay to the Presidio, the adobe-walled fortress town on the edge of a mesa which, though cut by sharp canyons, spreads eastward to the foothills of the coastal mountains. The owner and supercargo of the *Louisa* had rented a house in the Presidio, and staffing it with stewards from his vessel, proceeded to take part in the social life of a little settlement which though far removed from the main stream of civilization was beginning to spill over onto the sandy plateau below the hill.

Years later Davis recalled the deep impression all this had made on him:

It was quite a lively town. At our house, which was a building of six or eight rooms, we entertained many beautiful Spanish women at dinners, and also at dancing parties. The location of the Presidio was chosen from a military point of view, to protect the citizens of this miniature city, from the ferocious and savage Indians of those days. In the town the inhabitants, soldiers and citizens numbered between 400 and 500. Quite a large place. There was a great deal of gaiety and refinement here. The people were elite of this portion

EVEN TO MEXICO, knowledge of its territory of Upper California was limited to the coastal area, as shown in José Narvaez' map of 1830. A line running along the crest of the mountain range appeared to be the eastern boundary of the four districts. The Central Valleys were indicated as being vast swamps.

3

of the department of California. In the garrison were some Mexican and not a few native Spanish soldiers.

These were the Californians, or *Californios*. There were only about 4700 of them in all of the territory known as Upper or Alta California, mostly living close together in small pueblos and presidios, and existing by trading in hides of their own and selling the furs of coastal sea otters to American ships engaged in the China trade. They shared common lands for raising their crops and grazing their cattle. Much of the rest of the coastal regions—twelve million acres of the rich mesas and valleys of California—was still held by Franciscan missionaries in trust for the Indians in accordance with old Spanish law and custom.

The time was 1831. Nine years before, Mexico had won its independence from monarchial Spain and the *Californios* had reluctantly raised the Mexican flag over the adobe walls and buildings of the Royal Presidio of San Diego. Their spiritual and ancestral ties with the Old World had been very strong. Many of them were first generation descendants of the original Spanish Royal expeditions led by Gaspar de Portolá, Fr. Junípero Serra and Juan Bautista de Anza. Capt. Portolá and Fr. Serra had come up from Lower California in 1769 to establish a chain of Franciscan missions, to settle a territory that had been neglected for centuries. A few years later Capt. Anza led the first colonists up from Sonora, in northern Mexico, to found San Francisco.

But independent Mexico, torn by revolution and continuing political disorder, was able to maintain only a tenuous control over the vast territory of Spanish America which had embraced all of the area of what is now Southwestern United States. The American-Mexican War that brought California into the Union was fifteen years away.

The Presidio of San Diego was the principal garrison for the protection of a district which for many years included the four missions of San Diego, San Luis Rey, San Juan Capistrano and San Gabriel, which were strung on a 125-mile line a day's march apart from San Diego to Los Angeles, and three smaller missions, or rather *asistencias*. The San Diego Mission maintained one at Santa Ysabel, in the mountains, while San Luis Rey Mission had two, one in the upper San Luis Rey Valley and the other to the north at Las Flores, near the coast.

There were twenty-one missions in all, from San Diego on the border to Sonoma north of San Francisco. By 1830 they already were beginning to decline, though they watched over the lives of more than 15,000 Christianized Indians, and their ranchos and

*Presidio as it looked
at its height*

farms were able to furnish enough food and goods to also support the dwindling military garrisons of California.

The *Californios* looked upon the lands held by the missions and knew that the mission era was coming to a close. All soon would be theirs. They would be kings of their own empires stocked with thousands upon thousands of cattle. The meat would be left to rot and the hides shipped around the Horn to Boston to provide the leather for the population of an expanding United States.

Behind San Diego and the other southern coastal settlements rose the mighty coastal ranges, and behind them were the harsh wastelands of the Colorado Desert. The coastal region was temperate though semi-arid, but the mountains, with some of their peaks rising more than 6000 feet, were blanketed with snow in the winter. Their flowing western slopes were green and inviting; their eastern sides were steep, rocky, dry and hot. Mission ranches were located along the creeks of upland valleys or along the few rivers which sliced through the coastal mesa and except in the rainy season usually disappeared beneath the sands. A season's rainfall could vary from a few inches to more than twenty-five, and generally it fell within a few months during the winter, sometimes almost all at once. Life was simple for the cattle *rancheros* but stubborn for the cultivators. The canyons and steep hills were to mock the builders of roads and the dreamers of cities.

There are four passes through the mountains into Southern California, two of them easily visible from great distances, and they had been sighted by the earliest exploring missionaries moving up from northern Mexico. In almost three centuries of Spanish rule they had been pierced only a few times. Anza had led the first colonists for California across the Borrego Desert in northeast San Diego County and up Coyote Canyon through San Carlos Pass lying between the San Ysidro and Santa Rosa Mountains.

In the early 1800's the frontier of the United States was being pushed ever Westward. Adventurers and traders were crossing the plains and the deserts and, coming up to the mountains, they eased their way through the passes, to cast envious eyes upon a fertile country that seemed to bask in eternal sunshine.

In 1827, trapper Jedediah Smith and his men left their winter quarters high in Utah, followed river routes southward, crossed the Mojave Desert and went up through the 3800-foot Cajon Pass, usually wind-swept and often snow-covered, to reach San Gabriel Mission, east of the present city of Los Angeles, and then down the Mission Road to the Presidio of San Diego.

Two years later trapper James Ohio Pattie and his party left New Mexico, crossed into Arizona and followed the Gila River to

El Camino Real, the original mission trail joined the Californias.

5

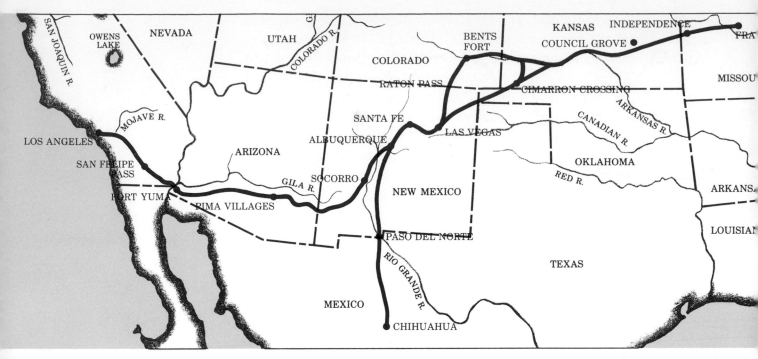

THE SANTA FE TRAIL was the first trade route into the Far West, running originally from Missouri to New Mexico and then south to Chihuahua, in Sonora, Mexico. Eventually it was extended along the Gila River to the Pacific Coast.

its junction with the Colorado, and went down the Colorado into its delta, crossed the peninsula of Baja California amid great hardships, and finally reached San Diego by way of *El Camino Real*, the King's Highway, connecting Lower and Upper California.

They were trail blazers. Then came the traders. Far to the east in Missouri, in the territory of the United States, Capt. William Becknell as early as 1821 had loaded pack mules with stocks of goods and headed for Santa Fe, New Mexico, where he found trading with the Mexican colonists so profitable he returned the next winter with loaded wagons. This was the beginning of the Santa Fe Trail. From Santa Fe the trail south led to Chihuahua in north central Mexico. In time, it was extended to the Pacific Coast, by way of Pattie's old trail along the Gila River, then across the Imperial Valley and up through the 3500-foot high San Felipe Pass in San Diego County, and down to the pueblo of San Diego or north over rolling valleys to Los Angeles. Ewing Young led an expedition in 1829 which left New Mexico with forty men. Among them was a young man named Christopher Carson, the Kit Carson of history. They also made their way to the California coastal plain through Cajon Pass.

Active trading with the Mexican settlements on the coast began in 1829-1830 with the opening of the Old Spanish Trail between

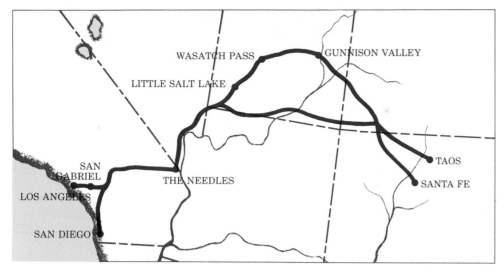

COMMERCE BEGAN TO MOVE across the Western deserts in 1829 by way of the Old Spanish Trail which in later years became known as the Caravan Route.

New Mexico and California. It ran farther north than did the Santa Fe Trail and eventually became known as the Caravan Route. It swung north from Santa Fe, or Taos, crossed Utah by two different routes to Little Salt Lake, and then turned southwest to the Colorado River. The first expedition was led by Antonio Armijo. His party of thirty-one men and a caravan

Southern California was settled largely by Southerners who came over the bitter Gila Trail and by-paths in immigration which began with the Gold Rush.

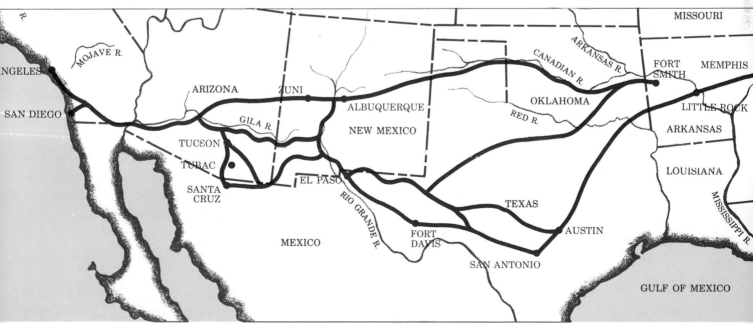

loaded with merchandise left the Colorado at The Needles and also made their way up through Cajon Pass to Mission San Gabriel, where they traded goods to the Californians in exchange for mules and horses. In 1831, Young led another party to California along the old Pattie Trail and with them was one Jonathan Trumbull Warner.

The old Spanish route up from Mexico through Sonora and Arizona had been closed for half a century because of troubles with the warlike Apache and Yuma Indians, and Warner was to write:

> There could not be found in either Tucson or Altar—although they were both military posts and towns of considerable population—a man who had ever been over the route from those towns to California by way of the Colorado River, or even to that river, to serve as a guide, or from whom any information concerning the route could be obtained, and the trail from Tucson to the Gila River at the Pima villages was too little used and obscure to be easily followed, and from those villages down the Gila River to the Colorado River and from thence to within less than a hundred miles of San Diego, there was no trail, not even an Indian path.

In all the wanderings of these intrepid men, none of them used the lowest pass of the Southern California mountain barrier, San Gorgonio, which lies between the coastal mountain peaks of San

THE SONORA TRAIL was first supply road to California. It followed the original Anza Route into Southern California. One branch led through San Felipe Pass to San Diego; later another through San Gorgonio Pass to Los Angeles.

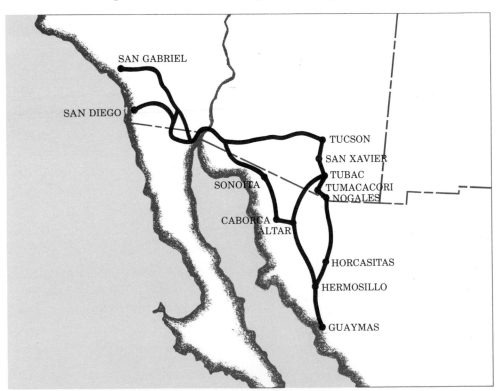

Jacinto and San Gorgonio at the upper end of Coachella Valley. At its desert gateway now lies the playground of Palm Springs. Though its highest elevation is less than 2500 feet, it must be approached through a waterless waste.

By the 1830's a few adventurers and traders again were making their way to California over the old Serra trail from Lower California as well as by the Anza route from Sonora. John Forster, who was born in Liverpool, England, came to Southern California by way of Mexico. An uncle who had amassed a fortune as a merchant captain had asked John's father to "lend me one of your sons." Of the seven sons, John was chosen, and thus he began a life of adventure that led to vast holdings in a new land. He first came to California by sea with a trading expedition from Guaymas, a small port on the mainland on the Gulf of California, with $50,000 worth of goods imported from China, which he sold off at San Diego and at Los Angeles in 1833. He liked what he saw. After returning to Guaymas, he started back, not by sea, but by land, crossing the terrible deserts of Sonora and Southern California as had Anza so many years before.

An even stranger odyssey was that of a Yankee schoolmaster, Hall J. Kelley, who entered Mexico at Veracruz and crossed the continent to the port of San Blas, from where he obtained passage to La Paz, on the gulf side of Baja California. From there he walked the length of El Camino Real to San Diego, in the footsteps of Fr. Junípero Serra. At San Diego, he obtained passage on the hide ship *Lagoda* for San Pedro, from where he proceeded to Los Angeles and finally to Monterey and on into Oregon. Kelley was one of California's first boosters. His glowing descriptions of the country were published by the United States Congress in 1839, and they did a great deal to heighten interest in Westward expansion.

These explorations and expeditions were the stirring of empire. But for a score of years the sea was the only open route and ships brought the goods that enriched life in a remote and isolated land. The hides, tallow and furs of California were traded for the silks and wares of China, the household goods and tools of New England and the church bells of Lima.

Benjamin Hayes, who arrived at San Diego during the Western migrations after the American conquest of California in the war with Mexico, and an indefatigable gatherer of historical information, put down the memories of the old families who had lived through the days of the primitive simplicity of the Mexican era:

The arrival of a ship was more than a sensation. Its date served the memory to reckon ordinary events thereafter, and cold the heart not to relish the gaiety

Juan Forster

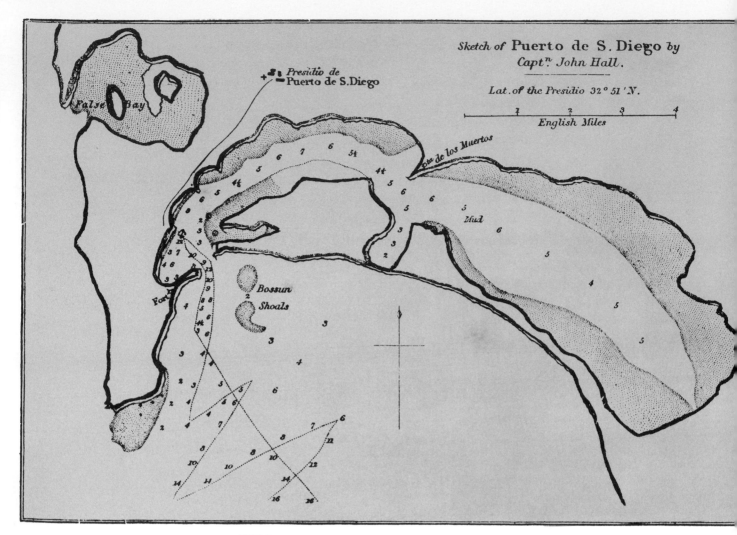

THE PORT OF SAN DIEGO was becoming well-known to foreign sea captains. This map by the English skipper John Hall is an accumulation of early knowledge of its shape and depth, and location of the fort, presidio and town in 1839.

and enjoyment that flowed by dropping the anchor at La Playa. The vessels spent a considerable time in the harbor. Liberality on one side, unbounded hospitality on the other, contributed to gild and prolong the festival hours. It is a lively picture of a venerable lady . . . "ah what times we used to have." Every week to La Playa, aboard the ships — silks . . . *rebozos* . . . music . . . dancing . . . frolic. There was to be met the prettiest of women, one has said, whom time touches lightly. When I was a girl 'twas the reign of prosperity and plenty."

The rich and hot blood of Andalusia coursed through the veins of many of the finest sons of Spain who came to California with the Spanish Army. The ranks of the later military units, unlike the earlier Spanish regulars or the trail-blazing Leatherjackets, were filled out with riff-raff gathered up from the frontiers of northern Mexico or from the scum of fetid ports. Many of them

10

took Indian wives and their children melted into a mixed and rugged generation. The unwanted of Mexico were sent to Upper California to seek new homes and new lives. Mexico neglected its distant territories and the Presidio which had been the symbol of Spanish power swiftly washed away. On a shelf of land just below the hill, and barely above the flood plain of the San Diego River, the *Californios* began to build the low, rambling, thick-walled homes which have lived in the romantic memory of what is now historic Old Town.

How Casa de Pico appeared in early days.

There is nothing in the records to show when the first person moved down from the Presidio but it was sometime in the 1820's and even before that Capt. Francisco María Ruiz, a frontier soldier born in Loreto, the capital of the peninsula of Lower California, had a garden and small structure on the "bench," as they called it.

As his father had been killed by a mountain lion, he had been educated by a Jesuit missionary. He enlisted in the army in 1780 and though a man of strong opinions and violent temper, and at times irregular in conduct, he rose rapidly in the military service and in 1816 he was recommended to the last Spanish governor of California by an officer of the Department of San Blas, with the following words:

This is an old American, one of the few true men met with in America or the world. He may have some faults as all men have, but all are outweighed in the balance against his natural honesty; by the justice that in the midst of his great popularity with his soldiers he deals out so as to make himself respected by all; and by his unbounded love for Fernando VII, our monarch, in whose honor he often assembles his soldiers, ordering them to play, dance, drink, and shout Viva! Spain! Viva Fernando VII! Long Live the Governor! Viva! Viva! Viva-a-a-a!

After the revolution, and the collapse of the Spanish empire, he learned to salute and respect the Mexican flag, and though he never married he laid the foundations for at least three of the houses in which much of California's early history was made. In 1823 he was granted the first private rancho in San Diego County, Los Peñasquitos, over the protests of the mission fathers.

The founder of the most numerous branch of the Carrillo family of California, Joaquín Carrillo, came up from Lower California sometime after 1800, and served as a soldier for more than twenty years. His daughter Josefa eloped to Valparaiso, Chile, in 1829 with a Protestant, though freshly baptized, American sea captain, Henry Delano Fitch, to the dismay of Catholic San Diego. In time the couple took over the large Carrillo home on what is now Calhoun Street and Capt. Fitch became a prosperous merchant. To Richard Henry Dana Jr., the young mariner who came to California on the hide ship *Pilgrim* and wrote "*Two Years Before the*

Mast," Capt. Fitch was a big, vulgar shopkeeper and trader, but an examination of his business records and correspondence reflects an honest and patient man to whom Californians were a strange and generally untrustworthy lot.

The Carrillo house may have been the first *casa* built below the Presidio, as there are indications it was standing as early as 1821.

Casa de Estudillo

When Sgt. José María Pico, the founder of the Pico family of Southern California, who had come up from Sinaloa, Mexico, in 1782, died in 1819 at San Gabriel Mission, at least part of his family of seven sons and three daughters returned to the Presidio of San Diego. By 1823 they had saved enough money to build their own home, the Pico House, facing along what is now Juan Street.

By about 1824 houses had been completed by the Picos and by Juan Rocha. A year later Juan María Marrón had built his first house, this one on the Plaza, as had Rafaela Serrano, while María de los Reyes Ybañez, widow of an old cavalry sergeant, Cristóbal Domínguez, had come into possession of a house started but not finished by Capt. Ruiz. Here Alfred Robinson, author of "*Life in California*," lived while serving as an agent for Boston hide ships.

An historic town was beginning to take shape. José Antonio Estudillo and Juan Bandini were granted house lots in 1827. Estudillo, born in Monterey, well educated, of excellent character, and with considerable influence throughout all of California, was the son of a soldier of Spain and became a captain in the presidial company of San Diego. He built the Estudillo House and in American fiction it has become identified as Ramona's Marriage Place of the enduring romance written by Helen Hunt Jackson. It was a large and fine home, fronting along the entire south side of the town Plaza and its great hall served as a chapel for the town for several years. It had a tower with a round balcony from which the family and friends could watch the bull or bear fights in the square or where musicians could play for the many fiestas and religious festivals.

The home or *casa* most mentioned in all the accounts of visitors was that of Juan Bandini, a descendant of a high Italian family, whose father was born in Spain but migrated to Peru and then came to California.

Alfred Robinson wrote of his visit to San Diego in 1829:

On the lawn beneath the hill on which the Presidio is built stood about thirty houses of rude appearance, mostly occupied by retired veterans, not so well constructed in respect either to beauty or stability as the houses at Monterey, with the exception of that belonging to our "administrator," Don Juan Bandini, whose mansion, then in an unfinished state, bade fair, when completed, to surpass any other in the country.

THE FINEST OF ALL THE HOMES in Old Town, according to visitors as well as tradition, was the Bandini House. It later was rebuilt, second story added.

The Bandini home southeast of the town Plaza was the social center of Old San Diego, and Don Juan was as gracious a host as he was a wily instigator of revolutions and the principal author of the plot to destroy the California missions.

While Estudillo's house had twelve rooms, Bandini's perhaps had fourteen, with a kitchen and two storerooms separated from the main house by an *arcada*, or arcade. Servants' quarters were to be in an adjoining structure which may never have been completed. The Pico house grew to ten or twelve rooms. The large houses had tile roofs and planked floors, and the adobe walls were coated with white plaster.

The tall, haughty and reserved Don Santiago Arguello was born at Monterey in 1791, and also became one of the military *comandantes* at San Diego. He was the father of twenty-two children. The town home of the Arguellos, who were connected by marriage to most of the leading families of early California, was situated at the intersection of Mason and Jefferson Streets. The houses of Francisco Alvarado and Rosario Aguilar were built about the same time as those of Bandini and Estudillo, sometime before 1830. By 1833 Marrón had built another house near the river.

Juan María Osuna, born in California before 1800, was a poor man, a soldier and corporal in the San Diego company. After leaving the service and settling in San Diego, he rose rapidly in politics, becoming an *alcalde*, though his house evidently was not a large one, as his will read:

I declare having a house in this pueblo, situated near the house of Don Enrique Fitch, deceased, said house is composed of one hall, one room, kitchen, corral and dispensary.

Apolinaria Lorenzana was a foundling named after the Archbishop of Mexico, as was the custom at the asylum where she lived, and about 1800 she and a large group of men, and women and children were sent to California by the Viceroy of Mexico, to be distributed among families "like dogs." She spent her days helping the fading missionaries administer to the Indians who were swiftly dying away of the white man's diseases and of neglect, and was known as *La Beata*, the pious.

With the growth of a little settlement outside of the mud walls of the Presidio, the residents of San Diego petitioned to end the long military control of San Diego by formation of an official *pueblo*, or town, and election of an *Ayuntamiento*, or town council. The petition to Gov. José Figueroa was signed on February 22, 1833, by José Antonio Estudillo, Juan María Osuna, Francisco María de Alvarado, Manuel Machado, Ysidro Guillén and Jesús Moreno "in the name of all the residents of the port of San Diego."

At the time Santiago Arguello was military *comandante*, though he was soon to retire, and as he often was at odds with his fellow San Diegans, the petitioners to the governor perhaps had him in mind when they wrote that:

> It is sad to know that in all the pueblos of the Republic the Citizens are judged by those whom they themselves elect for this purpose, and that in this port alone one has to submit himself, his fate, fortune and perhaps existence, to the caprice of a military judge, who being able to misuse his power, it is always easy for him to evade any complaint which they might want to make of his conduct . . . and there is no other formula than the imperious words of I command it.

The unfortunate citizen, the petition stated has no "other choice than to suffer, and humble himself in his degradation, for they always fear to provoke further the wrath of the one who rules them." The wind of independence which had blown so hot through Mexico was now beginning to sear the distant shores of California.

Gov. Figueroa agreed with the petitioners, and he held that the population of San Diego, 432 persons, was sufficient under Mexican law and therefore, on May 4, 1834, he forwarded his favorable recommendation to the Territorial *Diputación*, and though San Diego requested the right to elect four *regidores*, or councilmen, only two were allotted. Organization of the pueblo was formally undertaken on December 21. Juan María Osuna was chosen *alcalde* over Pío Pico. Juan Bautista Alvarado was elected first *regidor* and Juan María Marrón, second *regidor*, and Capt. Fitch, *sindico procurador*, or town attorney. A total of thirteen votes were cast by the electors in San Diego's first election.

The boundaries of the new pueblo were vague. Santiago Arguello testified almost two decades later, before a United States Land Commission, in identifying a map drawn by Capt. Fitch,

Santiago Arguello

14

that the pueblo lands extended "north from San Diego to the Soledad, south to the Choyois, a watering place, west to the point of the hill; east to the well of the Mission of San Diego. These points were designated by myself previous to the survey. I have known them since the year 1818."

This described an area roughly embracing the upper part of San Diego Bay and what is now a major portion of the city of San Diego. From Soledad Valley, the common grazing lands, on the north, the line ran southeasterly passing just west of Mission San Diego, to the border of Rancho de la Nación, or the government grazing grounds, now the site of National City, and then southwesterly along a line near Chollas Creek, across the bay and out over the ocean, to include Coronado and North Island, to the tip of Point Loma. The vast holdings of the Mission, almost 3000 square miles, lay to the east of the pueblo boundary.

The *alcalde* was instructed by the governor that his political power was not to extend beyond the Presidio settlement, as each mission, when the time came for its secularization, or confiscation, was to have its own *Ayuntamiento*, though his administration of justice was to embrace Mission San Luis Rey, once the largest and most prosperous of all the missions, thirty-eight miles north of San Diego and six miles east of the present town of Oceanside.

The *alcalde*, or village judge, was a position coming down from the Arab-Moorish invasion of Spain. His insignia of office was a cane of light wood with a knob of silver or gold. Below the knob were holes through which was drawn a black silk cord with tassles. According to William Heath Davis, in his book, "*Seventy-Five Years in California,*" the *alcalde* carried his cane on all occasions, especially when about to perform an official act, such as ordering an arrest, and was always received with great respect and deference. He could intervene in the personal lives of inhabitants, usually upon request, and when he could not be present at official functions he would send his cane.

On January 1, 1835, the authority of the new *Ayuntamiento* became effective, and its members got down to the business of establishing civil law and order in the little frontier settlement and to provide for the regulation of trade and commerce. In its proceedings of January the *Ayuntamiento* ruled that the carrying of small arms was to be prohibited, that all cattle were to be kept out of the pueblo under pain of fine, and all vagabonds, drunks, bill posters, and the rest, whether neophytes or "*gente de razón,*" or people of reason, would suffer the full punishment in accordance with constituted law, and those who stole amounts from one *real* to one dollar were to suffer fifteen days' labor on public works. No

William Heath Davis

15

hides were to be delivered to vessels without the knowledge of the Judge of the Plains, under pain of loss of the hides, and merchants and others must present their measures and measuring sticks for approval.

Bonifacio López, who had built a large home on the slopes of what is now Stockton Hill and had laid out below Presidio Hill a corral almost a block in area, was designated Judge of the Plains to oversee the rodeos and *matanzas*, and settle disputes over ownership of cattle allowed to graze over the hills and valleys being broken away from mission control. Bonifacio López was popularly known as "The King," and his corral as *el corral del rey*, or the king's corral.

Going to Town

But a pastoral calm was coming to an end. The unsettled conditions in Mexico were reflected more and more in California, and the *Californios* were eager to get on with dividing up the territory among themselves, as had been assured as the result of the revolution. Hints of great changes were in the air.

A decree of the Mexican Congress had opened the way for the confiscation of the mission lands at the climax of a long struggle between church and state and between the settlers and the padres. The mission churches were to be secularized, or reduced to parish churches, with the missionaries to be offered posts as priests. The mission buildings were to be converted into Indian pueblos, and the Indians were to receive enough land to assure their support and well-being. But this was not to be.

On September 20, 1834, Mission San Diego, the "mother mission" of the California chain, was transferred from Fr. Fernando Martín to Juan José Rocha, who had been appointed commissioner for that purpose, and the inventory included all church goods and even sacred vessels. The last mission report at the end of 1832 had listed 1445 Indians, 4500 cattle, 13,250 sheep, 150 goats, 200 horses and 80 mules. In April of 1835, Joaquín Ortega was named administrator with a salary of $50 a month to be paid from income from mission property. An inventory signed by Fr. Martín placed the value of the mission church and its buildings at $4777.37; listed its debts at $531, and noted that $18,816.75 was owed by the military for supplies requested or confiscated over the years.

More than seventy years of the missionary domination of California thus came to a close. The old missionary dream that the San Diego Mission would become a self-supporting Indian pueblo died along with the end of the Franciscan era. An Indian pueblo was formed, as promised, in San Dieguito Valley, in November of the same year, with just 113 Indians. When Mission San Luis Rey was conveyed to Capt. Pablo de la Portilla, and after Pío Pico was

16

RANCHO SAN DIEGUITO, now Rancho Santa Fe, was one of earliest grants and this diseño shows where the Osuna family located their houses and corrals.

named administrator, two more little Indian towns, at San Pasqual and Las Flores, were organized. But the great majority of the Indians were turned loose to become as one historian wrote, homeless wanderers upon the face of the earth.

By 1835 the Presidio was all but abandoned except for the *comandante* who still lived in the main building, and a garrison of a dozen ragged soldiers. Five years before, the presidial company had totalled 120 men. Now there were between twenty-five and thirty-five soldiers scattered on guard duty over much of what is now Southern California.

Into these changing and tumultuous times came more American and other foreign settlers and traders. They dropped off at coastal ports from ships engaged in the hide and fur trade, some as deserters.

As far as is known Capt. Fitch was the first American to settle permanently in San Diego. His romance and marriage with Josefa Carrillo, which had stirred all of California, ran onto the rocks of trouble. Josefa was a compulsive gambler, and in one card game alone she lost $1000. On December 18, 1835, Capt. Fitch appealed to the *alcalde* for a separation from his wife. As a divorce of course was not possible in Catholic California, a temporary separation was ordered, but when Josefa acknowledged the gambling, and begged the pardon of the *alcalde* and her husband, and promised to deport herself well in the future, all was forgiven.

Young William Heath Davis, who wrote the description of life in the old Presidio, returned a number of times as a sailor and supercargo, or agent, and finally walked off a ship and never went back. In 1833 there came Thomas Wrightington, a shoemaker by trade from Fall River, Massachusetts, who left the hide ship *Ayacucho*; and Joseph Snook, an English mariner who had been along the coast since 1824, and after being naturalized, became master of the Mexican brig *Catalina*. John C. Stewart, second mate of the hide ship *Alert* and a shipmate of Richard Henry Dana, saw San Diego in 1833, and went ashore in 1838, to remain for good. Allen B. Light, a Negro, jumped a Boston ship and became an otter hunter.

A half million acres of fertile land lay waiting. A trade that so many of the Spanish Dons had neglected held promise of wealth and influence. And the daughters of the Dons were attractive and available.

CHAPTER TWO

"Good old rule — the simple plan —
That they should take who have the power,
And they should keep who can."

THE LASH OF GREED

The Californians fell upon the property of the missions and divided into quarreling factions. Revolutions were followed by uprisings of Indians released from mission control or being driven from ancestral lands. In the San Diego and San Luis Rey Mission districts, less than two years after secularization, eighteen ranchos had been carved out of former mission lands, or lands claimed by the missions, though seven had been occupied for some years. Santiago Arguello and José Antonio Estudillo, both former military *comandantes*, had acquired three ranchos each.

Many of the missionaries remained at their posts doing what they could to help the few Christian Indians who elected to remain at the missions, where many of them had been born and lived all their lives and were needed to maintain the fields, gardens and stock. Conditions grew steadily worse and at a meeting of the *Ayuntamiento* in January, 1836, it was decided to appeal to the territorial government for assistance against the Indians. The little adobe settlement of less than 500 persons, backed up against the sea, faced more than 10,000 Indians—Diegueños, Luiseños, Cahuillas and Yumas, living in the vast territory stretching all the way to the Colorado River, and comprising one of the most thickly populated regions of aboriginal America. The *Californios* were fortunate indeed that these Indians lacked the sustained courage and organization of the American Plains Indians.

INDIAN TROUBLES reached a climax when the Leiva sisters were kidnapped from Pío Pico's Jamul Rancho and sold to Yuma chieftains down the Colorado.

21

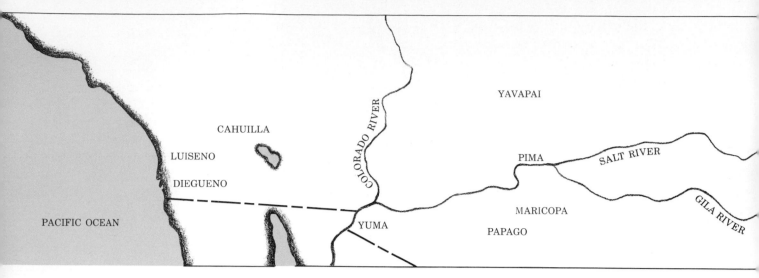

THIS MAP SHOWS the distribution of Indian peoples in one of the most thickly populated areas of aboriginal America. There were more than 10,000 Indians alone in a southern area stretching from San Diego to the Colorado River.

Arguello, who had succeeded Osuna as *alcalde*, insisted that an armed force must be sent to Santa Ysabel in the mountains, fifty miles from San Diego, as had been done once before. A *junta* of prominent citizens was called to list the damages being inflicted on all of the ranchos in the southern area. They said they no longer felt secure in their property, and even in the town itself. They could not count on the garrison for protection because the men were so badly paid and so poorly equipped.

Several days later *Alcalde* Arguello informed the military *comandante* of San Diego that the people were about to move out of town because of Indian thievery, that even then there were few men left to meet any attack, and he asked that the "violent" cannon be brought down from San Luis Rey. A month later Arguello instructed Capt. Pablo de la Portilla and his soldiers to proceed against an Indian force which was assembling in the mountains. The campaign was not successful, and Portilla laid the blame on the citizens for failing to provide sufficient help. Arguello was indignant at the accusation and replied that he looked "with contempt upon whatsoever calumny which he may impute to me."

In the midst of the Indian troubles, Leandro Serrano was accused of stealing cattle from San Luis Rey Mission, having been found in possession of twenty-nine hides bearing the mission's brand, and he was forced to turn over twenty-nine cattle. An Indian was found hanging from a peach tree in a garden, and according to custom, the first *regidor* and the secretary of the *Ayuntamiento* looked upon the body, asked it three times, in the name of the true God, who had killed it, and receiving no answer, they proceeded to examine the body, and being satisfied he had hung himself, they ordered it cut down and carried off to a cemetery.

In Mexico, a new revolution had overthrown the constitution of 1824. In faraway Texas, American settlers who had come to dominate a large territory of Mexico, after seeking vainly to ease restrictions imposed by Mexico, raised the Lone Star flag and moved toward independence. Many of their heroes died in the fall of the Alamo before the Mexican troops of the revolutionary general, Santa Anna.

In California, the North and the South contended for political domination, and San Diego and Monterey fought over location of the customs house, the chief source of revenue for the province. The question of loyalty to the government in Mexico City and the new centralist constitution further divided the state.

In one year after José Figueroa's death California had four governors. Before his death Figueroa divided the political and military commands, with Lt. Col. Nicolás Gutiérrez as military leader and José Castro as *jefe político*. The South protested that the political leadership belonged to Estudillo of San Diego, as senior *vocal* of the *Diputación*, though he had been frequently absent from Monterey because of illness. The Northerners conspired against him and maneuvered the election of José Castro. In retaliation, José Antonio Carrillo, provisional deputy in the Mexican Congress, had Los Angeles instead of Monterey designated as the capital. The *Diputación* formally recognized Castro and refused to move from Monterey. In the midst of the continuing dissension, Castro in January of 1836 transferred the *jefatura* to Gutiérrez, a maneuver that Bandini charged was designed to withhold the governorship from Estudillo.

Bandini had a plan; he always had a plan. He and others presented a memorial deploring the decay of the missions since secularization, the decline of trade and agriculture, and the lack of courts of justice, and suggesting that a general assembly of civil, military and missionary representatives should be called to reorganize California affairs without waiting for approval from Mexico. A record of the meeting was sent to Gutiérrez along with assurances of the loyalty of San Diegans. But Gutiérrez already was on the way out.

In April of 1836, Col. Mariano Chico came up from Mexico City as the newly appointed Mexican governor of the rebellious province, and assuming office in May announced that the new centralist constitution was now in effect. On May 29, the ceremony of swearing the bases, or the taking of oaths of allegiances, was carried out in San Diego by the *Ayuntamiento* as follows:

This was done by the President and immediately after by the other gentlemen who are members of this corporation, this being witnessed by the majority of the citizens to solemnize this act, at the conclusion of which demonstrations of cheer and acclamations for the happiness and prosperity of the Supreme General Government and its worthy representatives were made; this act being solemnized with a salvo of artillery followed by a powerful ringing of the bells, it being ordered that same be repeated at noon and at sundown followed by corresponding illumination.

The happiness didn't last very long. After taking office Chico promptly issued an order prohibiting retail trading aboard foreign ships and requiring all goods to be sold in California to be landed at Monterey. He reported to Mexico City that armed foreign vessels, mostly American, were ignoring the national laws, slaughtering sea otters as they pleased, landing men and killing cattle, and attacking native fishermen.

Conditions generally were chaotic. Bands of rustlers from Sonora in northern Mexico were crossing the Colorado River and ranging over all the South, stealing cattle and horses and plundering ranches. Murders were common. There was no force to impose law and order, and no courts of justice.

Embittered and impoverished by the turn of affairs, Bandini accused Chico of being "scandalously avaricious." Gutiérrez was sent to San Diego to investigate the situation and succeeded in making himself well hated. Bandini was never considered a true Californian, as he had been born in Lima, and was in disgrace with many Californians because of a conviction for smuggling while serving as collector of customs.

Events were treating him rather harshly. He wrote a letter to Mariano Guadalupe Vallejo, military *comandante* in the North, lamenting the persecutions and injustices he said he had been suffering, and that injury had been added to insult by the theft by Indians of his cattle and horses from his Tecate Rancho, which was situated about fifty miles southeast of San Diego just below the present United States-Mexico border. All he had left, he wrote, were two mules and two horses:

Terrible sorrows and tragedies are besieging our beloved land . . . and it is best not to write it down in pen and ink. Many tears are being shed, but some day, the Supreme Power will shower us again with blessings.

In subsequent letters he begged for assistance:

. . . send me what wheat and other things, which are used directly toward preserving life itself. To feed my family, is all that I worry about. My misfortune is such that I can no longer sleep and work ceaselessly to no avail. Yes, my dear friend, provide for this unhappy friend some leftovers or wastes from your abundant crops, and the generosity based on this request, will forever be engraved in my heart.

Vallejo sent orders of flour, wheat, *manteca*, beans, horse mackerel, 120 *pesos* in money, and a draft on the Hudson Bay Company for another 400 *pesos*.

Pío Pico saw that unless conditions were quickly corrected the country would be beset with endless troubles. In his own correspondence with Vallejo, he wrote that:

> ... so many rumors of war, so many fantastic tales have produced their effect, the Indians who before were satisfied with their lot and who worked with much pleasure, have turned evil and instead of taking care of the cattle, they slaughter it and sell the hide and the tallow ... If the Californians were united, in a very short time this country would present a very praiseworthy aspect and instead of being worthy of only pity, we would be the most envied of all the inhabitants of the states that form the confederation of the Mexican Republic ...

News from Texas that Gen. Santa Anna had been defeated and captured, and that Texas had won its independence from Mexico, reached California and deeply stirred the American settlers and traders who were swiftly moving into public affairs.

When Chico requested troops from San Diego because of political troubles in the North, they were refused on the grounds that Indians were ravaging the Sonora frontier and threatening San Diego. Chico's day was almost done. With him when he came to California was a mistress whom he had introduced as his niece. When he tried to force her upon the society of Monterey, the Californians chased both of them aboard a ship, and with Chico

MONTEREY, as seen by William Rich Hutton, the American sailor. Its adobe buildings still reflected the pastoral days of Spanish and Mexican domination.

Juan Bautista Alvarado

shouting he would "bring up crows to peck your eyes out," they sailed for Mazatlán. He had lasted three months.

When Gutiérrez stepped back into office, the residents of Monterey also decided they had had enough and that California was entitled to choose its own governor in its own way. Juan Bautista Alvarado, then only 27, began a new revolution. He had been born in Monterey and was a relative or friend of nearly all *Californios*. His small force of Californians, carrying lances and with fife and drums, was reinforced by Americans, Mexicans and Indians led by an American hunter named Isaac Graham, who had settled in the North and built a distillery, an indispensable asset for a California revolution.

After marching his men around and around to make them appear more formidable than their numbers justified, Alvarado attacked Monterey on November 4, 1836, fired his single cannon ball at the governor's mansion, and that was it. Gutiérrez joined Chico in Mexico. The province was declared to be independent as the "free and sovereign state of Alta California." Though a Lone Star flag was raised by American volunteers, California was not to be another Texas and the Mexican flag continued to wave over the capitol. What the Californians desired was for Mexico to abandon its centralist ideas and return to the federalist constitution, and an end to the sending of unwanted governors. Alvarado was installed as governor, Monterey was recognized as the capital, and the *Diputación* transformed into a "constituent Congress."

The Southerners, or *Sureños*, more loyal to the government of Mexico City, were not enthusiastic over these developments, particularly in Los Angeles, and a revolutionary fever boiled through the countryside. The San Diego *Ayuntamiento* was summoned to meet on November 22 and Bandini and Santiago E. Arguello, son of the *alcalde*, were named to go to Los Angeles and confer with representatives of Los Angeles and Santa Barbara on forming a provisional government of their own, one loyal to Mexico, and avenge the national honor. Majordomos at the San Diego and San Luis Rey and San Juan Capistrano Missions were requested to supply horses and whatever else they needed to speed them on their way. On their return they reported all were in agreement and full of loyalty and brave determination.

San Diego named three electors, Bandini, Santiago E. Arguello, and Juan María Marrón to participate in choosing a political leader. Pico was substituted later when Bandini became ill.

Los Angeles reported it was in fear of attack from Gov. Alvarado and appealed for help. The San Diego *Ayuntamiento* on January 11 instructed *Alférez* Juan Salazar, at the Presidio, to send aid, but, as he was a friend of José Castro, who had been named by Gov. Alvarado to lead a citizens' army, he interposed many objections, claiming that he lacked supplies and would need six horses, two wagon wheels, a wagon, six blankets and twelve *pesos* in *reales*. The troops stationed at San Luis Rey as well as those at San Diego also refused duty, insisting that if they were going to do any fighting they expected their pay, which was long overdue. Pío Pico promised to lend aid if they returned to their posts and did their duty like soldiers.

His efforts evidently were successful as he and *Regidor* Francisco M. Alvarado started north with a force of twenty men and expected to pick up more on the way. It was later charged that Capt. Fitch had supplied them with moist powder.

When the San Diegans reached Los Angeles, it was too late, perhaps fortunately. The promised resistance to Alvarado and his forces had melted away. A temporary truce was struck with an agreement for election of a new legislative body and a petition to Mexico City for the restoration of federalism and to allow California to govern itself.

As for the San Diegans, Gov. Alvarado dismissed them as braggarts who would do nothing but talk and to whom "the Supreme Being had denied the gift of veracity." The soldiers who had marched north with Pico and *Regidor* Alvarado disbanded and never returned.

Pío Pico, José Joaquín Ortega and Martín S. Cabello informed San Diego that they had done all in their power to retain "the fundamental laws of our sacred charter" and now was the time to assure public tranquility. San Diego was left alone and feared the worst. The residents accused their representatives of having compromised them. When reports were received that Alvarado's "army" was about to march on San Diego, the remnants of the old Presidio cavalry company fled into Lower California, where they joined Capt. Agustín V. Zamorano, a former governor and a political refugee from the North.

In a letter to the Mexican Minister of Relations, from his ranch at "Ti Juan," also below the present international border, written on March 6, 1837, the elder Arguello begged the government to dispatch troops to California on assurance that the rebel army most certainly wouldn't fight. He stated that the administrators of the San Diego and San Luis Rey Missions had been friendly with the rebels and their cause, and that in the North, Alvarado had sold a house to raise money for the purchase of 500 shotguns and munitions in the Sandwich Islands which was to be accomplished through two foreigners.

Juan Bandini, in his later years

Henry Delano Fitch

27

Arguello wrote:

This is not surprising of the Americans who reside in the Sandwich Islands . . . for it is known that there one lives without any obedience to any government. They have contracted an American schooner-brigantine called *Loriot* and another they hope to purchase called *Leonidas*, and have placed their own administrators in the missions to kill all the cattle they possibly can, securing for this purpose the most perverse and the worst thieves possible who have distinguished themselves in this type of plundering, so that the only means this country has will be devastated; this has already begun.

The *Ayuntamiento* had other problems with which to concern itself for a time. Up for decision was the question of whether San Diego most needed a church or a jail. The jail won. It was decided that the people would be asked to contribute to the construction of a "*casa consistorial*" which would be used as a jail, courthouse and town hall. On March 18, the *Ayuntamiento* in a solemn session formally decided not to recognize Alvarado as governor, as he had failed to submit necessary proof of his right to the office, nor any other governor not named by the Territorial *Diputación*. Judge Benjamin Hayes, who copied the original document from the old San Diego Archives, noted that it was conspicuous by the precautionary lack of signatures.

A little later came a report that 200 Sonorans, Indians and Americans were advancing on California from along the Colorado River, and though it proved to be false, Alvarado sent a force to San Diego with orders to remove or spike all guns, leave not a single horse between San Diego and San Gabriel, and redistribute supplies and rations so they would not fall into the hands of enemies, whoever they might be. The records on this incident are not clear.

Santiago Arguello in his correspondence refers to an event of about the same time, when he wrote that when a militia of fifty men from Los Angeles, under the command of Eugenio Montenegro, was reported approaching, most of the population abandoned San Diego. The militia, however, was seeking enlistments and finding the town virtually deserted, proceeded to walk off with the "violent" cannon on the Plaza and all the ammunition they could find. They loaded it on the brig *Catalina* to be taken North. Subsequently, according to Arguello, Montenegro united his militia with Castro's forces at San Gabriel. In a report dated April 24, Estudillo said that Montenegro had seized the secretary of the *Ayuntamiento*, José María Mier y Terán, and the town attorney, Domingo Amado, apparently in connection with the *Ayuntamiento's* action of March 18 in refusing to recognize Alvarado as governor. The two San Diego revolutionists managed to escape and flee across the border to join the other refugees.

Judge Benjamin Hayes

Presumably most San Diegans trickled back to their homes except for the fighting opposition which rallied at a place called Campo de la Palma, on the Arguello ranch about seventeen miles inside Lower California. Under the leadership of Arguello, Zamorano, Nicanor Estrada, Antonio María Zavaleta, Bandini and José María Mier y Terán, they counted forty men, among them eight cavalrymen from the old San Diego company and some twenty volunteers.

Agustín Zamorano

The military commander at La Paz, José María Mata, reported to the Minister of War that he had dispatched troops to the frontier, though only to protect Lower California from the Northern rebels.

At this hour, the Indians decided to strike in force. Serious trouble had been building for more than a year. Marrón's rancho, Cuero de Venado, had been attacked in the spring of 1836, though several of the raiders were killed by Christian Indians. A mission creamery in El Cajon Valley, where the padres made cheese, was raided and three Indian helpers killed. Efforts to establish a garrison at Santa Ysabel had been unsuccessful, though several punitive expeditions were sent into the mountains, and at one point Don Silvestre de la Portilla, brother of Capt. Portilla, offered to conquer the Indians at his own expense if allowed to keep any captives as servants. The Diegueños of San Diego and some Yumas from the Colorado River joined in raiding and plundering nearly all the ranchos, burning buildings, driving off livestock, and even plotting to capture San Diego and kill its inhabitants.

The most tragic incident occurred at the Jamul Rancho of Pío Pico, about twenty-five miles southeast of San Diego. There are a number of versions of this attack and all vary in some degree as to details, even as to exact date. It was in April of 1837. Two of the most detailed stories were related in later years by Doña Juana Machado, widow of the American sailor, Thomas Wrightington, and by Apolinaria Lorenzana, in her *Memorias*, as she was living at the time on her nearby Jamacha Rancho. Pío Pico was not at Jamul, being busy with other San Diegans in revolutionary plotting. His widowed mother, Doña Eustaquia López, and his unmarried sisters, Feliciana, Jacinta and Ysidora, were at the ranch, however, according to the story of Doña Juana Machado. As she had never learned to write, as was common among women in Spanish and Mexican days, she dictated a narrative which follows in part, to Thomas Savage, in Old Town on January 11, 1878:

Early one afternoon an Indian woman named Cesarea came to where Doña Eustaquia was sitting at the door looking toward the street and in a loud voice asked her for salt. The mistress ordered that salt be brought her, but the Indian

Pío Pico, in his later years

29

woman, by sign, gave her to understand that she wished to give it to her, herself. The mistress got up and the Indian woman followed her. Arriving at a secluded spot the Indian woman in a tongue which Doña Eustaquia understood well, told her that the Indians were going to rise, kill the men, and make captives of the women.

Doña Eustaquia with much prudence went to the room where her daughters were sewing; she told them to leave their work, take their *rebozos* (all of the women wore *rebozos* at that time), and go for a walk along the edge of the cornfield, saying she would soon follow them.

With much secrecy she called the *mayordomo*, a relative of hers named Juan Leiva, and told him what Cesarea had revealed to her and saying besides that she herself had for some days noticed things among the Indians which had made her suspicious, although these had not been great.

Leiva assured her there was no danger, advising her to calm herself, and said he had men and twelve firearms. She urged him to place her and her family in safety, and when he still refused, she ordered him to bring up a *carreta* with oxen and she drove down the road, picked up her daughters, and arrived in the middle of the night at the Jamacha Rancho of Doña Apolinaria. After warning her of the imminent danger, she and her daughters continued to San Diego and reported to *Alcalde* Estudillo.

Doña Juana Machado continues:

The Indians did not attack the same night, but the following; of a sudden they fell upon servants at the ranch; who were the *mayordomo*, Juan Leiva, his son, Antonio, a youth named Molina, and another from Lower California named Comancho. They killed all at the cornfield, except Juan Leiva, who broke away towards the house to defend his family.

When he went towards the gun room an Indian cleaning woman of the house who had locked that room and put the key in her pocket, mockingly showed him the key, saying that there were no hopes in that direction.

Leiva ran to the kitchen and with coals of fire defended himself for a while; but at the end they killed him and threw his body into the hall of the house. Afterward they overcame his wife Doña María, a little son named Claro, and his two daughters, Tomasa and Ramona (15 and 12 years old respectively).

The Indians were going to kill Doña María and the boy when the supplications of Doña Tomasa made them desist. They took off all the woman's clothes and those of the boy, and in spite of the screams and moans of all the family they carried off the two girls towards the Colorado River. Before starting they removed everything from the ranch, taking with them horses, cattle and all other things of value; and burned the house.

Poor Doña María covered her nakedness with grasses and thus reached Mission San Diego, which was in charge of Fathers Vicente Pasqual Olivas, and Fernando Martín.

One story says that the attack became known when the mother, naked and almost out of her mind, was found wandering toward San Diego with her young son. She never recovered and died of grief.

Arguello appealed to Alvarado for military help but there is no record that it was forthcoming. Mexican troops along the frontier came up from Lower California, under Sgt. Macedonio González, who is believed to have been an uncle of the girls and, joined by others from San Diego, a search for the kidnappers was begun. Entering the mountains they sighted the two girls atop a rocky hill, guarded by Indians. Their bodies were smeared with white paint and their hair was cut in Indian fashion. They called out to the men, while the Indians tried to cover their mouths to keep them quiet. Though the soldiers attacked and managed to kill some of the Indians, the first attempt at rescuing the girls failed.

A member of the expedition was Vicente Romero, a saddler who had been born in Loreto and was serving at the time as a soldier on La Frontera, guarding the Lower California missions of San Vicente, San Tomás and Descanso. He said Gonzalez' force consisted of eighteen regular soldiers and thirty friendly Indians under the noted chief Jatanil, and they started from Descanso, about fifty miles below the pueblo of San Diego.

They passed, he said:

. . . Through Tecate, Las Juntas, Milquatay, Jacum, Matacawat, Guatay, Cuyamaca Valley, and round to Valle de las Viejas, being out four months. During this time we had several encounters with the Indians, and killed many of them; but, finally, at a place known as Matadera, in the Jacum mountains, our ammunition having fallen into the hands of the Indians, by a surprise of the guard, we abandoned our horses at night and returned to the presidio at San Diego. In this battle were Yumas from the Colorado as well as Cuyamaca Indians.

Romero's testimony was given many years later before a United States surveyor-general for California in connection with conflicting land claims over Cuyamaca Valley, and his affidavit makes no mention of the expedition having ever seen the two girls. Macedonio, however, told the story of seeing the girls to Mrs. Wrightington.

The expedition came up through northern Lower California to Tecate, on the border, swung eastward along the age-old Indian trails that led through mountain passes at Jacumba, from where they split off into the desert regions, and turned north in a wide arc through the Jacumba, In-Ko-Pah and Laguna Mountains, then westward through Pine Valley to Guatay and then up into Cuyamaca Valley, where the Indians, who had never come under the influence of the missionaries, had their principal rancheria "in a pile of rocks just north of a sharp-pointed peak." This was 5000-foot Stonewall Mountain. From there they doubled back on a hopeless quest.

Apolinaria Lorenzana heard it said that the Indians had taken the girls to be sold at the Colorado River. She thought that Tomasa was 18 or 19 years of age and Ramona 10 or 12. A few years later one of her servants, by the name of Muñoz, wished to go to Sonora and during his absence his wife and son died. Upon his return, he assured Apolinaria that on his way back he had seen the younger of the two Leiva girls sitting in the back of a house, and that when he greeted her, she answered in Spanish and told him of her capture, and begged him to take her back. He didn't dare do so, he related, because he had only one "beast," or horse, and it was too tired to make the journey with two persons, and the Indians would find them and kill them both. The girls were never seen again, though there were reports over the years that they had been taken as wives by Indian chiefs.

The Jamul Ranch has remained almost intact through the years. The ruins of the original Pico house lie at the point of a broad, gently sloping promontory at the foot of Jamul Mountain, overlooking the junction of Jamul and Dulzura Creeks. The ruins, about fifty feet above the valley floor and visible from the Otay road, include stone and mortar foundations, mounds of washed down adobe, a small reservoir, and traces of several thousand feet of aqueduct. Treasure hunters have potted the area with holes. The surrounding hills, with the exception of the north slope of the San Ysidro Mountains across the valley, are dry and quiet.

San Diego itself was in danger of a massacre. In her *Recuerdos* dated Jan. 26, 1878, Felipa Osuna, daughter of Juan María Osuna and widow of Juan María Marrón, related that she began to notice

THIS IS THE EARLIEST KNOWN SKETCH of San Diego, still a Mexican village when Lt. William Emory, of the U.S. Topographical Engineers, made this drawing in 1846, just after the American occupation. The landscape was barren.

the frequent visits of a group of Indians with one of her Diegueño servants named Juan, and that upon eavesdropping on their conversation, as she knew their language, she learned of a plot to rob the store of Capt. Fitch, who was away on a business trip, to kill an American there by the name of Lawrence Hartwell, and kidnap Fitch's wife, Josefa Carrillo de Fitch, and herself. She identified two of the other Indians as being from the Fitch household, and one as a cook of the Estudillos. Arrows had been hidden in the ruins of the old Presidio. The attack was to begin while *Señora* Fitch was preparing to make her bread during the evening.

The plan was allowed to run its course. When Josefa started to roll her dough, two tall Indians entered and blocked the doorway. Hartwell and Felipa's husband, Marrón, who had been hiding in the building, attacked the Indians who offered no resistance. The next morning, Sgt. Macedonio González and his men arrested all the Indians suspected of being in the plot, together with Fitch's servants and the cook, Juan Antonio, from the Estudillo house and shot them. Señora Marrón's own servant, Juan, had gone to get wood early in the morning and never returned.

Much of what actually took place lies buried in old memories. Doña Juana Machado recalls that she believes the plot was first overheard by *Señora* Fitch's Indian maid named Candelaria. The only men present in San Diego were Bandini, Arguello, Estudillo and a Spaniard named Don Rafael, known as El Gachupín. It was decided that the women should go to the huts, or hide houses, at La Playa, used by the Boston ships, to where they would be nearer *El Castillo,* the old fort on Ballast Point. She recalls:

We arrived there at sunset and passed the night there, the Picos, my family; we were many. The foreigners were some eight or ten who protected us. The morning following they came with us to the pueblo and remained on guard for a week, more or less, until the Indian ringleaders had been shot.

It was painful to Felipa Osuna to see Gonzalez' men running after the Indians as hunted animals. Some were forced out of houses, others, running wildly about trying to get away, were lassoed. One sought refuge in her house, but he too was taken. Felipa relates that she felt terribly guilty and that other women of the town were saddened at what was happening to the Indians, and turned against her for informing on them. But what else could she have done, she asks? Wasn't it her duty to inform on this terrible plot endangering the lives of others? What would have been the lot of the women of San Diego, if the Indians had started kidnapping them?

Another version of the "sad night" was provided by William Heath Davis, in his book, *"Seventy-five Years in California."* He said the Indians taken from the various houses all expressed the desire to die as Christians, and after their confession, they were shot and their bodies rolled into pre-prepared graves. One Indian accused of being a spy had one of his ears cut off, and was threatened with the immediate loss of the other and that he would be mutilated little by little, unless he confessed. He did. As he was a non-Christian he was shot without ceremony.

When the Indian troubles seemed to be subsiding, Juan Bandini, who had been advised to keep out of sight, as only native-born Californians were being allowed to "dance at this ball;" Santiago E. Arguello and Pico, were joined by Capts. Portilla and Zamorano. They advanced on San Diego, where on May 21, 1837, in conjunction with the *Ayuntamiento*, they proclaimed a new Plan of San Diego to recognize the authority of Mexico and to treat those who participated in the Monterey rebellion as "erring brothers worthy of pity and forgiveness."

Bandini and Santiago E. Arguello were selected to present the San Diego Plan to friendly conspirators at Los Angeles, and on May 26, 1837, Bandini and Arguello led a small force quietly into the northern pueblo, the few soldiers there being surprised at a game of cards. They quickly surrendered and gave up the "violent" cannon that had been taken from the Plaza at San Diego. The report of more Indian troubles sent Bandini and Arguello hastening back to San Diego with the captured cannon, and they were welcomed as heroes and conquerors.

The situation in California, and especially in San Diego, remained chaotic. Capt. Zamorano wrote to the Minister of War from San Diego, on June 5, 1837, that the people of San Diego were still loyal and that he was in temporary command while Capt. Portilla campaigned against the Indians. Reports had been received from an Indian spy that a large band of Indians had gathered two leagues away and planned to attack San Diego at midnight. Most of the men were away, and only fifteen were available to defend the town. At the request of Capt. Fitch, the hide ship *Alert*, then in the harbor, supplied ten sailors, and the force of twenty-five drove the Indians back into the mountains. A few additional details were published later in the Sandwich Island Gazette, Dec. 2, 1837, apparently on information obtained from the crew of the *Alert*. This report said the Indians fled when the *Alert* fired some of its guns.

Upon learning that Castro and eighty men had reached Los Angeles, the San Diegans recalled their troops from the campaign against the Indians, made grape shot for their cannon and bullets for the muskets, and, gathering up seventy men, prepared for war.

34

Victor Eugene August Janssens, a Belgian who had come up from Mexico as a colonist, was sent out to recruit as allies a band of Indian traders from New Mexico led by a crippled French-Canadian named Chalifoux. In his "The Life and Adventures in California," Janssens noted that the business of Chalifoux and his Chaguanoso Indians was to trade for horses "but they stole more than they traded."

Janssens found the group encamped in a woods at Agua Caliente, now Warner's Hot Springs, and came near being shot by a couple of their sentries as he approached the camp. Chalifoux agreed to help and promised Janssens at least twenty-five armed men from his group. The night before they were to march for Rancho Los Nietos, now the site of the town of Downey south of Los Angeles, where the force was forming, the Indians wanted permission to go purchase some extra supplies. Janssens says they were allowed to go in groups of five. They all got drunk on brandy and Janssens had to load them into carts to start for Rancho Los Nietos.

Each of the Chaguanosos was armed with a good rifle, a hatchet, a dagger and a bow and arrow. Janssens says they volunteered to lend their assistance without pay, that they were eager for the fight but that Chalifoux exacted strict discipline and obedience from the Indians.

The unexpected appearance in San Diego of Capt. Andrés Castillero, who had fled California with Gutiérrez, changed the course of events. He presented himself as commissioner for the Mexican government and had brought with him a copy of the new centralist constitution. It was posted in San Diego on June 12, and all the people enthusiastically swore to uphold it. The Plan of San Diego was abandoned, but not the campaign. Castillero joined Bandini and Capt. Zamorano and at San Luis Rey, the Army of the Supreme Government of Mexico, now grown to 125 men, and with Capt. Portilla in command, started North.

Castro hurled defiance at Bandini and Zamorano from his camp at Santa Rita east of Monterey:

Let the Californians alone and they will come out all right. If you continue among them you will cause the country's ruin and that of their families and persons. If Don Pío Pico, Andrés Pico or the Arguellos were leading that division everything would be settled, but you are very evil men, you have no prestige, nor a cent of money. If I say nothing about Don Pablo de la Portilla it is because he is a very good man. Watch out, I am not far from you, and if I did not have good intentions, it would be another thing. We shall soon see each other.

When the column encountered a Castro force at Rancho Santa Ana, they attacked, and the enemy fled. Portilla's main force

WILLIAM RICH HUTTON, an American sailor, drew this watercolor sketch of Los Angeles while it was still a pueblo, but the old ways were swiftly changing.

dropped the pursuit at Los Angeles, which they entered on June 16, but Chalifoux's Indians pursued the enemy all the way to San Fernando.

Castillero and Alvarado met at Santa Barbara. Alvarado agreed to take an oath of allegiance to the new constitution and restore California to the republic. Alvarado was left in control of California, though the idea of independence had vanished, and Bandini, after some reflection, decided he had been "vilely deceived" by his pretended friend and ally, Castillero.

Thus, Alvarado, once he was convinced that all political power was safely in his hands, passed easily from one constitutional position to another. But Mexico City was yet to be heard from.

The bitterness over the failure of the military to protect San Diego continued. In late June, the elder Arguello told the *comandante* that he had lost hope of getting any aid, that he had not even received any answers to his remonstrations, and that now it was his duty to help assure the town's defense. He outlined a plan to form a guard to maintain a constant surveillance. Ten days later, in the early morning hours of July 6, 1837, Indians fell upon the Rancho of St. Bernardo, one of the San Diego Mission

36

properties, killing the corporal, a soldier, and a shepherd, and wounding the "juggler's son." A few days later Arguello protested the summary execution by the military of two Indians accused of being "*asesinos*," one at La Soledad and the other at San Dieguito.

Later, that summer, frontier soldiers handed over to *Alcalde* Estudillo a gentile, or non-Christian Indian by the name of Claudio who was suspected of having led the raid on St. Bernardo Rancho, and a band of natives from the Indian pueblo of San Pasqual asked that Claudio be turned over to them, to be killed as nine others of his band had been killed in the attack. Estudillo hoped that this would be done because he was not sure that he would be able to hold Claudio a prisoner for very long.

In August, the elder Arguello sat down and wrote a letter to his brother, Gervasio, in Mexico, in which he accused Pío Pico of having aided and abetted Alvarado, and in commenting on the kidnapping of the two girls, something that had never happened before in California, charged that "you will be amazed at this barbarity, for do you know that the rebels of Monterey gave this plan to the Indians . . . there is no doubt, my brother, the very same Indians have declared it . . ." He told of the enemies he had made and described "the Carrillos as the principal agents of revolution."

He warned that unless help arrived from the Supreme Government "California will become foreign, as North American military personnel already were numerous and more were arriving, from Cape Mendocino to the Columbia River. You must not keep this information from the government, keep it very much in mind as I fear that California will follow the example of Texas."

The Carrillos—not the family of Joaquín Carrillo of San Diego, but a related branch—now entered deeper waters of California politics.

José Antonio Ezequiel Carrillo, once a San Diego school teacher, a former *alcalde* at Los Angeles and more recently territorial congressman in Mexico, appeared in California with the news that his brother, Carlos, had been appointed governor, an objective for which José Antonio had been maneuvering for a long time.

Castillero, however, on his return to Mexico City submitted a report in which he described Carlos Carrillo as a man of little character who craved money and always sought the winning side, and as for his brother, José Antonio, he was the worst man in all California, had no morals and no good habits, and took part in every revolution that came along. Alvarado was described as a man of good habits but very ambitious. As for Juan Bandini, the

South American, he was the one who sowed the seeds of revolt and always controlled the authorities.

As Alvarado had no intention of surrendering the governorship to a Carrillo, he stalled, waiting for the effects of Castillero's report to possibly produce a change of attitude in Mexico City.

Carlos took the oath as governor at Los Angeles on December 6, and the action was ratified at San Diego three days later. San Diego, however, was finished as a self-governing pueblo. Because of a lack of sufficient population, San Diego henceforth would be a part of the prefecture of Los Angeles and entitled only to a justice of the peace, and this would go into effect on January 1, 1838. Estudillo, who had been *alcalde*, became the *juez de paz*. Carrillo, however, issued a decree establishing the custom house at San Diego which San Diego most desired. Trading was more important even than politics. Everything was quiet for two months, but with Alvarado still showing resistance, José Antonio Pico took a body of San Diegans to Los Angeles, where they joined more men under Carrillo and marched northward to lay siege to Santa Barbara. The Santa Barbara garrison joined the Alvarado forces under Castro and the two "armies" squared off at San Buenaventura. Castro captured Rincon Pass, lobbed cannon balls into the Southerners, and it was all over. Carrillo retreated. One of Castro's men was left dead on the battlefield. Castro pursued the fleeing Southerners, captured seventy of them, including Andrés Pico, and entered Los Angeles in triumph on April 1.

Up from Sonora, by the overland route, came Capt. Juan José Tobar, renowned Indian fighter, to take command of the demoralized forces at San Diego. A force of 100 composed of volunteers from San Diego, refugees from Los Angeles, and frontier adventurers, marched northward again. After passing Mission San Luis Rey, and in the vicinity of its *asistencia*, Mission Las Flores, seven and one-half miles north of the present city of Oceanside, they heard that Castro was approaching. An adobe building was converted into a barracks and three cannon were mounted in a corral. Hides and saddles were used to protect the gunners. Bandini and both Carrillos were present. On or about April 21, Castro's force of about 200 men pulled up in formation in front of the improvised fort. Several cannon shots were exchanged and then a flag of truce was raised by one side, with a demand, not for surrender, but for negotiation. Tobar was anxious for action. Carlos Carrillo forbade any more shooting and was accused of cowardice. Tobar withdrew in disgust and with many of his companions crossed back into Mexico. After several days of talking, Carrillo agreed to disband his troops and continue the conversations at San Fernando.

Gen. José Castro

38

This virtually ended opposition to Alvarado, except at San Diego. In November he received word that Castillero's report as to the character of the Carrillos had been very effective. Carlos was out of the picture and he, Alvarado, a Californian, at long last was the recognized governor. Reports reached Santa Barbara of a renewed revolutionary spirit in San Diego, and Castro and twenty-five men were sent to San Diego. They arrived at the Plaza at midnight, on Christmas night, and a celebration was going on in Bandini's grand house. Some say it was a ball; others, a *pastorela*. Castro surrounded the house, and the two Carrillos, two of the Pico brothers, and Joaquín Ortega were arrested, but Bandini and Estudillo escaped.

Benjamin Hayes, who gathered from the old residents the facts of what took place that Christmas period, writes:

In the year 1838, . . . Don Carlos Antonio Carrillo was at San Diego, where the population sympathized with his pretensions to the governorship. Gen. Castro arrived in this neighborhood during the night. From his spies he learned that a grand ball was going on at the residence of Don Juan Bandini. Don Carlos, cynosure of all eyes; Don José Joaquín Ortega was there; young Pedro C. Carrillo, too . . . Gallant Castro tarried "till nearly dawn; desvelados all," they fell an easy prey.

Don José Antonio Estudillo, then *juez*, or judge, was warned by Don José María Estudillo, through a window of the Estudillo house. Fearing the worst from Castro, even that he would be shot in the excitement, although they were raised boys together at Monterey, he took refuge in the loft above the great hall in which it was customary to hold the services of the church; it being arranged that the family should give out he had gone to La Playa, as the place was called where stood the hide houses, and the landing for the ships.
His intrepid wife, Doña Victoria, in the morning observed Gen. Castro on the Plaza, writing with his paper upon a saddle. She sent José María, then eight years old, to deliver the key of the *Juzgado* and tell him he could write there. Receiving the message, the general enquired, "and your father, where is he?" Soon he came to the good lady, with a like inquiry. Then the fire of her resolute nature burst into a flame. Those who know her, can imagine her reply. Her high spirit was shown at the right time. They did not undertake to search the house.
With his prisoners, Gen. Castro took the line of march for Los Angeles. He would have to pass San Luis Rey. Meanwhile an arrangement was made with Don Pío Pico, who was in charge of that establishment, to prepare him a banquet and give full play to his passion for the wine cup. On a certain night the *Diegueñ-os* (San Diegans) would join such force as Don Pío could gather in that vicinity.
Don José Antonio Estudillo led the party from San Diego and took post silently among the trees to the west of the mission. Notified by Don Pío of the auspicious moment, he relented, fearing to shed blood, and against their earnest appeals, conducted his men back to San Diego. Next day Castro with his "yellow jackets" marched on in triumph. To his natural goodheartedness, it is due to say, he could not withstand the tearful entreaty of Don Joaquín and released him soon upon leaving San Diego . . .

All the recollections of the incident differ. Eventually all of the prisoners were released, but not, however, until they had been taken to sea aboard ship and subjected to the cruel and unusual punishment of seasickness. At San Diego, to guard against future surprise attacks, on the highest point of the hill overlooking Old Town, earth was thrown up, a ditch dug around it, and two or three cannon taken from *El Castillo* at Ballast Point placed in position.

There wasn't much left for Carlos. Alvarado in his own history of California events says the President of Mexico ordered him to give Carrillo an island and send him off to live on it. Alvarado contemptuously added that he personally offered to provide a servant who would say every morning, "How has your Excellency slept?"

San Diego slipped deeper into a decline. A heavy storm with rain and snow in 1838 was very destructive to sheep. Indian troubles persisted through 1839 and few of the ranchos escaped plundering. José Antonio Pico, in a letter to Vallejo, said that nothing could be done as there was not a single soldier on duty, nor any ammunition. Except for the chapel, not a building was left standing in the old Presidio, and *El Castillo,* which once represented the power and glory of Spain, and was feared by all American fur smuggling ships, was disappearing. The heavy planking which had been brought down from the redwood coast was being stripped away to build shacks for foreign seamen and beach derelicts at La Playa. The remainder of the dozen cannon, which once sent shot through two armed American vessels, were sinking into the sand.

CHAPTER THREE

"Bring me men to match my mountains,
Bring me men to match my plains,
Men with empires in their purpose,
And new eras in their brains."

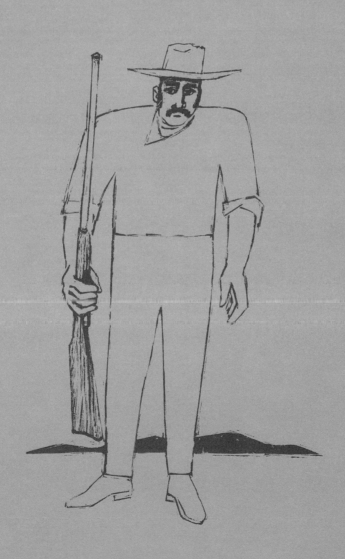

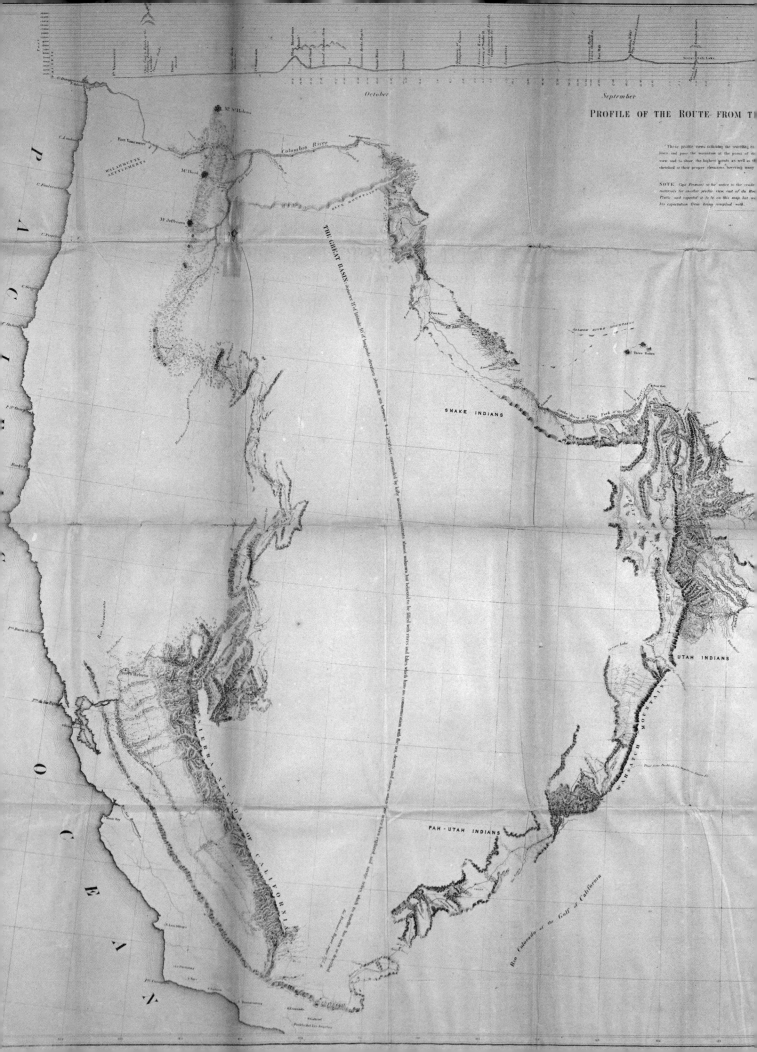

October

September

WINDS OF CHANGE

A few years of comparative peace settled upon San Diego and the *Californios* lived off the fading prosperity of the missions, and stocked their ranches with cattle stolen from the mission ranchos, or "borrowed" from them by the provincial government on one pretext or another, or acquired in the settlement of debts real and imaginary. For the missionaries, it was like "being martyred with needles."

An old Indian from San Juan Capistrano Mission, who had been let out to a rancher as a workman by the administrator, Santiago Arguello, got on a horse and rode to Monterey, where he was able to make a direct complaint to Gov. Alvarado:

I am not an animal that I should be made to labor for masters who are not to my liking. Thou canst do two things with me; order me to be shot if thou wilt, or give me my liberty, if thou art a just man. It is all the same with me.

In January of 1839, Gov. Alvarado appointed an inspector to look into the complaints of the Indians, that they were being robbed and abused, that the administrators and majordomos and their families were draining away the remaining wealth of the dying missions, and to report in general on the progress of secularization. He was William E. P. Hartnell, an Englishman who had come to California in the hide trade, had been naturalized, and was widely respected throughout the province. He began his inspections in San Diego.

JOHN FREMONT'S EXPLORATIONS opened more American knowledge of the Far West but left vast areas which, it was thought, might be filled with "lakes, rivers, deserts, oases and savage tribes which no man has seen."

After twenty-six years of serving the San Diego Mission, Fr. Fernando Martín had gone to his reward. He died on Oct. 19, 1838, at the age of 68. He had seen the mission structures slowly rise from the dust, prosper, and begin their swift decay. It was under his direction that a dam and aqueduct system, a marvel of early California, was built to bring water six miles down Mission Gorge to give life to the orchards and crops. He was born in Old Spain, and his remains lie beneath the floor of the present restored mission church. Fr. Vicente Pascual Oliva had come from San Luis Rey Mission to take over.

Hartnell found that the orchards and vineyards still were flourishing, with 8600 vines and 467 olive trees at the San Diego Mission and 8000 more vines at Rancho Santa Monica, or El Cajon Valley. Neglect had not yet brought them to ruin, though field crops were getting scarce and the Indians had fallen into a sad condition under José Joaquín Ortega, who had been appointed administrator in 1835:

At La Compasión, the people were reduced to utter destitution. All the Indians presented themselves and supplicated the government to remove the administrator and to return them to the care of the Father, not because they had any complaint against Ortega, but because they realized that the mission was not in a condition to maintain them.

At the little Indian town that had been established in San Dieguito Valley, with a handful of emancipated families, Hartnell reported:

. . . the Indians presented themselves and complained about Juan Osuna, the *alcalde* of San Diego, because he had taken from them the land which they had enclosed for their grain, and that he had left them nothing more than salinous soil which did not produce enough for their maintenance.

Pío Pico and his brother, Andrés, were having their troubles administering the San Luis Rey Mission, the Indians accusing them of all sorts of misdeeds. Pico complained to Hartnell that the Indians were running away and that the missionary father had not accounted for all of the property. Fr. Narciso Durán, President of the missions of the South, in a reply directed to Hartnell, wrote:

What about the hundred yoke of oxen and twelve carts? Does a friar conceal them up his sleeves that he should be made to give an account of them? It is Pico and not the missionary Father, who should be held to answer for, for it is he that enjoys the salary and appoints as majordomos whomsoever he pleases.

As far as he was concerned, Pico "ought to be thrashed from head to foot."

At San Gabriel Mission, Fr. Tomás Esténaga wrote that Juan Bandini, who had been appointed administrator, had assured him that during the whole month of February he with his entire family would be absent at his ranch:

Thanks to the Lord! that at this mission they furnish some bread, though not every day, a little meat, at noon only, wine and brandy, and that is all. Just now the "holy" family of Santiago Arguello and that of the Estudillos are arriving. They will make provisions still more scarce. During the last three months, the mother of the three Picos, with her daughter, niece, grandchildren, male and female servants, besides Señora Luisa, the wife of Agustín Zamorano, with her six or seven children, have occupied the mission in grand style. Just now two carts filled with grand people have arrived for the greater consolation of the poor mission and its missionary.

In transmitting this letter to Hartnell, Fr. Durán added that:

Now I ask what has Señor Bandini done with all his boasted activity? Why, with the abundant profit which he reaped, did he not purchase some cattle? The most incompetent friar would, by this time, have two or three thousand cattle.

A month later Fr. Esténaga wrote again that:

Thirty eight white people must be supported and are at home at this mission, without counting the male and female servants of the mission, nor those of the Arguellos, Estudillos, and the whole brood. This evening, Señor Bandini undeceived me, when he said that there was not a tallow candle on hand for a light, nor any tallow to make a candle, nor have the few cattle at the mission any in reality. What will happen in time if we are to continue thus?

Hartnell finally removed the Picos, under threat of force, and turned the management of the San Luis Rey Mission over to José Antonio Estudillo. Juan Osuna replaced Ortega at the San Diego Mission. At San Juan Capistrano, Hartnell appointed José Ramón Arguello, another son of Santiago, as majordomo, but the Indians complained about all of the Arguellos, and he too was removed and replaced with August Janssens, the Belgian who had aided the San Diegans in the rebellion against Alvarado. Bandini, however, was absolved by Hartnell of any serious wrongdoing at San Gabriel Mission, though he relinquished its administration and Juan Pérez was appointed majordomo.

In 1840 also Alvarado issued a new *reglamento* designed to correct some of the mismanagement, and to protect the fathers in their religious jurisdiction and the Indians from abuse.

The tide of bad feeling flowed back and forth but for the padres their day was drawing to a close. The future of so large and rich a territory could not be kept forever as a preserve for aboriginals who were culturally so far behind the invaders. Time, too, was pressing down on the *Californios* who were to labor not but deck themselves in silver and gaze on their cattle roaming over a thousand hills.

San Diego struggled back to life. In the district which included San Diego, and the mission areas of San Luis Rey and San Juan Capistrano, a census of 1840 showed only 150 white people, seven of them foreigners who resided at Old Town and had been naturalized or licensed to live in California. Most of the work was still being done by about 2250 Indian neophytes who lived at the missions or were in private service in town or on the ranchos.

The old Leatherjackets, army regulars and early settlers were dying off. Capt. Ruiz was disposing of property and land he had accumulated. He deeded his Old Town orchard to his godchildren, the children of Joaquín and María López de Carrillo who had been married in the presidial chapel in 1809. Just before his death Joaquín Carrillo attempted to sell the orchard, but his wife petitioned the government to prevent the sale as it was the only means of sustaining the family. The widow took her unmarried children to Northern California, to begin life anew. Capt. Ruiz came back to the pueblo from his ranch at Los Peñasquitos and died in the Carrillo home which was then occupied by Capt. Fitch and Señora Fitch, a Carrillo daughter.

On January 17, 1840, the remnants of the fort on Ballast Point were sold to Don Juan Machado for $40, though, from the evidence of what occurred at San Diego in later events, the remaining cannon were not removed from their sites. An investigation in 1839 had revealed the presence of nine cannon, two of them still serviceable, with fifty canisters of grape and 300 balls. The same year saw the wandering San Diego River finally close off its own channel into False, or Mission Bay, and pour its choking silt into the harbor that had so entranced all explorers since the days of its discovery by Juan Rodríguez Cabrillo.

The hide trade at the port of San Diego was shifting entirely away from the missions to the ranches. The English explorer Capt. Sir Edward Belcher reached San Diego on October 17, 1839, on Her Majesty's ship *Sulphur*, on a round the world voyage, remained for five days, and reported that "the port of San Diego, for shelter, deserves all the commendation that previous navigators have bestowed on it."

He remarked, however, on the heavy kelp beds which forced ships two miles out of their way to round the tongue of kelp and enter the harbor. An old sailor in port related that he had seen the whole bank of kelp forced into the harbor, by a southerly gale. The bank was three miles long and one-fourth mile wide.

Looking at the ruins of the mission, he thought it likely the whole country would before long either fall back into the hands of the Indians, or find other rulers:

During our visit they were very apprehensive for an attack and had been one night at quarters, their arms (in the Nineteenth Century) consisting of bows and arrows, inasmuch as they had no powder for any firearms they might have possessed. The garden, also famed in former days, has now fallen entirely into decay, and instead of thousands of cattle and horses to take care of them, not twenty four-footed animals remain . . . The trade of the port consists entirely of hides and tallow, but not, as formerly, from the missions; for they have long been fleeced . . .

He saw that Americans such as Capt. Fitch and Alfred Robinson, were marrying into the Spanish families, and thus moving in on the only real trade of the coast:

It is necessary that one of the parties should remain on the spot, probably marrying into some influential family, (i.e. in hides and tallow), to insure a constant supply for the vessels when they arrive. It is dangerous for them to quit the port, as some more enterprising character might offer higher prices and carry off the cargo.

The foreigners in California in some instances were becoming troublesome. Of the 380 listed in the census of 1840, fifty had come with overland parties and the rest by various sea routes. Gov. Alvarado turned on the Americans who had assisted him in gaining control of the government and seized Isaac Graham, the former trapper, and between fifty and sixty more foreigners, Americans as well as Englishmen. More were taken into custody at Santa Barbara and the arrest of others at San Diego was ordered. The records are not clear. An American, George Nidever, later related how he and several others escaped while their prison ship, the *Jóven Guipuzcoana*, was in San Diego Bay, and William Lumsden, an English pilot, was put ashore. In the end, about forty-seven foreigners, evidently none from San Diego, were delivered to authorities at San Blas, and released only after long negotiations with the United States and England. Taxes were imposed on the hide-salting establishments of foreigners at La Playa as had been done in 1834.

What had happened to the foreigners who had taken up new lives in the pueblo of San Diego, or had cast their lot with the riff-raff collected on the sands of La Playa?

Thomas Wrightington, the one-eyed shoe craftsman from Fall River, was operating a *pulperia* in Old Town, a competitive shop to the one maintained by Capt. Fitch. Thomas Russell, an American sailor who had been picked up at Santa Barbara by the *Pilgrim*, the hide ship of Richard Henry Dana, and installed at San Diego as beachmaster for its hide house, joined another American, Peter Weldon, in 1836 in a fruitless search for a hidden treasure in the ruins of the two missions on the Colorado River which had been destroyed when the Yuma Indians massacred a half hundred colonists and four missionaries in 1781. Upon their return Russell and Weldon were arrested when they failed to produce any gold. The legend of buried mission treasures persists to this day. Unnoticed, virgin gold sparkled in the streams and from outcroppings in the San Diego mountains, as elsewhere in California.

La Playa swarmed with the castoffs and half-breeds of a dozen lands who prepared the hides for the long voyages around the Horn. Richard Henry Dana, in his *"Two Years Before the Mast,"* wrote about Thomas Russell and this strange lot of beachcombers:

Of the same stamp was Russell, who was master of the hide-house at San Diego while I was there, but had been afterward dismissed for his misconduct. He spent his own money, and nearly all the stores, among the half-bloods upon the beach, and went up to the presidio, where he lived the life of a desperate "loafer," until some rascally deed sent him off "between two days," with men on horseback, dogs, and Indians, in full cry after him, among the hills. One night

FROM LIMA TO SAN FRANCISCO was the sea route traveled by the early coastal traders. This scene of Lima was sketched by U.S. sailor, Gunner Meyers.

View of Lima from Mount Christoval

48

he burst into our room at the hide-house, breathless, pale as a ghost, covered with mud, and torn by thorns and briers, nearly naked, and begged for a crust of bread, saying he had neither eaten nor slept for three days. Here was the great *Mr.* Russell, who a month before was *Don Thomas, Capitan de la playa, Maestro de la casa*, etc. etc., begging food and shelter of Kanakas and sailors. He stayed with us till he had given himself up, and was dragged off to the *calabozo*.

In December of 1837, Russell was banished temporarily from Old Town for escaping from jail.

There were so many sailors and Hawaiian natives, who were known as Kanakas on the beach, that the liquor business became important. A third store, identified as a dram shop, was opened in the pueblo by Andrés Ybarra and Rafaela Serrano, but they gave the authorities some trouble in refusing to pay their taxes and were threatened with the confiscation of their liquor. San Diegans in general kept a safe distance from La Playa, where, on Dec. 20, 1841, an outbreak of disorder resulted in one or two deaths.

The handful of foreign settlers at San Diego, however, began to take over the coastal shipping and merchandising that Californians had so neglected. Capt. Edward Stokes, another Englishman, who arrived by way of Honolulu, married Doña Refugio, the daughter of José Joaquín Ortega. From Lima in South America came Miguel de Pedrorena, who as supercargo of coastal vessels, became more and more involved in the affairs of San Diego. But it was Capt. Fitch who played the dominant role in the commercial life of early San Diego, both as a trader and merchant.

Trade was conducted over a vast area of the Pacific Ocean, from California ports to the Sandwich Islands, as the Hawaiian Islands were known, and as far south as Lima, Peru, and up through the coastal ports of Acapulco, Mazatlán and Guaymas on the Mexican mainland. Products from the Far East, the United States and Europe, from cotton to scissors, were sold and exchanged for the hides, tallow, soap, fruit and furs of California.

The West Coast of Mexico was still experiencing a richness of life brought by trade with China and the Philippines. As late as 1852, John Russell Bartlett, United States Boundary Commissioner, enroute to San Diego, found the stores of Acapulco stocked with Chinese silks, cotton, spices, aromatics, jewelry and jade. San Blas, farther north, the old supply port for the missions and the military garrisons of Lower and Upper California, was fading away. But Mazatlán, still farther up the coast, had a population of between 10,000 and 12,000 and the streets were lined with well-built houses. Bartlett wrote in his *Personal Narratives of Explorations and Incidents:*

San Blas

49

SAN DIEGO maintained many contacts with Mazatlán, on the Mexican west coast. Here is Mazatlán as sketched for the narrative of John Russell Bartlett.

We found Mazatlán considerably in advance of any town we had yet seen . . . the style is wholly that of Old Castilian, with short columns, Moorish capitals and ornaments. Many houses present long lines of colonnades. The richness of their goods vie with the fashionable stores of New York. The Spanish ladies are fond of dress; and I have no doubt the manufacturers of Lyons sell as rich a silk in Mexico as they do in Paris or London.

Next to Acapulco, he wrote, Guaymas, located far up on the Gulf of California, was the best port on the Mexican coast:

. . . the town stands close on the margin of the bay, occupying a narrow strip about a mile in length and not exceeding a quarter of a mile in width, when the mountains rise and hem it closely in . . . The houses are built of stone, brick and adobe. Those in the best part of town are plastered, which gives them a respectable appearance. There are several families of wealth here, whose houses are handsomely furnished and who enjoy the luxuries of residence near the coast. The streets are lighted at night, a convenience not noted elsewhere . . .

There were many large and well filled warehouses and department stores stocked with French and English, but not American goods.

The fur trade which had opened the ports of Spanish California persisted, though the waters were being hunted out. Among the hunters, who were financed by Capt. Fitch and other foreigners, were George Nidever and Allen Light, the Negro deserter from

50

the *Pilgrim*, who was known as "Black Steward." Sea otters were killed in expeditions to the Channel Islands and down along the coast of Lower California. Light eventually prospered to a point where he was able to finance his own expeditions. At times they had to fight it out with savage Northwest Indians employed as hunters by northern rivals.

In his voluminous business correspondence, preserved in The Bancroft Library of the University of California, Fitch writes of his many trading trips to the Islands and Mexico, and of the struggle to conduct a business dependent so greatly on barter and credit. His store evidently was located in the home originally built by Ylario Poinciano, on the west side of the Plaza, and which later was sold by his widow to Fitch in 1841. On one trip to the Islands, he left his store in charge of James Orbell, another English sailor who had dropped off at San Diego, and cautioned him to keep a sharp eye on a brother English sea captain, William Williams, who was in charge of the hide house in which Fitch stored his hides and furs:

Sir: During my absence, which in all probability will be about four months, I recommend to your care my interests which I have in your charge.

I wish you to tell every person that you have orders not to trust any one but you can always trust the persons whose names are on the list. I leave you from

THIS DRAWING OF ACAPULCO, an important seaport in the California trade, was made for U.S. Boundary Commissioner Bartlett's "Personal Narrative."

51

four to eight Dollars each. If you give any more it will be on your own responsibility and you will be answerable for the same.

In case there should be any danger from Indians or other causes I wish you to pack up the goods and take them to Mr. Celis' hide house on the beach and deposit them until the danger is over or if requisite, embark them on board of some vessel.

In time of danger you can assist with powder and ball any expedition that is sent out but give no more than is absolutely necessary and when it is over get back what is possible.

You can let my wife have what she wishes for out of the shop, charging me the same as any one else. You can also let her have what little money she might want for necessary expenses, bread . . . eggs . . . fruits, etc.

I wish you to keep a good look out for Capt. Williams' hide house and if Wm. Williams does not conduct himself properly you are authorized to put some person in his stead.

At present I have nothing more to advise you of. Hoping that you will do the best for my interest, I remain, Yours truly, H. D. Fitch.

Upon his return, the correspondence discloses, Fitch obtained from Orbell, a document, which, in part, stated:

I, the undersigned, do affirm that I have this day adjusted accounts with Mr. H. D. Fitch from whom I have received at several times goods to a considerable amount for sales or return on his account and I acknowledge myself deficient in, to the value of six thousand and one hundred and forty one dollars and four reales.

He agreed to make restitution, as best he could.

As the Americans and other foreigners prospered in trade, and as the Californians themselves experienced the beginnings of wealth in cattle and crops, their children were sent away to school, some to Mexico, or even to Spain; others to an American missionary school in the Sandwich Islands, and some even all the way around the Horn to New England or other Atlantic seaboard towns.

One son of Fitch was sent to Honolulu to be educated; two others were sent to a brother in Charlestown, North Carolina. From Charlestown, Fitch received a letter, dated July 4, 1841, in which the following was appended:

My Dear Brother: Having left a little space thought I would fill it up just to tell you we love your little boys dearly and Henry is called the best behaved boy in the village. I never had occasion to give him a sour word and as to strike him, I should as soon think of cutting my right hand off. He says the reason he did not use to give you an answer was because he was so frightened he could not; he says he likes the schools here, for they do not flog boys to make them learn. He says in San Diego it was "flog, flog, flog," all the time and he did not like to go. He nor Fred, have not the least desire to go back.

At times Fitch became discouraged with the lax and indifferent Californians, and in a letter to a business associate in 1842, from Los Angeles, he mentioned that he was sailing for the windward ports, or the Islands, and would touch at Santa Barbara, San Luis and Monterey, and try to make collections:

I am tired of running after them. I have been out to Williams', Bandini's, Palomares and . . . they all promise to pay but God knows when . . . I cannot conceive how you could trust so many vagabonds. There are upwards of forty, and some of them such as Leonardo Cota and others I think will never pay.

There were others, though, who saw over the horizon and envisioned the California to come. One of them was the young trapper Jonathan Trumbull Warner. He had been in California only a few years, when he returned to the United States and went on the lecture platform to describe for wondering Americans a new land lying beyond the deserts and mountains of the West. His remarks, in which he urged the construction of a railroad from Boston to the mouth of the Columbia River in the Oregon Territory, were printed and reprinted, even in London.

Warner warned that another harbor, presumably San Francisco, would be needed for the defense of Oregon:

Jonathan T. Warner

I am confident that unless Upper California is purchased of Mexico, it will cost the United States a greater sum to defend the Oregon Territory from the rivalry of California, than the purchase would now amount to. For we must not suppose that California is to remain stationary or under the control of the Mexican government, while all the parts of the earth are in movement, if not advancing. It must soon fall to some more enterprising nation than the Mexicans.

The New York Journal of Commerce commented:

Some of his views will perhaps seem extravagant, but extravagance itself can scarcely equal the onward march of civilization and improvement on this continent within the last fifty years, and in indulging his anticipations of the future, he is liable to no graver charge than at the commencement of that period would have been laid at the door of any man who had predicted what has since become a matter of history.

To Catholic California the biggest event of 1841 was the arrival of its first bishop, as a result of the separation of both Upper and Lower California from the jurisdiction of the Bishop of Sonora. Pope Gregory XVI appointed Fr. García Diego y Moreno as bishop and assigned him to San Diego.

The news of his impending arrival with his retinue of twelve aboard the English vessel *Rosalind* from San Blas, created considerable excitement and the *alcalde* ordered the streets of San Diego cleared of cattle.

The great day was December 10. The *Rosalind* dropped anchor at night and a friar went ashore to notify the military commander and to make preparations for a reception. Two cannons were fired to announce the good news to all who could hear. The Bishop went ashore the following day, and was borne in a sedan chair to the spacious home of Juan Bandini. The Bishop took a look around at the muddy pueblo and penned a note:

San Diego, December 12, 1841. My Son, Brother and most beloved Father—Yesterday I reached this insignificant town in good and sound health, thanks be to God . . .

With the Bishop came a number of school teachers and attendants, one of whom was Fr. Francisco Sánchez, whom Helen Hunt Jackson later made famous in her novel *Ramona* as Fr. Salvierderra. It was obvious that San Diego, with a population of perhaps 150 persons and with a mission church falling into decay, was no place for the seat of such a large diocese and the residence of the Bishop of California. After administering the Sacrament of Confirmation to 125 young people at the old presidial chapel, he departed by ship for Santa Barbara. He never saw San Diego again.

On one of his trips south, Capt. Fitch's trading ship put into Mazatlán and he learned about a new governor for California, Gen. Manuel Micheltorena, who had fought with Gen. Santa Anna in Texas, and had arrived at Tepic, near the port of San Blas, with a military force of convicts and some regular soldiers, who, presumably, were along to guard the convicts. "California," wrote Capt. Fitch, "will be in a devil of a mess after their arrival." The relative peace in California was about to come to an end. The central government of Mexico had begun to fear the growing domination of California affairs by foreigners and had decided to re-establish its authority over the distant provinces. Micheltorena was given extraordinary powers and even allowed to "select" the convicts for his "army." It was accompanied by the usual female camp followers.

The new governor and his army, beset by desertions, embarked at Mazatlán in four ships. The general arrived at San Diego on August 25, 1842. With him were Col. Agustín Zamorano, in a dying condition, and Capt. Nicanor Estrada, both of whom had played such leading roles in the rebellions in Southern California. The ships arrived separately over a period of nine days. Many of the convicts died on the long sea voyage and others were seasick or disgruntled. None of the reports agree as to how many actually reached here, the estimates ranging all the way from 300 to 600.

Alfred Robinson the American hide merchant, was at San Diego when the general arrived, and his own ship had to fire the salute as the guns of Fort Guijarros had been dismounted and there was no powder in San Diego. Five days later he watched the landing of the first ninety soldiers and their families:

I saw them land, and to me they presented a state of wretchedness and misery unequalled. Not one individual among them possessed a jacket or pantaloons; but naked, and like the savage Indians, they concealed their nudity

Gov. Manuel Micheltorena

54

with dirty, miserable blankets. The females were not much better off; for the scantiness of their mean apparel was too apparent for modest observers. They appeared like convicts; and, indeed, the greater portion of them had been charged with the crime either of murder or theft. And these were the *soldiers* sent to subdue this happy country! These were to be the enforcers of justice and good government! Alas! poor California! when such are to be thy ministers, thou art indeed fallen!

The Diegueños locked up their women and hid everything they could, but the ragged and hungry convicts stripped gardens and seized anything else they could find. Micheltorena managed to clothe them in white uniforms and tried to have them kept busy marching and drilling in the Plaza. It was a period of terror for San Diego.

At last, in late September, Micheltorena and his *cholos*, as they were contemptuously called, started northward, and after a long stay at Los Angeles they arrived at San Fernando, where they received some startling news — a United States fleet had captured Monterey and war was under way.

This unexpected turn of events had come about as the result of a report received by Commodore Thomas Ap Catesby Jones, USN, commanding an American fleet, that war had broken out between Mexico and the United States. Fearing that California might be seized by the English, he sailed north from Peru with the *USS Cyane,* a ship San Diego would come to know very well, and the *USS United States*. The men o'war put into Monterey harbor on October 19, 1842, and "captured" the town. Micheltorena fired a lot of angry words from the safe vantage point of San Fernando, and then prudently retired to Los Angeles.

At San Diego, when Capt. W. D. Phelps of the American hide ship *Alert* learned of the capture of Monterey, and heard that Micheltorena had dispatched a force of his ex-convicts to San Diego to seize the ship and its cargo and all other American property, he began loading 30,000 hides stored at La Playa.

Phelps, who was the author of the often-quoted *"Fore and Aft,"* described how the Americans spiked the guns of Fort Guijarros, in the following words:

> There were five beautiful long brass eighteens and three iron twenty-fours in the battery, but no garrison; therefore, to spike the guns, pick up a barrel of copper shot that would fit the ship's guns, and throw all the rest overboard, was not a difficult job.

The *Alert* had six guns placed in position to command the route to the fort along the high bank on the bay side of Point Loma. The next day five canoes of otter hunters, two Americans in each canoe, including George Nidever and "Black Steward," sought refuge aboard with $4000 worth of furs. Phelps remarked that they were

Hide Ship Alert

expert rifle shots. Half of the ship's cargo had been loaded when word came that the war had been a mistake. Commodore Jones had apologized, hauled down the United States flag, and restored Monterey to Mexico. But the die really had been cast and the American acquisition of California was not far away. Micheltorena assumed the governorship and found that the territorial treasury contained exactly twenty-five cents.

The first immigrant train started for California from Missouri in 1841, under the leadership of John Bartleson and John Bidwell. In later years Bidwell recalled how the members of the expedition had been stirred by the report of a trapper, Antoine Robidoux:

Robidoux described California as a land of perennial spring and boundless fertility, and laid stress on the countless thousands of wild horses and cattle. He told about oranges and hence must have been at Los Angeles or the Mission of San Gabriel a few miles from it. Every conceivable question that we could ask him was answered favorably. Generally the first question which Missourians asked about a country was whether there was any fever or ague. I remember his answer distinctly. He said that there was but one man in California that ever had a chill there and that it was a matter of so much wonderment to the people of Monterey that they went eighteen miles into the country to see him shake.

Nothing could have been more satisfactory on the score of health. He said that the Spanish authorities were most friendly, and that the people were the most hospitable on the globe. That you could travel all over California and it would cost you nothing for horses or feed. Even the Indians were friendly. His description of the country made it seem like a paradise.

More than 500 persons applied to go along but when the train finally was assembled west of present Kansas City there were only sixty-nine men, women and children, with teams of oxen, mules and horses, and $100 in cash. The expedition was pronounced "the most unheard of, foolish, wild goose chase that ever entered into the brain of man." It traversed the Western desert and forced a crossing of the Sierra Nevada Mountains in the cold of October, the people suffering terrible hardships, and finally reached the rich San Joaquin Valley.

In the South, the San Diegans were so busy building up their ranchos that in June of 1842, when another Indian uprising took place, there were only five men in the pueblo capable of bearing arms, and three of them were foreigners. In November, *Alférez* Salazar made his final report on the old presidial company. He had a total force of fourteen men without arms or ammunition to guard the vast territory of Southern California. Gov. Micheltorena did his best to win the confidence and the friendship of the *Californios*. He married his mistress and returned twelve of the twenty-one missions, including San Diego, San Luis Rey, San Juan Capistrano and San Gabriel, to the care of the friars. The church was to retain possession of any remaining property and lands but could not reclaim land that already had been granted. It was an empty gesture. Mission San Diego had only about 100 Indians in its care and San Luis Rey about 400, and the missionaries were old, tired and disheartened and no longer burned with missionary zeal.

But the *cholo* army was too much for California and a revolution broke out in 1844, upon which Micheltorena promised to send his convicts back to Mexico. He didn't, and aided by many Americans, he fought back and captured Los Angeles on January 20, 1845, in a battle in which several men were killed. A second battle followed on February 20 and 21, at Cahuenga Pass, near Los Angeles, in which two horses and a mule were the only casualties. When the foreign riflemen refused to help him, Micheltorena capitulated and agreed to leave California and take his *cholos* with him. The lines with Mexico now were almost completely severed and more Americans were streaming down through the mountain passes. Pío Pico, the old revolutionist from San Diego,

SIGNS OF DRAMATIC CHANGES were in the air when John Charles Fremont undertook his second and third explorations of the Far West for the United States.

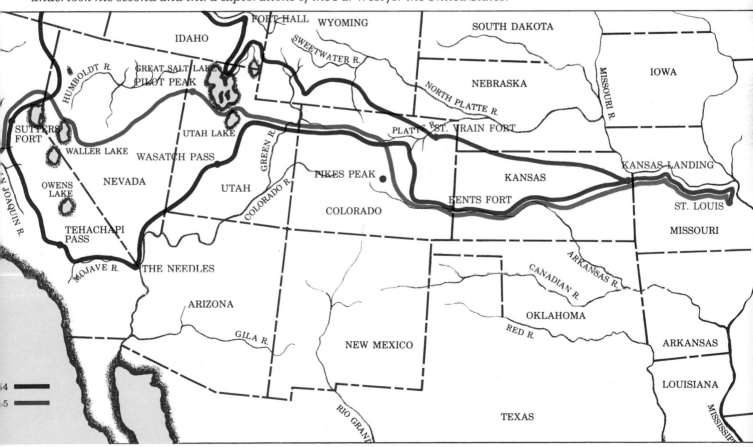

57

took over as ad interim governor and José Castro as military *comandante*. Juan Bandini was designated, for a time, as secretary of state.

The United States was showing increasing interest in the Far West. A young lieutenant of the Army Topographical Engineers, John C. Frémont, in 1842 led a mapping expedition to the famed South Pass in the Rocky Mountains. The next year, as a captain, he led a second expedition to explore the country south of the Columbia River and lying between the Rockies and the Pacific Ocean, in which he was joined by Kit Carson. On March 8, 1844, he reached the trading post and the fort of John Sutter on the Sacramento River. He went south into the great inland valleys, out through Tehachapi Pass and crossed the Mojave Desert and followed the Old Spanish Trail eastward. The next year he was back once more, with instructions to find a shorter route to Oregon, and again joined by Kit Carson, he crossed Utah and Nevada into Northern California.

CHAPTER FOUR

"Welcome was here with bright and lingering glow
Of happy care-free days of Mexico.
All doors were open, every table spread,
And ever, everywhere a waiting bed."

RISE OF THE RANCHOS

The warm sun of California lighted the flowering of a pastoral scene that would leave its magic and legends for generations yet to come. For 400 miles, from San Diego to Monterey, California became a vast, unfenced grazing ground. Silver ornaments from Mexico grew heavier on trappings of the horses which the landed Dons rode through the seas of wild mustard which drowned the hills in blazing yellow. They built rambling ranch houses and yet maintained their homes in the towns, and all doors were open to every visitor.

Alvarado and Micheltorena continued the policy of granting public lands, as was done throughout all of Mexico, in conformance with the old Spanish principle which had recognized the Crown as the owner of all colonial possessions. With Pico it was a problem of finding enough deserving people to reward.

Many land grants were held provisionally, others were claimed and then abandoned for one reason or another, and still other large sections were merely occupied and used, or, in some cases, token tracts granted to Indians for their maintenance were appropriated in exchange for liquor or sacks of goods.

The applicant for a land grant needed only to provide assurance he was a Mexican citizen, submit a *diseño*, or map, giving the approximate boundaries and describing natural landmarks, and promise to occupy the land, build a house on it, and stock it with

THE HIDE HOUSES at La Playa, and Old Town as seen from Point Loma, were painted in water colors by a sailor on the USS Cyane, *William H. Meyers.*

some cattle. No payment of any kind was required. The final act of possession was carried out by local officials. The taking over of the first land grant in San Diego, Los Peñasquitos, by Capt. Ruiz, in 1823, was described by Capt. Pablo de la Portilla:

> . . . I took Señor Ruiz by the hand and led him over it and made him take real and personal possession of said tract which he did take quietly and peacefully. I did cast stones to the four winds and made other acts of real possession. I, the above commissioned officer, ordered in the name of His Majesty, whom God may protect, that no one shall dispute in any manner the above mentioned Ruiz in his possession of said tract, called Peñasquitos, which the aforesaid Francisco María Ruiz has taken and which he shall not be dispossessed without being first heard and through legal right under the penalty of two hundred dollars the payment of which I now condemn whoever shall disturb him in possession . . .

The old Spanish league contained 4,439 acres, and a maximum grant was supposed to be eleven leagues. In time maps were not required. The only surveys were those made by "practical men" on horseback with lariats, sometimes only of fifty *varas*, or approximately 137 1/2 feet, in length, with stakes on each end. A horseman would plant one stake while another rode off at full speed to the length of the rope and set the second stake. This would be repeated until the land between natural landmarks was measured off. Landmarks were hills, conjunctions of creeks, groups of trees or even single trees. If natural markers were lacking, stones were placed in piles or sticks casually driven into the ground.

Wherever there was water there was a ranch, from the coastal mesas which are cut here and there by the intermittent streams of California, to the broad upland valleys which are enriched by mountain snows.

Los Peñasquitos Rancho, which followed the narrow Peñasquitos Canyon and Creek into the low foothills, and consisted of 8,486 acres, passed into the possession of Francisco María Alvarado, a builder of one of the earliest homes in Old Town, in 1837. Before his death Capt. Ruiz transferred it to Alvarado in compensation for board and care while in failing health. Alvarado also claimed, through a grant from the interim governorship of Carrillo in 1838, the town commons in Soledad Valley. Los Peñasquitos Canyon opens into Soledad Valley. This claim was never recognized, however.

Marriage was a route to plenty. John Forster, the English trader who came to California by way of Guaymas, married Doña Isadora Pico, one of the sisters of Pío Pico who had escaped the Jamul massacre, and in 1845 came into possession of the government ranch, La Nación, which had been used by José Antonio

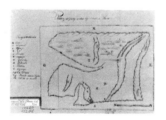

Rancho Los Peñasquitos, as claimed by Francisco María Alvarado

THIS QUAINT DRAWING depicts a California wedding party of 1845, and was made for the first manuscript of Davis' book "Seventy-Five Years in California."

Estudillo for grazing cattle for a number of years. It was a stroke of good fortune that his father-in-law was governor of California. This tract of 26,631 acres, lying on both sides of the Sweetwater River, adjoined the pueblo lands of San Diego on the south. The area now embraces the cities of National City and Chula Vista.

The Estudillo family held the nearby Otay and Janal Ranchos, two of the earliest land grants in San Diego, dating back to 1829 and the governorship of José María Echeandía. Janal Rancho had 4,436 acres and Otay Rancho 6,657.

The order by Micheltorena restoring some of the missions to the care of the padres, and which had left the San Diego Mission with the ranchos of El Cajon and Santa Ysabel, was ignored by Pico.

Miguel de Pedrorena, the sea trader from Lima, married María Antonia Estudillo, a daughter of José Antonio Estudillo. It was María and not Miguel, however, who in 1845 received El Cajon

63

Joseph Snook's Casa

Rancho San Bernardo, as claimed by María Antonio Snook

Rancho, the richest grazing ground of the San Diego Mission. This was a tract of 48,799 acres, embracing what is now El Cajon, Bostonia, Santee, Lakeside and Flinn Springs, between the eastern edge of La Mesa and El Monte Park, and lying, in part, along the San Diego River. Pedrorena became a rancher as well as merchant.

The English sailor Edward Stokes and his father-in-law, José Joaquín Ortega, acquired two large ranchos, Santa María Valley in 1843, and Santa Ysabel Valley, the site of the *asistencia* of the San Diego Mission, in 1844. Santa María Rancho, or Valle de Pamo, was a grant of 17,708 acres, and the present town of Ramona, thirty-eight miles from San Diego, is situated in its central portion. Santa Ysabel is a well-watered valley, and until taken from the Mission had a large Indian population. The grant contained 17,719 acres.

Jonathan Trumbull Warner, now back in California after his visit to the United States, acquired San José Valley, a property of San Luis Rey Mission known as Agua Caliente and now as Warner's Ranch. It had been held previously by Capt. Portilla and José Antonio Pico, another brother of Pío Pico, and divided into two ranchos. They apparently abandoned them because of continual troubles with the Indians, and so, in 1844, Warner filed a petition for the entire valley, or 44,323 acres. Warner never married into a Spanish-Mexican family. He became a Mexican citizen, however, taking the name of Juan José Warner, and married Anita Gale, the daughter of an English sea captain who had been left in the care of the Pico family while she was still a young girl. Warner went into business as a rancher and operator of a trading post and he soon found himself astride an important immigrant route. He became known as "Juan Largo", or Long John.

Another one of the English mariners, Capt. Joseph Snook, was naturalized in 1833 and while he was still engaged in the coastal shipping trade, had the foresight to marry María Antonia Alvarado, the daughter of Juan Bautista Alvarado. He was captain of the ship which transported Isaac Graham and his exiled hunters to San Blas and was at Monterey when it was "captured" by Commodore Jones. As early as 1842 he received a grant of two square leagues along the upper San Dieguito River, and three years later received an adjoining tract of the same size from Gov. Pico. With that, he quit the sea and settled down on his princely estate of 17,763 acres known as St. Bernardo Rancho, which stretched along the rolling land on both sides of what is now Highway 395, from north of Lake Hodges south to Peñasquitos Creek.

Capt. Snook's father-in-law held El Rincón del Diablo Rancho, 12,653 acres adjoining St. Bernardo on the north and now the site of the city of Escondido with its fine surrounding farm lands and citrus groves. He received it in 1843 from Gov. Micheltorena.

The Arguellos had cast their eyes to the south. Santiago, the elder, claimed a large acreage below the present international border, Rancho Ti Juan, his grant dating back as early as 1829. Here, in time, rose the squatter town of Tijuana and the resort area of Agua Caliente. During the Mexican years that area was considered the frontier and the ranch was abandoned from time to time because of lack of protection from the Indians. In one such period José Antonio Aguirre instituted proceedings to gain control of the property, but the governor gave Arguello six months in which to re-occupy the ranch, which he did.

His son, Santiago Emilio Arguello, was handed a section of Upper California by Gov. José Figueroa in 1833. This was Rancho Milijo, located along El Camino Real south of San Diego Bay, and evidently running into his father's property in Mexico, and which eventually became identified as La Punta. The home that he built appears on the first maps made by the Americans, but its hilltop site has been covered by the freeway from San Diego to Tijuana. He never was able to substantiate his right to this as well as to other properties. Rancho Milijo was estimated to have included more than thirty square miles. In the area now are the communities of Otay, Palm City, Nestor and San Ysidro. The Machado family of San Diego also came into possession of lands below the Arguello Ranch in Lower California.

Throughout so many of the grants in Southern California runs the name of Pico. Pío Pico had held Jamul since 1831, but as he was rarely there, it was left in charge of his brother, Andrés. The limitation on grants of eleven leagues was forgotten. In 1841 Pío and Andrés received from their old enemy, Gov. Alvarado, the largest grant of them all, Rancho San Onofre y Santa Margarita, consisting of 89,742 acres along the coast in northwestern San Diego County. Three years later, in 1844, they added another section known as Las Flores. They now had 133,440 acres stretching twenty miles along the Pacific Coast, from the city of Oceanside north to the Orange County line near San Clemente, and rising eastward into the coastal mountains. Las Flores was acquired by the Picos by the simple device of having a grant issued in the name of an Indian, Pablo Apis, who was living in the starving Indian pueblo of Las Flores, and then transferring title to themselves. The United States Marines were to acquire a large portion of the land during World War II.

After long effort Juan María Osuna, the first *alcalde* of San Diego, in 1845, was able to obtain absolute title to the San Die-

Rancho Santa Margarita and Las Flores, as claimed by Pío Pico

Juliana López Osuna used crayon to locate family home on San Dieguito Rancho

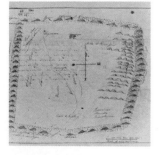

Rancho Cuyamaca, as claimed by Agustín Olvera

guito Rancho, the 8,824 acres which became known as Rancho Santa Fe, about twenty-five miles north of San Diego and inland from the sea about three miles. Osuna had obtained possession of the property in 1836, and provisional grants were made to him in 1840 and 1841. His daughter Felipa married Juan María Marrón, a son of a frontier settler, who always managed to hold a public post of some kind at one time or another, and who acquired the nearby Agua Hedionda Rancho, just south and east of the present town of Carlsbad and along US Highway 101. It contained 13,311 acres. Northward from San Dieguito Rancho was the grant of the dram shop owner, Andrés Ybarra, which was known as Las Encinitas Rancho. The one square league of 4,431 acres was inland from the coast and east of the present town of Encinitas.

Los Vallecitos de San Marcos, 8,877 acres of valley land west of El Rincón del Diablo Rancho, was granted to José María Alvarado in 1840 but eventually became the property of Lorenzo Soto and in modern times the site of the town of San Marcos. La Cañada de Los Coches, the smallest land grant in California, consisting of only 28.39 acres, on present Highway 80 just west of Flinn Springs and in the center of El Cajon Rancho, was granted in 1843 to *La Beata*, Doña Apolinaria Lorenzana, who also owned Jamacha Rancho. The mission fathers formerly watered their swine in dry seasons at a little spring arising from subterranean sources, thus giving it its name of Glen of the Hogs. Pauma Rancho, 13,309 acres southeast of the Pala Mission, and watered by the San Luis Rey River, was granted in 1844 to José Antonio Serrano. Buena Vista Rancho, 1,184 acres surrounding the present town of Vista, was granted to an Indian named Felipe, in 1845, but it was not to remain with him for very long. Cuca Rancho, 2,174 acres south of Palomar Mountain, was granted to María Juana de Los Angeles in 1845. In the same year Gov. Pico gave Cuyamaca Rancho, a mountainous area now embracing Cuyamaca State Park and Cuyamaca Lake, to Agustín Olvera who had married his niece, Concepción Arguello, but the boundaries were vague and much of the country was inaccessible in bad weather. Disputes over this territory were to last for many years. Olvera resided in Los Angeles and historic Olvera Street still bears his name.

Two Indians of San Luis Rey Mission, Andrés and José Manuel, were granted Guajome Rancho east of the Mission and lying between the present towns of Vista and Bonsall, in 1845. This grant of 2,219 acres soon passed into the hands of an American merchant, Abel Stearns, of Los Angeles, who married a daughter of Juan Bandini. The Bear Valley district northeast of Escondido, known as Rancho Guejito y Cañada de Palomía, consisting of 13,298 acres, was granted in 1845 to José María Orozco, who had served as a justice of the peace and collector of customs in San Diego. Juan López, who also built one of the early homes in Old Town, near that of his friend, Santiago Arguello, took over the San Vicente and Padre Barona Valleys, which lie south of Ramona and northeast of Lakeside. This tract of 13,316 acres was known as Cañada de San Vicente Rancho.

In a rare gesture of consideration, the government denied a petition of Bonifacio López for grazing rights in San Pasqual Valley, on the upper San Dieguito River, where a small band of Christian Indians had been re-settled in their own "pueblo" of mud and grass shacks after the secularization of the San Diego Mission.

Rancho Los Encinitos, as claimed by Andrés Ybarra

Juan Bandini was not fortunate with his property and he finally abandoned Tecate Rancho below the border and transferred his interests to areas north of San Diego and into Lower California. Pico reached down into Baja California to grant to Bandini the lands of the last mission built in the Californias, Guadalupe, fifty miles below Tecate and founded in 1834 by the Dominicans. It is now the site of a religious colony which fled from Russia. Bandini also was to lay claim to the offshore islands of Santa Catalina and Santa Cruz.

Other ranchos, and the owners or occupants, were: Cueros de Venado, J. M. Marrón; Jeus, M. I. López; Paguai, Rosario Aguilar; San Antonio Abad, Santiago E. Arguello; San Ysidro, José López, and Secuán, probably in Lower California, Juan López. Only one of these went before the U.S. Land Commission.

The end of the mission system had brought some fear to the Boston hide traders who had depended on the mission ranchos for the great shipments of leather for the factories of New England. Alfred Robinson, in his *"Life in California,"* wrote:

At first, the change was considered disastrous to the prosperity of California, and the wanton destruction of property which followed, seemed to warrant the conclusion; but the result, however, proved quite the contrary. Individual enterprise, which succeeded, has placed the country in a more flourishing condition, and the wealth, instead of being confined to the monastic institutions, as before, has been distributed among the people.

The liberality of the Californians, since their first opposition to Mexico, has induced many foreigners to settle in the country, and several hundreds of Americans may be already found located at different points. Their industrious habits have procured for them many very promising settlements, where the lands, under the judicious management, produce abundance, and contribute greatly to the beauty of the surrounding country.

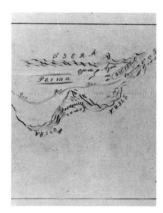

Rancho Pauma, as claimed by José A. Serrano

Nostalgia always has gripped those who looked back on this period in California's history. William Heath Davis, in his *"Seventy-five Years in California,"* wrote:

Rancho Cuca, as claimed by María Juana de los Angeles

Dress of the Señorita of 1820

When the rancheros . . . rode about, during the leisure season, which was between the marking time and the *matanza*, or killing time, and from the end of the *matanza* to the spring time again, the more wealthy of them were generally dressed in a good deal of style, with short breeches extending to the knee, ornamented with gold or silver lace at the bottom, with *botas* (leggings) below, made of fine soft deer skin, well tanned and finished, richly colored, and stamped with beautiful devices (these articles having been imported from Mexico, where they were manufactured), and tied at the knee with a silk cord, two or three times wound around the leg, with heavy gold or silver tassels hanging below the knee. They wore long vests, with filagree buttons of gold or silver, while those of more ordinary means had them of brass. They wore no long coats, but a kind of jacket of good length, most generally of dark blue cloth, also adorned with filagree buttons. Over that was the long *serape* or *poncho*, made in Mexico and imported from there, costing from $20 to $100, according to the quality of the cloth and the richness of the ornamentation.

The *serape* was always plain, while the *poncho* was heavily trimmed with gold or silver fringe around the edges, and a little below the collars around the shoulders.

They wore hats imported from Mexico and Peru, generally stiff; the finer quality of softer material—*vicuña*, a kind of beaver skin obtained in those countries. Their saddles were silver-mounted, embroidered with silver or gold, the bridle heavily mounted with silver, and the reins made of the most select hair of the horse's mane, and at a distance of every foot or so there was a link of silver connecting the different parts together.

Behind the saddle, and attached thereto, was the *anqueta*, of leather, of half-moon shape, covering the top of the hindquarters of the horse, but not reaching to the tail; which was also elaborately stamped with figures and lined with sheep skin, the wool side next to the horse.

The stirrups were cut out of a solid block of wood, about two and a half inches in thickness. They were very large and heavy . . . Their spurs were inlaid with gold and silver, and the straps of the spurs worked with silver and gold thread.

When thus mounted and fully equipped, these men presented a magnificent appearance, especially on the feast days of the Saints, which were celebrated at the Missions. Then they were arrayed in their finest and most costly habiliments, and their horses in their gayest and most expensive trappings. They were usually large, well developed men, and presented an imposing aspect. The outfit of a ranchero and his horse, thus equipped, I have known to cost several thousand dollars.

The styles of women's dress changed but little over many years until the rise in trade brought the latest styles from Mexico City. Families were large but there were plenty of servants. The women, though small of stature, exerted strong domination over family life. Pío Pico once said that until he was twenty-six years of age "I was in complete subjugation to my mother, my father being dead. When younger I could repeat the whole catechism from beginning to end, and she would send for me to do so for the edification of strangers." Children were almost as plentiful as the cattle on the range. Juan Bandini had ten children; Joaquín Carrillo, twelve; Santiago Arguello, twenty-two; José Arguello, thirteen; Domingo Carrillo, eight; José Antonio Estudillo, eight, and José María Ortega, eleven. There were Indians to serve as

THE FIESTA was a way of life in early California. This scene, of costumed horsemen and carretas was painted many years later by Alexander F. Harmer.

cooks and maids, to wash and clean, and to attend individually to the wants of even the youngest child.

Days were made pleasant with sports of various kinds. There was cock fighting, horse racing and bear hunting, and the Plaza in Old Town would be fenced upon occasion for days of amateur bull fighting and the cruel bear-and-bull fights.

The population of the San Diego district began to grow once more. By 1845 there were perhaps 350 white persons, native-born and foreign, in the area of San Diego. There were now probably forty or so houses in the pueblo and the larger ones had wooden floors and furnishings brought all the way across the Pacific Ocean from China and the Philippines, or around the Horn from Eastern United States. With military protection absent, a militia was organized under the command of Andrés Pico as captain. In the same year Upper California was divided into two districts, with the first district, Los Angeles, including everything from San Luis Obispo south and having three *partidos* of which San Diego was the third. Each *partido* was to have a sub-prefect, and for San Diego, the appointment went to Santiago Arguello. The sub-prefect succeeded to the authority which had been vested in justices of the peace who had continued, however, to be referred to as *alcaldes*.

The hide trade went on as before, Boston vessels taking as many as 40,000 hides at a time from the houses at La Playa where they had been cured and stored after being collected up and down the coast. With heavy imports, the market in Boston drifted up and down, and at one time, Alfred Robinson, who was in New York in 1844 in connection with his duties as a supercargo, or shipping agent, wrote that the ship *California*, which had sailed from San Diego, "still lies at the wharf in Boston, her hides unsold and the owners awaiting better prices . . . hides are worth from 10c to 10-3/4c." Generally shippers expected about one hide for each dollar they invested in wares to be sold in San Diego and other coastal ports.

American whalers appeared in increasing numbers. At least eight of them put into San Diego Bay, in the period from 1842 to 1845, for repairs and supplies, and, in some cases to sell merchandise to pay for outfitting before returning home. One whaler from New London, Conn., in 1843, received permission from the Prefect at Los Angeles to make repairs at San Diego but was refused a license to hunt whales in the bay. It did so anyway, evidently, for Manuel Domínguez, the justice of the peace, received a letter from the Prefect demanding to know who had granted permission.

The American settler who became the first United States consul at San Francisco, Thomas O. Larkin, and who often engaged in trading deals with Capt. Fitch, in a letter to the Secretary of State, wrote in 1844:

In all probability, within three years there will be six hundred American ships, with twenty thousand seamen, engaged in the whale fishery on the Northwest Coast of America. The ports of California offer many inducements to those thus engaged, to put in for fresh provisions and to recruit the health of sick on board.

Less than six months later, his prediction was confirmed, according to a letter he wrote, as a correspondent, to the *New York Journal of Commerce:*

By almost every newspaper from the United States and many from England we find extracts and surmises respecting the sale of this country. One month England is the purchaser, the next month the United States. In the meantime the progress of California is onward, and would still be more so if Mexico would not send every few years a band of thieving soldiers and rapacious officers . . .

Candle Lantern

70

the whole foreign trade of California is in the hands of Americans. There now (are) 500 to 1000 American whalers with 20,000 seamen in the Pacific. Half of them will be within twenty days' sail of San Francisco.

He noted that there were 1000 to 1200 foreigners in California:

Many of them never expect to speak the prevailing language of the country. At this . . . period a knowledge of the English language is to a merchant of more importance than the Spanish . . . A person traveling from San Diego to San Francisco . . . can stop at a foreigner's farm house almost every few hours, and travel without knowledge of the Spanish language . . . The laws of Mexico are but little respected, and observed only when they are for the interest of this country.

He saw the leading men of San Diego in a different light than did their political enemies. He described Juan Bandini as a man of wealth, information and influence, of good standing and studious disposition.

In a letter to Secretary of State James Buchanan, he wrote:

Ninety miles (by sea) south of San Diego there are some very extensive copper mines belonging to Don Juan Bandini. There is no doubt but that gold, silver, quicksilver, copper, lead, sulphur and coal mines are to be found all over California . . . the Indians always have said there was (sic) mines in the country but would not show their location; and the Californians did not choose to look for them.

Capt. Fitch, he wrote, was "a man of wealth, some influence, of medium information, not of a political character in general." John Warner "has much land and some cattle. A man of active life, good information, some influence, will have more. Addicted to politics." As for José Antonio Aguirre, the merchant and ship owner from Spain, he was "a man of wealth and information, correct and formal. Has much influence among the Spaniards in this country, the same with clergy. Converses but not connected in politics."

Larkin, encouraged by Buchanan and working secretly with a number of Californians, including Warner, sought to bring about in an orderly way an independent California which eventually could seek the protection of the United States. But other events were to intervene.

In Washington and Mexico City, the issue of Texas reached a climax. The independence of Texas had never been recognized by Mexico, and its admission into the Union late in 1845 triggered an outbreak of hostilities. On May 13, 1846, President Polk signed a bill declaring that a state of war existed between the United States and Mexico. A "Manifest Destiny" began to unfold.

Within four days rumors of the declaration of war reached Commodore John D. Sloat and a United States fleet then in the harbor of Mazatlán, Mexico. The ships slipped by a British fleet and headed out to sea.

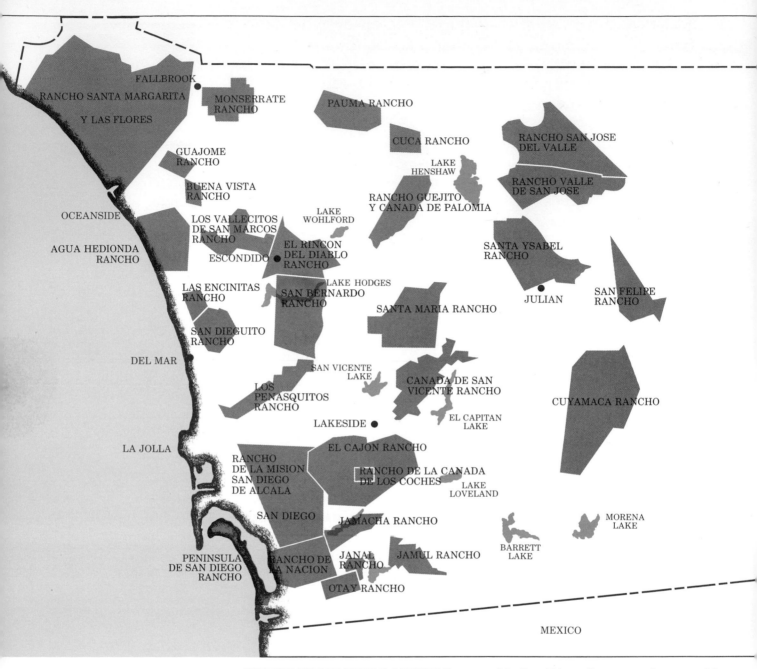

THESE WERE THE RANCHOS granted in San Diego County and patented by the United States. A number of other claims were rejected or never submitted.

Frémont, the American military officer supposedly engaged in exploration and mapping, moved his rugged adventurers too near the coast, in violation of a pledge he made to Gen. José Castro, and in June, in the charged atmosphere, a band of Americans led by a rawboned frontiersman named Ezekiel Merritt seized some horses that had been collected for Castro. In the ensuing excitement, settlers in the Sacramento and Napa Valleys began an insurrection in which they raised a crude Bear Flag at Sonoma and proclaimed the Republic of California. In less than a month the new "republic" had withered away.

Pío Pico, with history rushing upon him, had hastened to dispose of the rest of the mission properties. He auctioned off San Juan Capistrano Mission on December 4, 1845, to John Forster and James McKinley, for $710.

California Bear Flag

Five months later, on May 15, 1846, he gave away land many believed to be within the pueblo boundaries in granting Coronado and North Island to Pedro C. Carrillo, the son of Carlos Antonio Carrillo, who was *receptor* or collector of customs at San Diego and who had married Josefa, another daughter of Juan Bandini. The grant of 4,185 acres was known as Peninsula de San Diego Rancho.

The two islands are connected to the mainland by a narrow causeway of sand to form the protecting arm of San Diego Bay. They were covered with grass and wild poppies, and Carrillo said he needed them as grazing grounds for his cattle. They are now the site of the City of Coronado and the United States Naval Air Station.

Three days later, on May 18, the mission which Pico had helped despoil, San Luis Rey, once the most populous and most prosperous of all the missions of California, was sold to his brother, José Antonio, and Antonio José Cot, for $2437.

Monserrate Rancho, 13,322 acres south and east of Fallbrook, was granted to Ysidro María Alvarado, and San Felipe Rancho, 9,972 acres in San Felipe Valley, east of the mountains and on the old Sonora route from Mexico to California, was granted to an Indian by the name of Felipe Castillo, but eventually passed into possession of John Forster. Ramón Osuna, son of the first *alcalde*, tried to claim Valle de las Viejas, between Alpine and Descanso.

On June 8, Pico signed a deed conveying the mother mission of California, San Diego, and all its remaining lands, 58,875 acres from the pueblo boundary inland to El Cajon Valley, and from National City to Clairemont, now the major residential areas of San Diego, to Santiago Arguello in payment for past services, whatever they might have been.

After performing the last recorded baptism, on June 14, Fr. Oliva left the unhappy Mission of San Diego and retired to San Juan Capistrano. At San Luis Rey, Fr. José María de Zalvidea, who previously had toiled for twenty years at Mission San Gabriel, and was regarded by the Indians almost as a saint, was in his last days. Felipa Osuna de Marrón remembered how he pierced his feet with nails, until he hardly had any toes left, and knelt on the ground in the fields and taunted bulls to attack him. He died sometime in June and was buried on the gospel side of the main altar at San Luis Rey.

On June 30, Colonel Stephen Watts Kearny left Fort Leavenworth, Kansas, to lead the Army of the West on the Santa Fe Trail to California. On July 2, Commodore John D. Sloat arrived at Monterey from Mazatlán and after an unexplained delay of five days, disclosed to the Californians that war between Mexico and the United States had already begun, and proceeded to raise the Stars and Stripes. Two days later a courier brought the news to Frémont.

CHAPTER FIVE

"We're the boys for Mexico
Sing Yankee Doodle Dandy,
Gold and silver images
Plentiful and handy."

Cyane off the coast of California

A MANIFEST DESTINY

San Diegans went to Mass on the morning of July 26, in the chapel in the great house of José Antonio Estudillo, as they had done every Sunday since the abandonment of the little church in the Presidio. Only mounds of adobe marked the place where the first Christian service in California had been conducted by Fr. Junípero Serra in 1769.

They knew that Mexico was at war and that a time of change had come. No resistance as yet had been offered in California. A few had hoped that California would fall to England. Others had wanted independence. Most were apprehensive for the continued possession of the lands for which they had struggled against church and state for so many years. A few even saw themselves cast adrift as were the Indians. As for San Diego, it had been under American influence for several generations because of being the center of the hide trade for California. A dozen foreigners now resided in Old Town and at times a score or more of others lived in the hide houses and surrounding shacks at La Playa.

The turn of fortune had put at least four more Americans in the area at the time of the outbreak of hostilities. They were Albert B. Smith, Bill Marshall, Peter Wilder and Philip Crosthwaite. Smith's background and manner of arrival are not known. Marshall deserted the whale ship *Hopewell*, from Providence, R. I., took up life with Indians in the mountains, married a native girl,

THE USS CYANE, whose Marines and Naval officer raised the first American flag over San Diego, as sketched by William Meyers, a member of her crew.

John Drake Sloat

Samuel F. du Pont

and came to an end on a hangman's rope in the Plaza. Wilder may have been in the San Diego area for some years, before the first mention of his name appears. He may have been the "P. Wilde" who was hired to search for deserters by the captain of the hide ship *Admittance* in 1844. In June of 1846 he married Guadalupe Machado and purchased the house of Andrés Ybarra. Crosthwaite was a native of Ireland, and though his family migrated to America while he was still a child, he was sent to Dublin for his education. On his return to the United States he shipped as a crewman on a vessel which he later insisted he thought was sailing for Newfoundland. Instead, he was taken to the Pacific and either deserted or was allowed to leave the ship at San Diego. He was otter hunting in Lower California with Julian Ames and William Curley, when they learned war had begun.

The conciliatory Commodore Sloat had been replaced in command of the conquest by Commodore Robert F. Stockton whose proclamations and aggressive attitude were beginning to stir resentments. Pío Pico and Gen. José Castro convoked the territorial assembly in Los Angeles, and decided to organize a militia and call upon every man in California to do his duty. That was on July 24. Pico appealed to Juan Bandini to join the assembly but he pleaded ill health though affirming his patriotism as a true Mexican.

On that same Sunday, July 26, when San Diegans went to Mass in the dread of uncertain times, the twenty-two gun American corvette, *USS Cyane,* set sail from Monterey for San Diego. Capt. Samuel F. du Pont in a letter dated August 4, to his wife, wrote:

According to orders I sailed at 8 o'clock on Sunday morning, the time from daylight having been occupied in embarking, by means of all the boats of the squadron, the Cavalry Battalion of Major Frémont consisting of 165 American Arabs of the West . . . fifty of them have been his companions across the Rocky Mountains; the others, American settlers in the Valley of Sacramento . . . His party, of course, could not bring their horses but brought their saddles, packs, etc. Our own number on board is 120. You may conceive the condition of our decks, etc., with the addition of this motley group.

The group included the Bear Flag revolutionists, Kit Carson, and five Delaware Indians who had been serving with Frémont and Capt. Archibald Gillespie, of the United States Marines, who, disguised as a merchant, had carried secret dispatches from President Polk to Frémont and Larkin in California by way of Veracruz, Mazatlán and Hawaii. Frémont's instructions from Stockton were to advance by land, cut off any possibility of Castro's retreat by way of the Colorado River and aid in the capture of Los Angeles.

In his *"Memoirs of My Life,"* Frémont wrote:

My men were all greatly pleased at the novelty of a voyage in a man-of-war
. . . But like many prospective enjoyments this one proved to be all in the
anticipation. By the time we had been a few hours at sea we were all very low
in our minds; and there was none of the expected enjoyment in the sparkling
waves and the refreshing breeze, and the sail along the mountainous shore as
the ship rolled her way down the coast. Carson was among those who were
badly worsted by this enemy to landsmen, and many were the vows made to
the winds that never again would they put trust in the fair-weather promises
of the ocean.

The *Cyane* raised Point Loma on Wednesday, July 29, and Capt.
du Pont wrote:

As we approached the land at a distance of two miles we entered the kelp and
it was a remarkable and beautiful sight, as I remember seeing it . . . no language can convey an idea of this wonderful perfection of nature . . . the bright
sun reflected its striking though grave colors, being all shades of a beautiful
lightbrown and salmon. Though intent on watching the points of land and the
breakers, I could not keep from exclaiming occasionally at so novel and
brilliant a sight.

Capt. du Pont met with difficulty in entering the harbor. Owing
to the wind he could not reach the deepest water, and ugly shoals
could be seen under his lee. They put on more sail, and crossed
the bar with six inches to spare and put into the anchorage at
La Playa in gallant style. Du Pont said Frémont was so excited
he could scarcely breathe.

My orders were to send an officer to wait upon the authorities and propose to
them to hoist the flag. If they declined (which they did) I was to take possession
and defend the place. I dispatched Mr. Rowan with the marines; for I did not
like his going alone, the town of the Presidio being about four miles,
generally called five.

The log of the *Cyane* tells what happened:

At 3:40 the launch *Alligator* under command of Lieutenant Rowan, and the
Marine Guard under Lieutenant Maddox, left the ship to take possession of the
town of San Diego and hoist the American flag.

The two officers were Lt. Stephen C. Rowan, USN, and Lt.
William A. T. Maddox, USMC. It was Lt. Rowan who commanded
the raising of the flag.

More than three hundred years of history came to an end that
day. The green, red and white Mexican flag had flown over San
Diego for only twenty-four years, merely an interlude in the long
possession and occupation of California. San Diego Bay was discovered by Juan Rodríguez Cabrillo in 1542, but 227 years passed
before the Sacred Expedition of Fr. Serra and Gaspar de Portolá
arrived to raise the red and gold flag of Spain and bring Christi-

William Maddox

79

anity to the upper Pacific Coast. Now it was all over, and there were few to weep. Mexico had not been a good stepmother.

Du Pont said they arrived just in time to prevent the sailing of the *Juanita,* a hermaphrodite brig that had entered the bay with a Mexican pass, but immediately upon seeing the *Cyane* hoist her colors, had showed the Hawaiian flag:

> She gave out that she was bound for San Pedro but if the report that Castro is nine miles from here be true, my impression is that he was to have embarked on her this afternoon, if not, to go on board her at some near point on the coast.

He took possession of the ship to cut off Castro's retreat by sea. As soon as sufficient time had been allowed for the raising of the flag at the Plaza, Frémont was landed with a portion of his troops. From the ship, du Pont said they saw horses, some belonging to Americans, being driven away from La Playa by Andrés Pico and that he directed Lt. Rowan to secure him and offer him parole. Andrés evaded capture, though the horses were returned to La Playa. Horses, the captain wrote, are "the sinews of war in this country." Rowan returned to the ship:

> He reports the authorities are with us in feeling, but fearing to compromise themselves in case of the flag coming down, declined active cooperation. Great joy prevailed among women and children at the appearance of our people, they having been kept in constant terror by Castro.

John Charles Frémont

The rest of Frémont's men were landed on the following day, and a report of Castro being in the vicinity was contradicted, and "Andrés Pico left last evening, not having been seen except while the flag of truce was flying."

In a dispatch to Stockton on July 31, du Pont described how he went into the town and was waited upon by the civil authorities who said that while they were friendly toward the movement, they had received their offices from other powers and would have to resign.

> They proposed a meeting of the citizens to appoint their successors, subject to my approval; this, of course, I encouraged, and the meeting was held, but of the persons elected, Capt. Fitch, one of them, declined serving. The late civil authority is therefore at an end in San Diego; but the very small population, their quiet and orderly character, and their friendly feelings toward us, keep me from apprehending much trouble in consequence.

He said there was one exception to the general resignation from office:

> Don Pedro Carrillo, a very prepossessing person, speaking English fluently and a son-in-law of *Señor* Bandini, offered the hospitalities of his house and agreed to continue as administrator of the customs. The people of San Diego have resisted all the appeals of Castro's agents to join him, and are naturally in terror lest before the war be brought to a close, they should be left unprotected.

80

On the same date he informed Stockton:

On going to town Friday, I learned from Major Frémont he had been advised of the possibility of a night attack by Castro and his forces, under the impression the town was defended only by our Marine guard, his troops having reached it only after nightfall on Wednesday, previous to which Andrés Pico had left for the pueblo (Los Angeles). A messenger was immediately dispatched to the ship and in an incredibly short time a reinforcement of about 100 seamen, under Lt. Rowan, came into the town wholly armed and marching like regular troops. A detachment was also left with the launch and gun, to defend the hide houses near the beach. But the enemy did not appear, nor was it possible on reconsideration of the distance for him to have done so.

Don Andrés Pico

The first days passed pleasantly enough. Frémont scouted the interior to obtain horses, finally getting perhaps ninety, about half that were required for the projected march north to capture Los Angeles, and loaded oxcarts with supplies and saddles.

In his *Memoirs*, Frémont continues:

Exploring for horses, we became well acquainted with the general character of this district. Every farm or rancho had its own spring or running stream sufficient for the supply of stock, which hitherto had made the chief object of industry in California. In this neighborhood there are places of extraordinary fertility. Cultivation has always been by irrigation, and the soil seems to require only water to produce vigorously. Among the arid, brush-covered hills south of San Diego we found little valleys converted by a single spring into crowded gardens, where pears, peaches, quinces, pomegranates, grapes, olives, and other fruits grew luxuriantly together, the little stream acting upon them like a principle of life. This southern frontier of Upper California seems eminently adapted to the cultivation of the vine and the olive. A single vine has been known to yield a barrel of wine, and the olive trees are burdened with the weight of fruit.

While we remained between San Diego and Los Angeles during this month, the days were bright and hot, the sky pure and entirely cloudless, and the nights cool and beautifully serene. In this month fruits generally ripen—melons, pears, peaches, prickly-fig (*cactus-tuña*), and others of like kind—and large bunches of ripe grapes are scattered numerously through the vineyards, but do not reach maturity until in September. After the vintage, grapes are hung up in the houses and so kept for use during the winter. On one of these excursions we came upon a pretty spot where the noon-day heat enticed us into making a halt. It was in garden grounds, not far from the house of the rancho, where the water from a little stream was collected in a basin about fifteen feet across, around which ran a low cement-covered wall. Fruit trees, among them pomegranates, hung over the basin, making a cool, pleasant place with the water and shade. With a portion of lamb, which we got at the house and cooked ourselves, we had a hearty luncheon after our own fashion, with appetites the better for their later interruption by the sea.

*Andrés Pico's
Linen Jacket*

Du Pont became well acquainted with the leaders of San Diego:

Don Juan Bandini . . . has long been a friend to this province, but after trying in vain to induce Mexico to pay attention to its interests, by doing something for California . . . is now disgusted, and ready for the change. He is employed on the history of the country, has a good house, three grown daughters by a first wife (two married); has now a second wife much younger than himself, and quite handsome. His house has been thrown open to us, and is the resort of the other society of the place. The single daughter, Doña Isidora, plays well on the harp-guitar and with the ordinary one, they contrive to have music and dancing every night, the *sola diversión* in California. Don Juan, although over sixty, is the most infatigable and active of the dancers, saying it is *muy inocente*. His son-in-law, Don Pedro Carrillo, was educated in Boston and speaks English well. Don Miguel Pedrorena also speaks it fluently. These people are all intelligent and make it a much more agreeable place than Monterey where I saw no society whatsoever.

He visited the old mission, and found it in a mournful state of decay:

The miserable naked Indians were around the piazza. We were received most hospitably by the old padre, a Franciscan, a perfect Friar Tuck, who was what sailors' term 'two sheets in the wind.' . . . We looked at the dilapidated church and tattered paintings. Remains of gardens and vineyards were on either hand and near the latter were the Indians' thatched wigwams. A more miserable and naked sight I never saw. Under a dead bush stuck down to keep off the sun lay an object covered with a sheepskin; a silvery head peeked from under it, laying on the bare ground, the whole shriveled and shrunked half a man's size. It was an old Indian, 110 years old. They seem the last connecting link between the human species and the creation. Indeed the donkeys around their huts seem much more natural.

Frémont and his "American Arabs" left San Diego on August 8 with the major astride "an uncommonly beautiful" sorrel horse which had been presented to him by Bandini with its tail and mane plaited and tied with green ribbons. This was a strange "army." San Diegans have left no description of it but Lt. Fred Walpole, on the *USS Collingwood*, in his book, "*Four Years in the Pacific*," told of seeing Frémont and his men in Northern California:

Here were true trappers. These men had passed years in the wilds, living on their own resources. They were a curious set. A vast cloud of dust appeared first, and thence in long file emerged this wildest wild party. Frémont rode ahead, a spare, active-looking man, with such an eye! He was dressed in a blouse and leggings, and wore a felt hat. After him came five Delaware Indians, who were his body-guard; they had charge of two baggage-horses. The rest, many of them blacker than the Indians, rode two and two, the rifle held by one hand across the pommel of the saddle. Thirty-nine of them are his regular men, the rest are loafers picked up lately. His original men are principally backwoodsmen from Tennessee . . . The dress of these men was principally a long loose coat of deer-skin, tied with thongs in front; trousers of the same, of their manufacture, which, when wet through they take off, scrape well inside with a knife, and put on as soon as dry. The saddles were of various fashions, though these and a large drove of horses, and a brass field-gun, were things they had picked up in California. The rest of the gang were a rough set; and perhaps their private, public, and moral characters had better not be too closely examined. They are allowed no liquor . . . and the discipline is very strict.

Frémont never liked this description and took pains to refute its particulars in his own *Memoirs*.

FREMONT'S INDIAN GUARD and Volunteers are depicted entering Monterey in 1846. His force later was landed at San Diego, for the conquest of Los Angeles.

Instructions to sail for the north and not to leave any force behind, also had been received by du Pont:

> ...in consequence of which the inhabitants of San Diego were in great terror, and were left in a defenseless state. Fortunately, Gillespie remains for some days, until his men can get horses, or I know not how I could have got away from the kind people of the village, who should not have been left that way.

The records are vague. A lone guard, a Frenchman named Ancelin, was left at San Diego when Capt. Gillespie followed Frémont north. Commodore Stockton personally led the conquest of Southern California, landing at San Pedro with a force to meet Frémont. Los Angeles was captured on August 13, and Gillespie placed in command.

Bandini, who had assured Pico he was a loyal citizen of Mexico, and Santiago Arguello issued a joint appeal to their fellow Californians not to resist the Americans, that the separation of

California from Mexico had been inevitable, that a new government could bring the protection and stability necessary to prosperity, and anyway, events had progressed to where now it was a matter of self-preservation. Estudillo maintained a distant reserve. The Osunas, the Carrillos and the Marróns remained loyal to Mexico. The old families, though so closely intermarried, turned against each other, and a little civil war began. It was too late for Pico and Castro to turn back from their course, even if they had wanted to, and all that was left for them was flight.

In a proclamation to the people of California on August 10, Pico declared:

My Friends: Farewell! I take leave of you, I abandon the country of my birth, my family, property and everything that a man holds most dear, all to save the National Honor; but I have the sweet satisfaction that you will never favor the deceitful ideas of the crafty foe; that your loyalty and courage shall be the impregnable wall against which the machinations of the invaders shall fall to pieces. Conserve your honor at all cost, and observe that the eyes of the entire universe are fixed upon you, and that your . . . fidelity will gain the sympathies of the nations of the earth!

Castro slipped away through San Gorgonio Pass to the Colorado River and took the Sonora route into Mexico. He never saw California again. Pico went to Santa Margarita Rancho where he found his flight cut off by the advancing Americans. He was hidden by his brother-in-law, the Englishman, John Forster.

The governor's secretary, José Matías Moreno, hid out at San Luis Rey Mission, where Juan Osuna was serving as administrator for its owners. While Moreno rested in the living room, Osuna's daughter, Felipa Marrón, went outside and saw the arrival of Frémont who was scouring the countryside in search of the fleeing officials. She had Don Matías undress, tie a cloth around his head, and climb into bed. To Frémont's men, he was a "sick nephew." Felipa lamented in her memoirs that Frémont's adventurers stole food and goods and Gillespie also took, on account, twenty-five horses and never paid for them.

When the Americans had left, Moreno sent a note to Santiago Emilio Arguello, for a reason unknown to Felipa, as Arguello was with the Americans at the time. Soon after, Arguello and Gillespie appeared at the Mission, but Moreno evaded capture and slipped away to join Pico at Santa Margarita. Accompanied by Sgt. Macedonio González, who had led the search nine years before for the kidnapped Leiva girls, they managed to escape into Baja California, and finding West Coast ports blocked by American ships, they wandered in the desert and mountains for six weeks and reached Múlege, far down the peninsula on the Gulf of California, on October 22. Later, from Guaymas, across the gulf, Pico appealed to Mexico City for men and arms and money, but nobody even really bothered to answer his letters.

San Diego, its lot already cast with the Americans, heard reports of bands of Sonorans roaming the mountains, of a ruffian element of California organizing for action, and of Indians preparing to take advantage of circumstances. On guard was the lone French-born sentinel. Capt Fitch sent an appeal for help to Gillespie at Los Angeles and the frontiersman, Ezekiel Merritt, now a captain with the Volunteers, arrived with fifteen men on September 15. Gillespie aroused the Angeleños with restrictions on their conduct and pleasure. You could take the *Californios'* province but to forbid their pastimes, was something else. Sérbulo Varela led a band of semi-outlaws in an attack on the Americans at Los Angeles, and eventually Gillespie was driven out and allowed to retreat to San Pedro. A number of engagements followed in which the Californians were victorious, but more American forces were converging on rebellious Southern California. Frémont was marching south from Monterey with 300 men.

SAN FRANCISCO BEFORE THE GOLD RUSH and the American stampede was only a village. This shows the U.S. Naval Squadron at anchor in its bay.

Stephen W. Kearny, just promoted to brigadier general, had captured Santa Fe, New Mexico, on August 18, and leaving the larger part of his command there, had taken the Gila Trail to California with 300 men. Disaster lay ahead.

Gen. Stephen W. Kearny

The defeat of Gillespie at Los Angeles brought the disorder that so many had feared. All of Southern California was in turmoil. José María Flores assumed command of dissident forces and sent Francisco Rico and fifty men to recapture San Diego. John Bidwell, one of the Sacramento Valley settlers who had joined Frémont, had been left in charge of the San Luis Rey Mission and he hurriedly pushed a small cannon into a mud hole and with his handful of men fled to San Diego. There they joined Merritt's men, who had returned from reconnoitering in the vicinity of Agua Caliente, where, Bidwell later recalled, "the road from Sonora first strikes civilization and by which rumor said Castro might return with forces from Mexico, having heard of the country being in revolt . . ." Merritt and Bidwell decided to abandon San Diego, and accompanied by some Americans and *Californios* who had been supporting the conquest, including Santiago Arguello and Miguel Pedrorena, they boarded a small "smelly" old whaler, the *Stonington*, of New London, Conn., which had arrived in port with its supplies of food almost exhausted. Its captain, George W. Hamley, lost no time in enlisting his vessel in the war.

According to Bidwell:

> Several brass cannon spiked during some Mexican revolution years before were found near the entrance to the harbor. Two of these were brought on board the whale ship and the work of drilling out the spikes and mounting them began.

Thus at least two of the abandoned cannons at Fort Guijarros, which had been spiked in 1842 by the crew of the *Alert*, were placed back in service. The women remained, huddled together for protection behind the five-foot thick walls of the Estudillo House. Estudillo quit San Diego, retiring first to San Ysidro, near the border, then to the Cajon Rancho of his daughter and son-in-law, Miguel de Pedrorena, who was aiding the Americans. Estudillo was held in such high regard that his desire to be neutral was respected by both sides.

Rico and his men never arrived. They were recalled to Los Angeles after reaching Santa Margarita Rancho. But other Californians loyal to the flag of Mexico, and led by Sérbulo Varela, ransacked San Diego and the ranchos for guns, knives, lances and ammunition, and seized horses which Dupont had described as the "sinews of war."

More than 800 miles to the east, along the Rio Grande River south of Socorro, New Mexico, Kit Carson, bearing dispatches for President Polk from Stockton and Frémont, met the Army of the West. Gen. Kearny, upon reading the dispatches, dated twenty-six days earlier, that the conquest of California was all but over, ordered most of his men back to Santa Fe. He persuaded Carson to lead the remaining 110 men to the coast, and the messages of "victory" were entrusted to other couriers. Continuing west with Kearny were Lt. W. H. Emory and a detachment of Topographical Engineers. Emory has left a detailed record of the long march and the fateful events in their path. Considerably behind Kearny was the Mormon Battalion, well on its historic trek to open a military wagon road from Council Bluffs, Iowa, to San Diego. In return for volunteer military service, the 500 members expected to be allowed to re-settle in California. On the Pacific Coast, however, the Americans were precariously holding only the ports of San Diego, Monterey and San Francisco.

While the *Stonington* cruised off the coast, and with food becoming more and more scarce, Bidwell and a crew of four, and accompanied by Russell, the ex-beachcomber of La Playa, sailed a small boat to San Pedro, to seek assistance and supplies of Capt. William Mervine, USN, in command of the *USS Savannah*. They arrived about October 7 or 8, but Mervine was not there. Merritt and his men returned to the whaler, after a hazardous storm-tossed voyage down the coast in which they lost all the food and supplies they had obtained at San Pedro. There was no recourse except to go ashore and fight it out, and Bidwell recalled:

The cannon were taken ashore the next day and twenty-five men including some of the sailors of the whale-ship began the march to retake the town of San Diego three miles distant. The road lay all the way through soft sand, the dragging of the cannon was very difficult, requiring most of the way all the men to move a single piece. When about half way our movements were discovered. Flores came out with his men in line of battle. All were mounted.

But our march continued without the slightest hesitation, one of the brass pieces being hauled a hundred yards or so was left in charge of three or four men and while they were aiming and firing, the rest went back to bring up the other and so on alternately, loading and firing till Flores fled with all his force and we entered and took possession of the town, raising the flag where it has floated from that day to this.

At that time all the country between San Diego and Monterey was in a state of revolt. Stockton also had failed to repossess Los Angeles and the flag floated at no place south of Monterey except at San Diego.

Varela's guerrillas retreated to positions of safety on the hilltops, along the line of the ridge from the Presidio to what is now known as Fort Stockton, from where they could fire down upon the Plaza.

SHIPS OF THE PACIFIC NAVAL SQUADRON which took part in the war with Mexico as sketched at sea in water colors for the journal by Gunner Meyers.

The *Stonington* then sent its whale boat back to San Pedro, with Pedrorena aboard, and Midshipman Robert C. Duvall entered the following in the log of the *Savannah* under the date of October 12-13:

> . . . at 10.AM a whale Boat from the whale Ship *Stonnington* at San Diego arrived with Don Miguiel de Pedrorena 40 hours from said place having despatches from Captain Merritt saying that he had landed with his men about 40. in all, and had retaken the place in the face of 75. of the Enemy all mounted and having also one piece of artillery which he succeeded in capturing the Enemy cowardly deserting it and leaving it charged to the muzzle with grapshots he then took up his quarters in the edge of the town conveniant to water, where he was determined to remain at all hazzards until he could be reinforced. fearing that the Enemy would increase their force, he asked for Fifty men and then bid defiance to all California to unplace him.

At San Pedro, the whaler *Magnolia*, of New Bedford, Mass., was chartered by the United States Government and Lt. George Minor, two midshipmen, including Duvall, and thirty-five sailors and fifteen Volunteers were ordered to proceed to San Diego to the aid of Merritt. The *Magnolia* arrived on the 16th, and that night, the men were landed near the mouth of the San Diego River, or at least near the outlet of one of its smaller channels, and selecting a site near boggy ground, where the enemy would have difficulty in advancing, they began building a fortification.

They were constantly harrassed by the gunfire of the *Californios* who refused an open encounter, and Duvall wrote:

> The first two or three weeks were employed in getting Guns from the old Fort and mounting them, in our Barracks, which was situated in the west end of the town on the edge of the Bank bounding the Plane, and conveniant to

Water, our forces being too weak to admit of being divided, in occupying the Hill or East end of the town, the Enemy frequently visiting that end of the town by night and appeared to be content to appear on the Hill and fiering into us at long distance, especially when our Flag was hoisted and lowered, but always avoiding our efforts to engage them and as they were mounted, of course, the distance allowed between us was left entirely to their own wishes, in addition to our Barracks we carried adobes from the town and built Two Bastions at the two corners commanding the town and the Plane in the rear, in which we mounted six Brass nine pounders, from the old Fort.

From the movements of the Enemy we soon found out the manner in which war would be waged, which was to drive into the mountains all the cattle & removing from the adjacent Ranchos every kind of subsistence and by that means starve us out, and they are certainly entitled to credit for having performed their intentions so effectively. They kept sentrys by day and night on the Hills over looking the town, and on the different roads and passes leading into the country, and by that means prevented us from sending out "spys" to asscertain where we might manage to obtain supplys. For a time our situation was extremely precarious being reduced to almost the last extreme.

An Indian whom Duvall said was the chief "of a numerous tribe" agreed to go thirty-five miles down the coast, into Lower California, where many sheep had been reported, and drive them up to the bay and onto a sandy island which was connected with the mainland at low tide. This may have been North Island, Duvall writing under the impression it was an island more than part of a peninsula. A few days later a fire on the island signaled the return of the Indian. He had driven 600 sheep up the coast, though a companion had been captured and killed. The harassed garrison was aided in transporting the sheep to their barricades by the crew of the *Stonington*, which also had been taken over by the government, and to which "we owe in great measure our success."

Duvall tells of several expeditions to the southward, "using the whale ship *Stonington* to land our forces at different places along the Coast, and succeeded in getting both cattle and Horses, though the Horses were very poor." Many years later, in a civil suit involving Pío Pico and John Forster, Pedro C. Carrillo signed a deposition which included information that one of these expeditions, commanded by Merritt and which included Carrillo, Pedrorena and Santiago E. Arguello, went as far south as San Vicente, 200 miles below the border, and raised the American flag, whereupon the people swore allegiance to the United States.

The siege continued for thirty or forty days, the men sleeping with their guns at their side, waiting for help they were sure would come. San Diego was kind of a no man's land. Judge Hayes recalled that Manuel Rocha, son of Don José Juan Rocha, called down from the hill to his aunt, Doña Victoria, and mischievously asked her to send him some clothing and chocolate. Nor did they deal in words only. Hayes wrote that:

One day A. B. Smith, climbing the staff on the Plaza to clear the flag, hurried down, feeling the propinquity of a bullet. The shot came from Don José María Orosco, reputedly a famous shot.

On one occasion this was rather annoying to Capt. Miguel de Pedrorena, who was escorting Doña Felipa Marrón and was recognized by his red uniform jacket as they passed out of the gate of Doña María Ybañes' residence into Juan Street to her own residence. Two pretty close shots he stood, taking off his hat and politely waving it to the hill; the third from Orosco's rifle (as were the others) hurried his steps, but after all disappointed Orosco who "merely wanted to see if he could make Miguel run!"

Varela's men began to melt away and Gen. Flores sent Ramón Carrillo and Leonardo Cota to take command at San Diego. Forster, the Englishman, later told of a council of war being held at Rancho Santa Margarita, under a sycamore tree that was still standing in 1963. He recalled that an expedition to re-take San Diego was to be led by Cota and José Alipás.

The situation changed at the beginning of November. The USS *Congress* rounded Point Loma on October 31, bringing Commodore Stockton and Capt. Gillespie with forty Marines and California Volunteers. The *Congress* struck attempting to cross the bar, and though managing to slip off, was forced to anchor outside the harbor. Stockton was disturbed by the desperate condition of the garrison and its defenders, the men having abandoned the town to serve with one side or the other, leaving the women and children dependent on the Americans. On the day of his arrival the enemy attacked, and Duval wrote:

> The Enemy sudenly appeared to the Number of between 80 and 100 and knowing that we would be reinforced by the *Congress*, charged on us headed by José Antonio Carrillio, one of their *Bravos*, but were repulsed, their loss not asscertained, one of them had his foot shot off (the end of his heel being found) by a 9 lb shot passing also through his Horses Body, which ran into our ranks with his entrails dragging the ground. The man afterwards died with 3 others we know of.

The San Diegans who were supporting the Americans had been given military ranks in a Volunteer battalion, and in his manuscripts, Hayes put down their recollections as to the events and the roles they played in the engagements that eventually drove the enemy into the interior:

> On the eighth day of the "seige," a company of soldiers, under command of Capt. Santiago E. Arguello, ascended the steepest declivity of the hill, rapidly and gallantly.
>
> One ball from the fort slightly wounded Capt. A. in the leg. This did not stop his progress. The Californians were forced to withdraw down the northeastern slope. They planted themselves behind the adobe ruins of the Presidio at the distance of a few hundred yards, and continued firing at the Americans. In a short time, they retreated through the valley toward the Mission.
>
> It appears their leader was a native of Sonora, and commonly known by the name of Hermosillo: considered to be a *militar*. Don Ramón Carrillo had joined

Robert F. Stockton

90

him, with a party of men . . . The greatest part of his force he had left at the rancho of Peñasquitos, eighteen northwest miles from San Diego.

A company under Capt. Miguel de Pedrorena, was sent in pursuit. About a mile up the valley, he encountered the small Californian advance guard, headed by Don Leandro Osuna. Several shots were exchanged, before they fell back. The main body was concealed from view of the Cañada de la Soledad a mile short of the Mission: so that in the approach of the Mission, an enemy at first was not visible. An American soldier, going to water his mule at a well . . . was fired at and killed. Capt. Pedrorena at once charged the Californians, who were behind the old walls. The affair was soon over. A shot from Carrillo whizzed past Pedrorena. He returned a "Roland" that barely grazed behind the sword belt of Carrillo. Capt. Pedrorena brought back prisoners, Carrillo and others.

The Cañada de la Soledad mentioned by Hayes was Murphy Canyon which is west of the Mission and leads up toward the mesa and to Soledad Valley or Sorrento, where the padres going north turned into El Camino Real.

If Ramón Carrillo was taken prisoner, he soon escaped as Americans were to see much more of him. Duvall's log of events also gives a different picture, both as to the battle on the day of Stockton's arrival, and of subsequent incidents:

On this day the volunteers proved themselves as on evry other occasion to be worthless, having left the Barracks, where they were stationed at the Guns in case of an attack and took to the old Houses and Brush fenses. Mr. Morgan, myself and 40 Marines & Sailors receiving the Enemy fire and preventing them from charging into the town. A party afterwards succeeded in getting from us about 40 head of cattle, after this they were seldom seen around us.

On one of the Expeditions one of our men was Lanced and died shortly afterwards. He had strayed off before day light for the purpose of giving his horse some water (with one other who escaped), about 300 yds. from the camp, where some of the Enemy were in ambush, and succeeded in Lancing him.

While the *Congress* took Stockton back to San Diego, the Marines routed the enemy from their positions on the hill and extended their operations in an ever-widening circle. A small force was sent out to intercept some *Californios* who were reported driving a large number of cattle and horses through the countryside about twenty miles south of San Diego. The enemy learned of their approach, abandoned camp, and disappeared.

Duvall commented:

We afterwards found out the reason for their having left their intended camp so suddenly, which was through the treachery of an Englishman who had been allowed to come and go out to his family at his pleasure on Parole, alledging that should he remove his family from his Ranch the Enemy would destroy his property, a fair specimen of an Englishman's sincerity & feelings toward us.

The Englishman has gone unidentified.

Commodore Stockton returned on November 18, to prepare for an advance on Los Angeles from the south, and Hayes wrote:

Don Juan Bandini and family received the Commodore elegantly at their mansion and entertained him sumptuously. A portion of his men were quartered in the house of Doña María Ybañes; another, at the Arguello house, on the west side of town. The women and children were collected within the strong walls of the Estudillo house for greater safety, in event of battle. Rations were served out to the inhabitants.

One morning, along the road from the mission, came *Alcalde* Juan María Marrón, the husband of Felipa Osuna, carrying a white flag. He wanted to visit his wife. Pedrorena took him into custody, but Stockton finally gave Felipa and her husband a pass through the lines, to go to their rancho. With their children they walked all the way to San Luis Rey Mission, where another band of *Californios* seized them and threatened to shoot Marrón for having collaborated with the Americans. They released him but stripped his Agua Hedionda Rancho of horses and cattle.

Though many *Californios* were giving up and wandering into San Diego, the main bodies of insurgents were organizing and re-equipping, and Flores planned to re-capture San Diego as soon as enough powder could be made available.

Gillespie ranged the valleys and low mountains searching for Andrés Pico and José Antonio Carrillo, whom Flores had placed in charge of two of his three "armies." Pico's was known as "*Los Galgos*," or the Greyhounds, and Carrillo's as "*Los Hilachos*," or the Ragged Ones. Each had about 130 men at his command.

On one of these expeditions Gillespie seized and arrested "Long John" Warner, who operated a trading post at his rancho in San Jose Valley and had aroused suspicions by failing to join other American-born settlers though passing in and out of San Diego, and through the *Californio* lines, with impunity. This seemed strange in view of Warner's known advocacy of American occupation of California and his service to Larkin, the United States Consul at San Francisco, but Gillespie, a number of years later in a letter explaining the imprisonment, said Warner had expressed himself as against the war, as unnecessary, had denounced President Polk, had excited the enemy against them, and had helped in driving horses and cattle into the mountains to prevent their capture by American forces. He later was released and evidently exonerated. But for years he was plagued by an unfounded charge that he had tried to lead Gillespie's men into a trap in Sonora.

The Americans, preparing for a long defense of San Diego, began building a fort on the hill at the site of the one first laid out in 1838 for protection against the *Norteños*. It was named Fort Stockton and is now a historical monument. The guns could sweep the broad mesa to the east and be pointed down on the town below.

Duvall provides a detailed description:

SOLDIERS TOILED FOR THREE WEEKS to build Fort Stockton on the hill overlooking Old Town. It had a moat, drawbridge and a solid ballproof house.

The Commodore now commenced to fortify the Hill which over looked the town by building a Fort constructed by placing 300 Gallon casks full of sand close together, 30 yds by 20 square throwing a Bank of earth and small gravel up in Front as high as the Top of the casks & running a Ditch arround the whole. In the inside a Ball Proff house was built out of Plank lineing the inside with Adobes, on the top of which a swivel was mounted. The entrance was guarded by a Strong gate having a draw Bridge in front, the whole fortification was completed in about 3 weeks. Guns mounted and evry thing complete notwithstanding the Plank, etc. had to be carried by the men near a mile and the ditch cut through a solid strata of gravel and rock, with but indifferent tools to do it with. It is a monument of the most excessive hard Labor our forces have as yet performed and notwithstanding they were on short allowance of Beef and wheat for a time without Bread Tea sugar or coffee, many destitute of shoes but few complaints were made.

Though the nights were turning cool, the days were pleasant, the enemy no longer threatened the little village, and the Californians who had defied their countrymen to aid the Americans began to resume the pastoral existence they had known most of their lives.

Judge Hayes wrote:

The population breathed freely; re-opened their pleasant dwellings; and quick gave rein to their natural inclination for enjoyment of life. "Stockton's band" with sweet notes contributed to their amusement. To this day they speak exultingly of that music; and say: the band had many Spanish musicians . . . It in fact was composed . . . of Italians — thirty-seven in number. The private band of the Commodore, paid by himself, and sailing with him in the frigate *Congress*. Every evening they placed themselves around the flagstaff on the Plaza, and played and supplied the music for the "Bandini *bailes*."

While the band played on, the normally rather docile Luiseño Indians of the San Luis Rey Valley, who had been driven from their lands, and who no longer could turn to the padres for counsel and help, became ugly and emboldened, and began to roam the countryside, demanding food and wine and threatening the whites. At San Fernando Mission, above Los Angeles, and at Santa Margarita Rancho, where Andrés Pico's men maintained headquarters, the *Californios*, still lacking guns and powder, shaped long lances out of laurel and ash and tipped them with long blades fashioned out of scrap iron or old razors. At San Diego, on December 3, a strange courier arrived with a message for Commodore Stockton. He was clad in a black velvet English hunting coat, black velvet trousers cut off at the knees, with white drawers showing, and wore long, clanking spurs. He was Edward Stokes, the English sea captain and rancher from Santa Ysabel. He brought a message reporting the arrival of Gen. Kearny at Warner's Pass. The same evening, at 8 o'clock, Capt. Gillespie left the pueblo with a force consisting of Capt. Samuel Gibson's Company of Mounted Riflemen, Volunteers twenty-seven strong, and Lt. Edward F. Beale, of the *USS Congress*, with a four-pounder known as the Sutter gun, and Passed Midshipman James M. Duncan with ten Carbineers. A lieutenant in the Volunteers identified by Gillespie as "Lt. Rhusan" probably was Hiram Rheusaw who served in the California Battalion throughout the war. The Sutter gun once was a Russian cannon at Fort Ross, the Russian fur trading post north of San Francisco. The American trader John A. Sutter, of New Helvetia, came into possession of the gun when he purchased the abandoned fort, but later the gun was captured in one of the California revolutions and then seized by the Americans.

From the large Pico house Mariquita, sister of Andrés Pico, watched the men file out in the cold, sharp night and take the padre road up Mission Valley in the direction of El Cajon. She scribbled a warning note and sent it to her brother. The word of the arrival of new American forces in California also passed from Indian to Indian from the Colorado River to Soledad Valley, where Pico was encamped with his *Californios*.

CHAPTER SIX

"Farewell: we have left thee: companions in arms;
Our lives may be joyful or filled with alarms,
Whatever our joy or our sorrow may be,
We'll remember the graves by the lone willow tree."

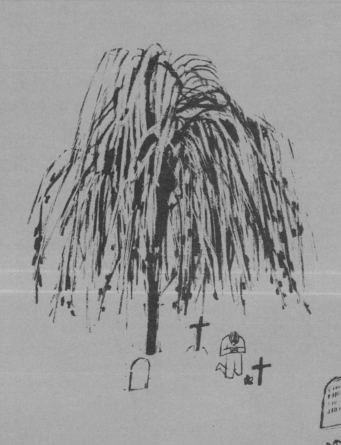

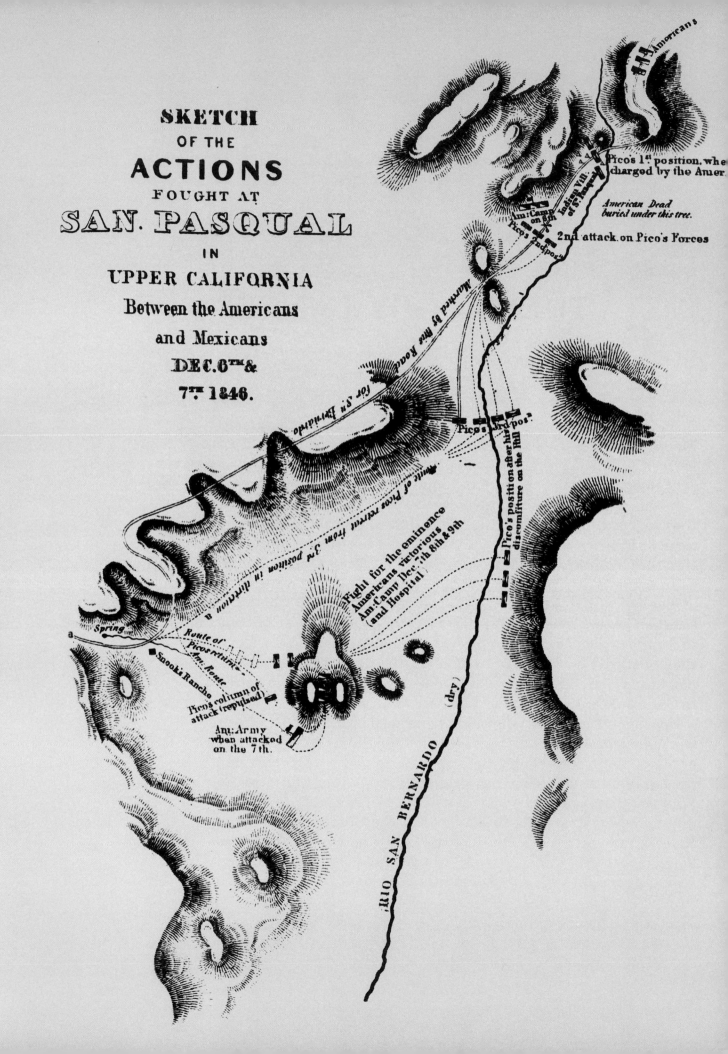

SKETCH
OF THE
ACTIONS
FOUGHT AT
SAN. PASQUAL
IN
UPPER CALIFORNIA
Between the Americans
and Mexicans
DEC. 6TH &
7TH 1846.

THE BLOODY LANCES

A cold December wind was whipping off the snow on the Cuyamaca Mountains when Gen. Kearny and his weary Army of the West arrived at Warner's Ranch, dragging their two mountain howitzers along the ground as they had done since leaving New Mexico.

It was while they were approaching the Colorado River that they learned that the situation in California had changed drastically since they had met Kit Carson and been assured by him that the *Californios* would never fight.

First they encountered a group of Mexicans with a large band of horses, which, it turned out, belonged in part to a band of Sonoran horse thieves and in part to couriers of Flores on the way to Sonora to plead for help in the war against the Americans. Next, they captured a Sonoran in whose saddle bags were found dispatches to Gen. Castro describing in detail all that had transpired in California since his flight.

Kearny and his men were not discouraged. The First Dragoons were one of the proudest units of the United States Army and veterans of the frontier, and Kearny himself was a respected and proven commander. They had originally set out for California to fight the enemy, and now, no matter their tired and tattered condition, they were anxious to get about it. They forded the Colorado River a mile and a half south of the Gila junction on November 25, where it was 1500 feet wide, camped, and the next morning, wrapping bundles of grass behind their saddles, and taking "the

THE AMERICANS SUFFERED HEAVY LOSSES in the Battle of San Pasqual. How the actions were fought is shown in Lt. Emory's sketch of the battlefield.

ONE OF THE WORLD'S LONGEST MILITARY MARCHES was that of the Army of the West which General Kearny led all the way to San Diego.

great highway between Sonora and California," rounded the base of the white drifting sand dunes just below eastern Imperial Valley, and began crossing the bed of a lost sea at places more than two hundred and fifty feet below sea level. It was the worst stretch of their march of 1600 miles.

The second camp was made at Alamo Mocho, twenty-four miles from the river, south and east of Mexicali, in Lower California, where they had to dig for water. The night was made horrible by the cries of hungry mules. The next day they headed for a salt lake thirty or forty miles away, despite the warnings of the captured Sonorans. The lake evidently was one of the salty flats which occasionally filled with flood water from the Colorado.

Emory wrote:

The heavy sand had proved too much for many horses and some mules, and all the efforts of their drivers could bring them no farther than the middle of this dreary desert. About 8 o'clock, as we approached the lake, the stench of dead animals confirmed the reports of the Mexicans and put to flight all hopes of our being able to use the water.

The basin of the lake, as well as I could judge at night, is about three-quarters of a mile long and half a mile wide. The water had receded to a pool, diminished to one half its size, and the approach to it was through a thick soapy quagmire. It was wholly unfit for man or brute, and we studiously kept the latter from it, thinking that the use of it would but aggravate their thirst.

One or two of the men came in late, and, rushing to the lake, threw themselves down and took many swallows before discovering their mistake; but the effect was not injurious except that it increased their thirst.

A few mezquite trees and a chenopodiaceous shrub bordered the lake, and on these our mules munched till they had sufficiently refreshed themselves,

Well in the Desert — Alamo Mocho

98

when the call to saddle was sounded, and we groped silently our way in the dark. The stoutest animals now began to stagger, and when day dawned, scarcely a man was seen mounted.

With the sun rose a heavy fog from the southwest, no doubt from the gulf, and sweeping towards us, enveloped us for two or three hours, wetting our blankets and giving relief to the animals. Before it had dispersed we came to a patch of sun-burned grass.

The weary column had swung north and crossed into what is now the United States, probably just west of Seely, and finally entered the wide gap that led to Carrizo Spring, the first step in a slowly rising climb through the mountains.

The short way to the port of San Diego lay directly over the mountain ridges, but they were impassable for military equipment and wagons. The route for Kearny led a long way around through the Carrizo Corridor, which took them in a northwesterly direction up through dry canyons into a broad green pass that lifted up to Warner's. Here, several circuitous and difficult trails led to San Diego. From here also a trail led northerly through a series of rich, comparatively flat upland valleys to lush Temecula, from where the trail again branched, one southwest, back toward the San Luis Rey Mission and down to San Diego, and the other going north through open country to Los Angeles.

Emory continued:

When the fog had entirely dispersed we found ourselves entering a gap in the mountains, which had been before us for four days. The plain was crossed,

THE LONG, WEARY ROUTE of Gen. Kearny's Army to San Diego was sketched in detail by Lt. William Emory, of the U.S. Topographical Engineers. His descriptions formed the basis of San Diego's hope of being the terminus of the first transcontinental railroad. The dream faded and so did San Diego for many years.

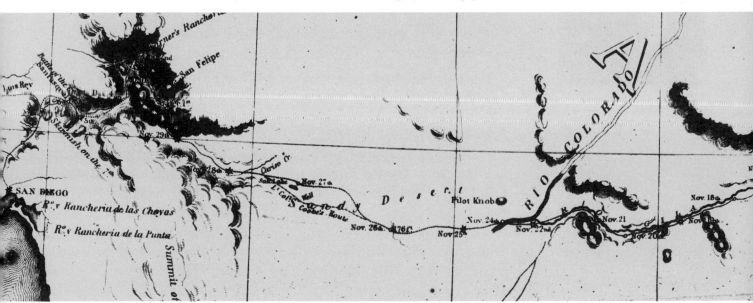

but we had not yet found water. The first valley we reached was dry, and it was not till 12 o'clock, m., that we struck the Cariso (cane) creek, within half a mile of one of its sources, and although so close to the source, the sands had already absorbed much of its water, and left but little running. A mile or two below, the creek entirely disappears.

They had made fifty-four miles in two days.

Many animals were left on the road to die of thirst and hunger, in spite of the generous efforts of the men to bring them to the spring. More than one was brought up, by one man tugging at the halter and another pushing up the brute, by placing his shoulder against its buttocks. Our most serious loss, perhaps, was that of one or two fat mares and colts brought with us for food; for before leaving camp, Major Swords found in a concealed place one of the best pack mules slaughtered, and the choice bits cut from his shoulders and flanks, stealthily done by some mess less provident than others.

On November 29 they followed the dry sandy bed of Carrizo Creek, riding many miles through thickets:

The day was intensely hot, and the sand deep; the animals, inflated with water and rushes, gave way by the scores; and, although we advanced only sixteen miles, many did not arrive at camp until 10 o'clock at night. It was a feast day for the wolves (coyotes) which followed in packs close on our track, seizing our deserted brutes and making the air resound with their howls as they battled for the carcasses.

They reached the "little pools" of Vallecito, where they refreshed themselves on water that was slightly salty, killed a horse for food, and rested for a day. Gen. Kearny conducted the last review of the Army of the West. Capt. Abraham Johnston, who had not long to live, wrote in his notes that "Our men were inspected today. Poor fellows! They are well nigh naked — some of them barefoot — a sorry looking set. A Dandy would think that; in those swarthy sun-burnt faces, a lover of his country will see no signs of quailing. They will be ready for their hour when it comes."

There were no complaints from such men as Capts. B. D. Moore and Johnston, Lts. Thomas Hammond and Davidson, all of the First Dragoons; or from Lts. Emory and W. H. Warner, of the Topographical Engineers, or Maj. Thomas Swords, of the Quartermaster Corps, and Dr. John S. Griffin, an assistant Army surgeon. The desert and the enemy held no fear, either, for Antoine Robidoux, the trapper and guide, and four other Mountain Men.

For the next two days they trudged through dry Mason and Earthquake Valleys, always over rising land, and drew up into San Felipe Pass, between snow covered mountains. The winter had brought unusually heavy snows, and far to the north, in the Sierra Nevada, the Donner party of immigrants, who had left Independence, Missouri, without knowledge of the start of war, were trapped by blizzards. Thirty-four out of seventy-nine died.

William H. Emory, as a brigadier general

100

Many of the survivors fell to eating the dead. On the night of December 2, Kearny and his force arrived at Warner's Ranch. At that time Warner lived in a house, which may have been begun by Silvestre de La Portilla or José Antonio Pico, when they had claimed the valley, and it stood a short distance from the hot sulphur springs.

Emory wrote:

> Our camp was pitched on the road to the Pueblo, leading a little north of west. To the south, down the valley of the Agua Caliente, lay the road to San Diego. Above us was Mr. Warner's backwoods, American-looking house, built of adobe and covered with a thatched roof . . .

Leather Shield

Warner grew his crops in the vicinity of his home and grazed his cattle down the valley along the upper stream of the San Luis Rey River, on lands now partly covered by Lake Henshaw.

Warner was not there. He was in custody at San Diego, and Bill Marshall, the deserter from a whaling ship, was in charge and provided the Army with the first fresh meat and vegetables they had had in many weeks. The Englishman Stokes was summoned from Santa Ysabel, and though he proclaimed himself a neutral in the war, agreed to take a message to Stockton asking that reinforcements be sent to meet Kearny somewhere along the road to San Diego.

Sixty miles away and near the coast, Andrés Pico led his seventy to seventy-five men out of Soledad Valley on the road to San Pasqual. They wore the traditional rich and ornamented costumes of the Dons, with leathern cuirasses to protect their bodies, and a *serape* over one shoulder, and a few perhaps carried the old leather shields with their Castilian heraldry. Gay pennants fluttered from medieval lances. The sight always had awed the Indians, and a little native girl, Felicita, who witnessed the Battle of San Pasqual, related years later to Elizabeth J. Roberts, how they feared the *Californios*:

> When I was a child I lived here in San Pasqual. Our village was by the Lagunas and the river. There were days when the Mexican soldiers rode through San Pasqual on their beautiful horses. They came from the Presidio at San Diego and carried swords and lances. At sight of them women and children ran to hide in the brush and rocks of the hills, for these men counted our lives of little worth, and we feared them.

In a clear and cold moonlit night Gillespie and his Volunteers pushed their horses and mules over the rolling mesa between Mission and El Cajon Valleys. He, as Kit Carson, had little respect for the *Californios* as fighters, and had informed the Secretary of the Navy that they had a "holy horror of the American rifle" and "will never expose themselves to make an attack."

101

Much of what is known about the events of those days is found in his official report to Commodore Stockton.

At 3 o'clock A.M. of the 4th, we arrived at the Rancho in the Cajon Valley, where we encamped to rest and await daylight, to commence the ascent of the mountains, the trail being rocky and of difficult passage for a Field piece. Although it had been reported that the enemy were in considerable numbers about this place, we saw no signs of them, and at 9 o'clock on the 4th, commenced our march for the hills. For the first three leagues, our road passed through pretty valleys, covered with wild oats, here and there interspersed with Oaks and Sycamores of great size and age; it then crossed a ridge of high mountains, completely covered with rocks and stones, a species of white granite. Towards sunset we descended the east side of the mountain, and entered upon the pretty valley of Santa Maria.

They camped that night at the ranch home of Stokes situated on the east side of the valley.

Kearny left Warner's on December 4, in a heavy rain, camping that night at Santa Ysabel, the site of the abandoned *asistencia* of the San Diego Mission and of the ranch home of Stokes' father-in-law, José Joaquín Ortega. The Indians from neighboring tribes met with Kearny and offered to aid the Americans. He told them it was best for them to remain neutral. The march was resumed the next morning, with the majordomo of the ranch, a "Sailor Bill," pressed into unwilling service as a guide. "Sailor Bill" was Bill Williams, the former English sea captain who had been employed by Capt. Fitch in 1841 and later became an Indian agent and was a claimant to Viejas Valley. In the cold of the San Diego mountains "Sailor Bill" preferred his liquor to a long march.

On the same morning Gillespie left Santa Maria Valley, headed east into the higher mountains:

Much rain had fallen during the night, and as we began the ascent of the mountains, with direction for Santa Isabel, it poured in torrents, effectually drenching our party. When about half the distance between Sta. Isabel and Sta. Maria, the weather cleared; and at one o'clock, one of the advance returned, reporting that Lieut. Rhusan had met with Gen'l Kearny's advance, & had proceeded forward to report my approach. Our Flag was immediately given to the breeze, and displayed for the first time upon those distant mountains; cheering the way-worn soldiers with the sight of the "Stars and Stripes," where they least expected to meet them.

I soon joined Gen'l Kearny, was received with great kindness by himself and officers, and reported to him what you had ordered; giving him all the information in my power, in relation to the state and condition of the Country, and also, said to him, that a force of insurgents under Andrés Pico, was reported to be at San Pascual, and that you advised him "to beat up their camp," should he feel so disposed. This proposition was received with great pleasure by all parties, particularly, Capt. Moore of 1st Dragoons, who was extremely desirous to meet the Enemy as soon as possible.

While Gillespie grazed his horses, Kearny's men moved down into Santa Maria Valley and camped in a grassy, oak-covered val-

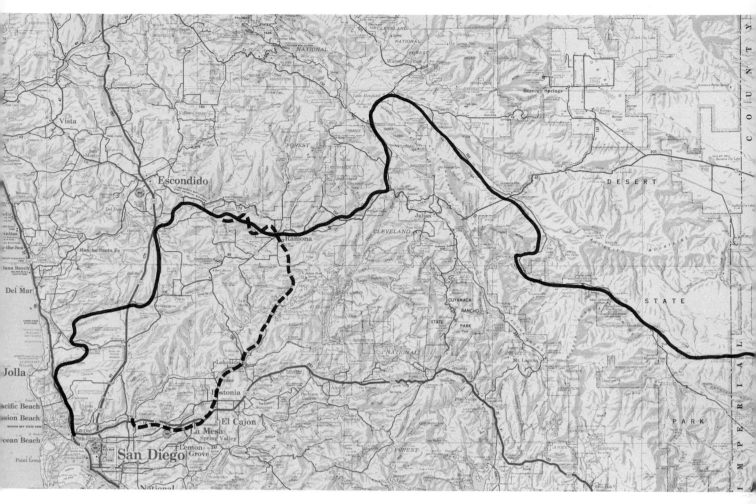

THE ROUTE TAKEN BY GEN. KEARNY through San Diego County is shown by the solid line. Dotted line indicates the route of Capt. Gillespie, whose Volunteers joined with Kearny's men and took part in the Battle of San Pasqual.

ley, presumably at the head of Clevenger Canyon, through which now descends the highway into San Pasqual Valley. Gillespie found them there at night:

> . . .many of the soldiers were lying upon the wet ground, notwithstanding the heavy rain, almost exhausted by their long and arduous march; indeed, the whole force, save the officers, presented an appearance of weariness and fatigue, rarely, if ever, met with upon any other service. The men were without any exception sadly in want of clothing; that which they wore was ragged and torn; they were almost without shoes; and although we were constantly accustomed to much privation and suffering, my men considered their own condition, superior to that of these way-worn soldiers, whose strength and spirit seemed to be entirely gone.

Far below them, in San Pasqual Valley, Pico's men slept around camp fires at the squalid Indian village, located along the edge of the hills on the north, convinced that a report of American forces being in the vicinity was false, and that Gillespie had gone out to capture horses and cattle and would drive them back along the San Pasqual road to San Diego, where they could be intercepted and the enemy engaged. Not all of the *Californios* with Pico have been identified, though it is known that they included Leonard Cota and Tomás Sánchez, as officers, and Ramón Carrillo, Leandro and Ramón Osuna, and José Antonio Serrano.

There were two routes from Santa Maria to San Diego. One led over the lower mountains to Lakeside and Santa Monica, or El Cajon Valley, and then down through Mission Valley, the route over which Gillespie had come. The other led a half dozen miles across rolling hills to the edge of San Pasqual Valley, down the valley to the present area of Lake Hodges, then south across San Bernardo Rancho to Los Peñasquitos Creek, west into Soledad Valley, and then up over Miramar Mesa back of Torrey Pines and down Rose Canyon to the pueblo. Although both routes had been in use for some time, the San Pasqual route was preferred to the Lakeside route because it was less rocky. Both routes had difficult climbs, the San Pasqual route at San Pasqual hill and the Lakeside route in the last mile before reaching the Ramona Valley. Gillespie reported the hill covered with rocks. Rocks were hard on horses' feet and broke the wheels of wagons.

On this cold, wet night, one route was open, the other blocked by an enemy force. Kearny sent a small detachment under Lt. Thomas C. Hammond and a native scout, Rafael Machado, attached to Gillespie's command, to reconnoiter Pico's camp and determine the number and disposition of his men. The bark of a dog alerted a guard and his shots aroused the sleeping camp. Hammond and his men, swords clanking in the still night, galloped back up the hill. The element of surprise now was gone, but Kearny was determined to move out and engage the enemy and "beat up his camp" as Stockton had suggested. The order to mount was given at 2 o'clock in the morning. His Dragoons went to the head of the column, and Gillespie's Volunteers, to their disgust, were ordered to the rear, to help guard the baggage. Gillespie tells the story of what followed:

The weather had cleared, the moon shone as bright as day almost, but the wind coming from the snow covered mountains, made it so cold, we could scarcely hold our bridle reins.

Our road lay over a mountain which divides the valley of San Pascual from that of Santa Maria, and is about six miles in length. The ascent is quite regular, the road smooth, and has been used by the native Californians for carts. As day dawned, we arrived at the top of the hill, which immediately overlooks the Valley of San Pascual; a halt was ordered and preparations made to engage the Enemy. General Kearny addressed the Dragoons and Riflemen, telling them to "be steady and obey implicitly the orders of their officers; that their Country

104

JEEP TRAIL now follows in part old carreta road from Ramona to San Pasqual over which Gen. Kearny's Army descended to face Californians' lances.

expected them to do their duty; and that one thrust of the sabre point, was far more effective than any number of cuts."

The General told me, that Capt. Moore would direct the charge, and had orders to surround the Indian Village; in the performance of which duty, he wished me to cooperate all in my power; to follow Capt. Moore, and if possible capture every man; to shoot any who might resist or attempt to escape, but make exertions to capture man and horse. Lieutenant Davidson, 1st Dragoons, in command of the Howitzers, was ordered to follow in the rear of my command. Major Swords with his command had not yet come up. The order to march is given. We proceeded down the mountain. The clang of the heavy Dragoon sabres, echoing amongst the hills upon this cold frosty morning, and reverberating from the mountain top back upon the Valley seemed like so many alarm bells to give notice of our approach. The grey light of morn appeared as we approached the valley. We were marching by twos; and as the advance, commanded by Capt. Johnston had reached the plain, the General gave the order to "Trot," which Capt. Johnston misunderstood for "charge;" a shout, and off dashed the Dragoons at the charge, as fast as their tired, worn out mules and horses could

Next Page, THE LANCES OF THE CALIFORNIA HORSEMEN took a terrible toll of Gen. Kearny's Army of the West, as shown in painting by Walter Francis.

W. FRANCIS

be urged; whilst my command was still upon the hill side, and more than a half mile from the Indian village; the boundaries of which, were clearly shown by the fire that was opened upon the advance, by the Enemy posted in a gulley at the side fronting our approach.

The charge led down a long hog-back ridge that slopes into the valley to a point about two miles west of the bridge across the Santa Ysabel Creek which becomes the San Dieguito River a few miles further west.

In the valley the alarmed *Californios* had rounded up their horses, and in a disorganized state awaited what might come. Felicita, the little Indian girl, saw the start of the action:

> . . .we heard the sounds of voices shouting on the mountain side toward Santa Maria; we ran out of our huts to find the cause. The clouds hung so low that at first we could see nothing for the mist, but soon there came the figure of men, like shadows, riding down the mountain. As they drew nearer we saw that they too were soldiers, wearing coats of blue.
>
> The Mexican soldiers were sitting on their horses, holding their long lances in their hands; they now rode swiftly to meet the soldiers in blue, and soon there came the sounds of battle. But the Indians, in great fear, fled again to the mountains. When we had climbed high above the valley, we hid behind the brush and weeds. Then we looked down and watched. One of our men who had lived at the mission, told us that these strange soldiers from the hills were Americans and that they were fighting to take the land away from the Mexicans. The Mexicans had not been good to the Indians, so we were not sorry to see the new soldiers come against them.

Kit Carson

The first man to fall was Capt. Johnston who had led the charge down the hill. A bullet from the gun of Leandro Osuna struck him in the forehead and he fell dead from his horse. The Americans driving down the hill virtually moved over their dead and wounded and slammed into the lances and bullets of the Californians. Kit Carson's horse, plunging down the hillside, stumbled and threw Carson to the ground, breaking his rifle. Though Kearny realized a mistake in command had been made, he knew it was too late to change it, and he followed his men into the swirling battle in the half-light of the morning. After a brief but bloody encounter the Californians suddenly turned and retreated across the valley and reorganized behind the little hill on which the San Pasqual Battle Monument now stands.

Capt. Moore, believing the enemy to be in retreat, ordered a second charge. As the Americans followed in a long disorganized line, the *Californios* swept out from their hiding place. The American Dragoons were cut to pieces. Alone in front, Moore ran up against Andrés Pico, fired one pistol shot and then slashed out at him with a sabre. Leandro Osuna and Dionisio Alipás closed in on Moore and pierced him with their lances. He fell from his horse and was finished off with a pistol shot by Tomás Sánchez.

Lt. Hammond, following close upon Moore, went down with lance thrusts between his ribs. The rifles of the Americans failed to fire because of wet cartridges. Some of the Dragoons were lassoed and hauled from their mules and horses, to be stabbed to death. Their tired mounts could not cope with the fresh and spirited California horses.

Gillespie tells the story:

After a pursuit of over a mile and a half, the Dragoons came upon the Enemy in the open plain, where they made a stand, evidently having observed the scattered position of our force. As we came up, I saw a party of some twenty-five or thirty Dragoons, slowly turning before a superior force of the Enemy. Sword in hand I dashed forward to them crying, "Rally men, for God's sake rally, show a front, don't turn your backs, face them, face them, follow me," but to no effect; their brave leader had fallen, pierced by many lances; their travel worn horses being incapable of any more exertion, themselves chilled by the cold, their limbs stiffened by their clothing, soaked by the rain of the night previous; and being almost surrounded, they were completely panic stricken; the best men of this command, having already fallen in unequal combat. Instead of the Dragoons heeding my efforts to rally them, they passed my left, when I fell in upon the center of the Enemy, and was immediately surrounded and saluted with the cry of recognition, "Ya, es Gillespie, adentro hombres, adentro." "There is Gillespie, at him men, at him!"

Gillespie was recognized as the American commander who had made life so unpleasant at Los Angeles for the pleasure-loving *Californios*.

Four lances were darted at me instantly, which being parried, the fifth and sixth quickly followed, accompanied by the discharge of an *Escopeta*, almost into my face. At this moment I noticed a lance "in rest" coming from the front and when leaning over the neck of my horse, parrying the charge, I was struck on the back of the neck by another lance, at the collar of my coat, with such force, as to be thrown clear from my saddle to the ground, with my sabre under me. As I attempted to rise I received a thrust from a lance behind me, striking above the heart, making a severe gash open to the lungs. I turned my face in the direction of my assailant, when, one of the Enemy riding at full speed, charged upon me, dashed his lance at my face, struck and cutting my upper lip, broke a front tooth, and threw me upon my back, as his horse jumped over me.

In the panic of those few minutes, Kearny, fighting alone, as were most of his men, was lanced three times, in an arm and in the buttocks, and was saved from certain death by Emory who drove off another attacker. One of the two howitzers was lassoed and hauled away. The Sutter gun and the other howitzer were brought into play and Gillespie managed to fire one himself by using his cigar lighter, before he collapsed on the field. The American retreat was halted, and the *Californios* temporarily scattered.

As day dawned, the smoke cleared away, and Emory wrote:

. . .we commenced collecting our dead and wounded. We found eighteen of our officers and men were killed on the field, and thirteen wounded. Amongst the killed were Captains Moore and Johnston, and Lt. Hammond of the 1st Dragoons. The general, Capt. Gillespie, Capt. Gibson, Lt. Warner, and Mr. Robideaux badly wounded.

The Indian village was scoured for the dead and wounded:

The first object which met my eye was the manly figure of Capt. Johnston. He was perfectly lifeless, a ball having passed directly through the centre of his head.

The work of plundering the dead had already commenced; his watch was gone, nothing being left of it but a fragment of the gold chain by which it was suspended from his neck. . . Captain Johnston and one dragoon were the only persons either killed or wounded on our side in the fight by firearms.

Gillespie reported that of the total American force of 153 men, not more than 45 had borne the brunt of the fight. Only one Californian, Francisco Lara, had been killed, though twelve had been wounded, one of whom later died. One was captured by Philip Crosthwaite, a volunteer who came with Gillespie's force. He was Pablo Vejar.

The Americans moved over to the north side of the valley, up on a long hill, and in the notes of Stanley, the artist-draftsman with the Kearny force, we find:

At first General Kearny thought to move on the same day. The dead were lashed on mules, and remained two hours or more in that posture. It was a sad and melancholy picture. We soon found, however, that our wounded were unable to travel. The mules were released of their packs, and the men engaged in fortifying the place for the night. During the day the enemy were in sight curveting their horses, keeping our camp in constant excitement. Three of Captain Gillespie's volunteers started with dispatches to Commodore Stockton. The dead were buried at night and ambulances made for the wounded. . . .

Late that night, the dead were buried in a single grave.
Emory wrote:

When night closed in, the bodies of the dead were buried under a willow to the east of our camp, with no other accompaniment than the howling of the myriads of wolves attracted by the smell. Thus were put to rest together, and forever, a band of brave and heroic men. The long march of 2,000 miles had brought our little command, both officers and men, to know each other well. Community of hardships, dangers, and privations, had produced relations of mutual regard which caused their loss to sink deeply in our memories.

Kit Carson escaped the lances, and years later, when his exploits were ridiculed in a cynical age, Lt. Beale came to his defense and wrote that "I remember when we lay side by side on the bloody battlefield all night, when you mourned like a woman, and would not be comforted, not for those who had fallen but for the sad hearts of women at home when the sad tale would be told."

The "wolves" to which Emory referred so many times were coyotes. With Kearny in great suffering, Capt. H. S. Turner, his aide-de-camp, took command and sent three couriers from the Volunteers to Commodore Stockton at San Diego, informing him of what had happened and asking assistance. Two of those sent were Alexis Godey and Thomas Burgess. The third probably was an Indian. Duvall in the log of the *Cyane* mentions that the Indian who had gone out and brought back the sheep for the besieged Americans at San Diego also was the one who later carried a message to Kearny, was captured by the Mexicans and badly treated.

The first inkling of the tragedy, however, was taken to San Diego by Capt. Stokes, who had heard reports while enroute back to his ranch. But he was vague as to details, and no alarm was sounded.

Stretchers, or ambulances, to carry the wounded were made of willow and buffalo robes, in frontier fashion, with one end suspended from a mule and the other dragging on the ground. In the morning the march toward San Diego was resumed, with Kearny back in the saddle and in command, the column passing along a route taking them over the hills on the north side of the valley. It was a painful day for the wounded. That mid-afternoon, after a trek of about five miles, they turned back toward the valley and reached Rancho San Bernardo and the ranch home of Edward Snook. It was deserted except for a few Indians. The site is just east of Highway 395 at the north end of the Lake Hodges crossing. Here they killed chickens to feed the wounded and rounded up some cattle.

After a short rest they moved into the valley. The enemy reappeared from a ravine, attempted an encirclement, which failed, and thirty or forty of them then took positions on a small hill commanding the road. Emory and six or eight men were sent to dislodge them, which they did, amid considerable gunfire. But the Army of the West could go no further. The cattle had been stampeded, and the wounded were in dire need of rest and treatment, and unless help arrived, they surely would all be lost.

Mule Hill, where Army of West made last stand

They dragged themselves up on the rocky hill, which can be seen from Highway 395, and barricaded themselves behind battlements erected with rocks. They bored holes in the river bed for water and killed the fattest of the mules for food. This rocky point now is known as "Mule Hill." The following morning a messenger with a flag of truce appeared and disclosed that Andrés Pico had captured four Americans and wished to exchange them for a like number of Californians. The three couriers to Stockton had gotten through but had been captured on attempting to return. As the Americans held but one captive, only Burgess was able to rejoin the Volunteers on Mule Hill. Pico also passed along some goods for Gillespie which had been sent out from San Diego with the couriers.

The message asking for help had been oddly matter-of-fact, lacking a sense of urgency, and while Stockton later said he had begun immediate preparations to send assistance, all available horses had been taken by Gillespie and some delay was necessary. On their way back to San Pasqual Valley, and just before their capture, Godey and Burgess committed the contents of the message to memory and cached the paper in an oak tree. It was found years later by one of Juan Bandini's *vaqueros*, and what is believed to be a copy is in the Huntington Library. It reads:

Sir: Your letter by Lt. Godoy communicating to me the sad Intelligence of the fight which took place yesterday at early dawn, reached me last night, and I would have instantly sent a detachment to aid you but unfortunately every horse that could travel had been sent with the riflemen, and left us without any means to transport our Artillery. We have not an Animal in the Garrison that can go two leagues, besides we have no conveyances or means of any kind to transport the wounded. Under these circumstances and especially because Mr. Godoy says you have effective force enough to defend yourselves in camp or to march to San Diego, I have thought it most wise to postpone the march of my men till I can hear from you again as they will only consume provisions without being of any use. Mr. Godoy returns to you Immediately with this. Faithfully, Your obt St. R. F. Stockton. To H. S. Turner, Captain U.S.A., Cmdg at Camp Near San Pasqual.

With the situation on Mule Hill now desperate, it was decided to send another plea for help. Kit Carson, Lt. Beale and an Indian volunteered to try and get through the enemy lines to San Diego, twenty-nine miles distant. An Indian had accompanied Beale from San Diego as a servant, and Frémont in his memoirs identifies him as the one who went with Carson and Beale.

Under cover of night they slipped out through the enemy lines. Carson's own story follows:

As soon as dark we started on our mission. In crawling over the rocks and brush our shoes making noise, we took them off; fastened them under our belts. We had to crawl about two miles. We could see three rows of sentinels, all ahorseback, we would often have to pass within 20 yards of one. We got through, but had the misfortune to have lost our shoes, had to travel over a country covered with prickly pear and rocks, barefoot.

During the day they remained in hiding in a gorge, perhaps Peñasquitos Gorge, and at night, when within twelve miles of San Diego, separated, to multiply the chances of getting in. The customary evening ball was under way at the Bandini house, and the band of the *USS Congress* was playing in the Plaza when the Indian servant reached Old Town with the sad news of Kearny's perilous situation. Carson arrived soon after. Beale came in later, in such a condition he had to be carried before Stockton.

Rocks formed defensive barricade on Mule Hill

Lt. Edward F. Beale

112

On Mule Hill, meanwhile, Sgt. John Cox died of his wounds and was buried on the hill and his grave covered with heavy rocks. The enemy attempted to drive a herd of wild horses through the camp and cause a stampede. The herd was turned aside but several were killed to provide a happy change of diet. The baggage was ordered destroyed to keep it from falling into the hands of the enemy. At the end of three days on the hill, Dr. Griffin thought the wounded had progressed enough where all but two could ride, and the order was given to resume the march the next morning. They were certain that Beale and Carson had not gotten through. During the night a guard heard voices — English voices.

Emory wrote:

It was a detachment of 100 tars and 80 marines under Lt. Gray, sent to meet us by Commodore Stockton, from whom we learned that Lt. Beale, Carson and the Indian had arrived safely at San Diego. The detachment left San Diego on the night of the 9th, cached themselves during the day of the 10th, and joined us on the night of that day. These gallant fellows busied themselves till day, distributing their provisions and clothes to our naked and hungry people.

In two days, on Dec. 12, the battered Army accompanied by Lt. Andrew F. V. Gray of the *USS Congress* and 180 men arrived at San Diego, and Emory wrote:

At this place we were in view of the fort overlooking the town of San Diego and the barren waste which surrounds it . . . the town consists of a few adobe houses, two or three of which only have plank floors . . . the rain fell in torrents as we entered the town, and it was my singular fate here, as in Santa Fe, to be quartered in the calaboose, a miserable hut, of one room, some 40x30 feet square. A huge old gun was mounted in this hovel, looking through an embrasure to the westward . . . we preferred the open air and the muddy plaza, saturated with all sorts of filth, to this wretched hole. . . .

The "calaboose" probably was the town hall in the Plaza. A different view of their arrival at San Diego was given by Dr. Griffin:

We all arose freshened with the idea of reaching St. Diego today, and thus finishing this long weary march. We left and marched into St. Diego around 4 p.m., where we received the warmest welcome and kindest attention from our naval friends. I found everything so far as it was in the power of the surgeon's post prepared for my wounded men, and every attention that a warm and generous heart extended to the poor fellows. The *Congress* and *Portsmouth* were laying at anchor in the bay and the town of St. Diego garrisoned by the crew and marines from these two ships.

To Gen. Kearny, San Pasqual had been a victory. The enemy had fled and the battlefield had been cleared. Two more Dragoons died in San Diego making twenty-one in all. One Volunteer also was listed as having been killed. As for the *Californios*, they divided into small bands and faded into the hills, a few of them giving up the fight and entering San Diego under flags of truce. Felipa Osuna Marrón tells how her husband became so embittered with his own people that he asked to be allowed to return to San Diego from his ranch at Agua Hedionda. With Felipa and her husband, under the protection of a white flag, came a number of men who had participated in the Battle of San Pasqual. One of them was her brother, Leandro Osuna, who had killed Capt. Johnston, and another was Jesús Machado. She said the flag of her brother's lance was stained with blood and at first the Americans seemed hostile, but nothing happened.

But, as Dr. Griffin wrote. The "enemy have the country and we have no communication with our friends in the north. The Sonorians are running off all the cattle and horses, and the fact is the country will have nothing in it after the war is over."

There was a sad aftermath to the tragedy of San Pasqual that left a legacy of sorrow in a little divided community. Hayes wrote:

> Some families of San Diego yet mourn for the relatives who were killed by the San Luis Rey Indians in 1846. The day is remembered only as between *dia de la Virgen* (December 8th) and that of *Guadalupe* (December 12th). It was immediately after the Battle of San Pasqual . . . it is unknown and inexplicable what may have led the Indians to strike this terrible blow at persons living amongst them, on terms of greatest confidence.

Men who had wet their lances with the blood of American soldiers themselves were slaughtered and certainly in a moment of savage retribution by Indians whose lands they had taken.

Fleeing from the field of battle, with the appearance of Lt. Gray's rescue expedition, a number of the *Californios* went to Pauma Valley, in the shadow of Palomar Mountains about forty-two miles northeast of San Diego, on the upper San Luis Rey River, four miles west of the Pala Mission and about fifteen miles southwest of Warner's. This was the ranch of José Antonio Serrano, though a number of other *Californios*, including Juan María Osuna, José Aguilar and Bonifacio López, had sent cattle there for grazing to keep them from falling into the hands of Americans.

A report reaching San Diego a few days later that Indians had killed eleven Mexicans was discounted, and Dr. Griffin in his diary noted that "the best versed in California affairs believe these men were killed in the action of the 6th, and that the Mexicans complained of the red skins to conceal their own loss."

Little by little the details began to come out. A small tribe of Luiseño Indians lived in the valley, with Manuelito Cota as their chief. Serrano, who understood a little of their language, overheard two women discussing an attack, and while he warned his companions who were resting at the ranch, he evidently didn't take it too seriously, and left that day with his son, Jesús, and his brother-in-law, José Aguilar, to join his family at Pala.

114

Eleven men were left at the ranch. Hayes wrote:

The well-known *General* Manuelito Cota, was supposed to have been at the head of this sudden movement of his people. The inmates of the ranch house were asleep, when he knocked at the door. Recognizing his voice, José María Alvarado opened the door, against every remonstrations of the rest. The Indians rushed in, seized their victims, took them . . . to Potrero and Agua Caliente, and put them to death in the most cruel manner. It is to be hoped the imagination of surviving kinsmen has exaggerated the terrors of this scene as it still is related by them.

The captured men were first put on exhibition at Agua Caliente, for the benefit of the Cupeños of Warner's, the Cahuillas of the eastern mountain and desert areas, and the Luiseños of the San Luis Rey Mission lands. Manuelito, in a change of heart, wanted to set the captives free. His companion, Pablo Apis, was against it. Here the story becomes more murky, obscured by legend and old hates. Counsel was sought from two persons, an American, Bill Marshall, the seafaring deserter of Warner's, and a Mexican renegade named Yguera who had married a Cupeño woman. It was Marshall who is believed to have influenced the Luiseños to kill their captives, by arguing that the American conquerors would be greatly pleased.

The disbelief that had failed to alarm Serrano and Aguilar turned to fear when they returned to Pauma and learned what had transpired. They picked up the trail and followed it to Agua Caliente, from where they sent an appeal for help to Bill Williams, at Santa Ysabel, and the chief of the Santa Ysabel Indians, Ignacio. Williams first sent an Indian with an offer to ransom the prisoners with cattle but, that failing, went himself and saw them lying bound around a fire. He was warned to be off, or he, too, might die.

There are two versions of the manner of their deaths. One is that they were forced to stand and then were shot full of arrows. The other is that they were lanced to death with spears heated in the fire. The story is told that young Santiago Alipás, only thirteen years old, alone remained calm in the face of death, and was rewarded with execution by gunfire. The bodies were piled in a heap and the Indians danced around them all night. The bodies, except those of Santiago Osuna, youngest son of Juan María Osuna, and Alvarado, were secretly buried. The persistence of legend is that the bodies of Osuna and Alvarado were turned over to an old Indian woman, who had been a servant for their families, and she buried them separately, and then walked to San Diego with the sad news.

The others who died were Manuel Serrano, brother of José Antonio; Ramón Aguilar, José López, his son-in-law, Francisco

Basualdo, two men from Los Angeles named Domínguez and Estacio Ruiz, Juan de la Cruz of Lower California, and an unidentified man from New Mexico.

There were attempts to link Kearny with the massacre, in regard to advice he had given to representatives of the Indians at Santa Ysabel, when they expressed a willingness to aid the American cause. He told them to remain neutral, though Manuelito insisted years later that Kearny also said they had a right to defend themselves from any acts on the part of the Mexicans. Marshall's part in the affair emerged only slowly, and his punishment was yet a few years away.

CHAPTER SEVEN

"Who cares to go with the wagons?
Not we who are free and strong;
Our faith and arms, with right good will,
Shall pull our carts along."

END OF THE PUEBLO

The conquest was nearing an end. The North had not joined in resisting the invasion, and the *Sureños* of the great ranchos of Southern California were dismayed by the loss of life at San Pasqual and in the Pauma massacre, and fearful of more Indian uprisings. The officers of Gen. Pico were divided by jealousy and bickering. With Col. Frémont's Volunteers threatening from the north, and Commodore Stockton and Gen. Kearny beginning final preparations for a march from San Diego, further resistance seemed hopeless, and then came the disheartening report from Indians that a large force of Americans with covered wagons soon would be at Warner's Pass. This was the Mormon Battalion.

The *rancheros* concealed their horses and cattle to prevent their seizure by Pico's Lancers who were made up largely of youngsters and riff-raff of the pueblos of Sonora. But a cry for revenge would take more lives and shed more helpless blood in the silent mountain valleys.

San Diego's destiny as a military city perhaps was written in the muddy little Plaza in Old Town. The *Cyane* returned to join the *Congress, Savannah* and the *Portsmouth* in the bay and add its marines and sailors to a force of 600 men being whipped into an "army" by hours of drilling in the Plaza. On November 23, Dr. Griffin noted in his diary:

We have but little bread only four ounces per diem. No vegetables, but plenty of fresh beef and mutton. I fear dysentery with this diet. The garrison is in a

THE WAR IN CALIFORNIA ENDED when Col. Frémont, left, and Gen. Andres Pico signed the Capitulation of Cahuenga; painted by Carl Oscar Borg.

119

wretched state . . . the quarters like all Mexican houses are ill ventilated, cold and damp. As to military affairs we had what I suppose was intended for a grand review yesterday, 20 dragoons on horses that would not have been used for anything else in the United States but for wolf bait; some 80 or one hundred marines; some 40 volunteer rifle men, and some 40 jacktars — all mounted on horses and mules. This presented certainly the most grotesque cavalry parade I have ever witnessed. All hands however got along remarkably well with their horses — except the marines. They either had the luck of getting the worst animals, or were the worst horsemen. A horse occasionally would become a little restless and give a slight kick, and off would roll the marine, bayonet and musket, then another would give a shake and off would go another marine.

USS Savannah, *here in Mexican War*

As fighting men, however, Dr. Griffin praised the marines as well drilled and healthy and as fine an infantry as could be raised in the United States. As for the sailors, he said jacktars didn't know what "back out" meant, were first rate in discipline, "and if they only had shoes, there is certainly no reason why they should not make first rate soldiers."

Their supply of horses had been increased with the return of the *Stonington* and Capt. Samuel J. Hensley of the California Volunteers. They had gone as far south as Mission Santo Domingo, 185 miles below San Diego in Lower California, and they had obtained 300 head of cattle belonging to Juan Bandini, 140 horses and mules, and some saddles and saddle rigging.

There were some hours of leisure and pleasure, despite the rather primitive surroundings, and Dr. Griffin wrote that "we had a fine ball last night, quite a turn out of good-looking women." Not all Americans were in agreement about such things. Gunner Meyers, who came to San Diego on the *Cyane*, noted that "for a description of the town, it is a miserable hole and the ugliest women I ever saw." He can be forgiven, perhaps, for of the many water color paintings this sailor made of the Mexican and California coast, he left two of San Diego, the only detailed sketch of the hide houses at La Playa and of Old Town as seen from across the bay.

Lt. Emory, the engineer, studied the coast as mapped on old Spanish charts published in Madrid in 1825 and the survey of the harbor made by Capt. Edward Belcher of the Royal Navy and published in his *"Voyage Around the World."* From the hill above the town he saw that the *Rio* San Diego originally debouched into False, or Mission Bay, "where meeting the waters rolling in from the seaward, a bar was formed by the deposit of sand, making the entrance of False Bay impractical."

As for San Diego Bay into which the river was now emptying:

Well grounded fears are entertained that the immense quantity of sand discharged by this river will materially injure, if it does not destroy the harbor of San Diego; but this evil could be arrested at a slight cost, compared with the objects to be obtained. At present San Diego is, all things considered, perhaps one of the best harbors on the coast from Callao to Puget's Sound, with a single exception, that of San Francisco. In the opinion of some intelligent navy officers, it is preferable even to this. The harbor of San Francisco has more water, but that of San Diego has a more uniform climate, better anchorage, and perfect security from winds in any direction. However, the commercial metropolis must be at San Francisco, owing to the greater extent and superiority of the country adjacent, watered by the rivers Sacramento and San Joachim, unless indeed San Diego should be made the terminus of a railroad leading by the route of the Gila to the Del Norte, and thence to the Mississippi and the Atlantic.

Though Stockton and Kearny fell into a dispute as to their respective authority in establishing civil government, the Army at last was ready to bid goodbye to San Diego. With Kearny in command of the troops under Stockton as commander-in-chief, and with some of Pico's irregulars watching from the hills, the 600 men, ill-clad and with shoes made of canvas, and oxen pulling heavily-loaded *carretas* marched out December 29th and camped that night in a heavy rain in Soledad Valley. Santiago E. Arguello went as captain of a Volunteer Battalion, with Luis Arguello as a lieutenant and Miguel de Pedrorena as an aide-de-camp to Stockton.

The next morning, Dr. Griffin wrote, they "marched as hard as our poor devilish, broken down animals could carry us." After camping the second night at Los Peñasquitos they reached San Bernardo Rancho. The day had been beautiful but the night was cold, the water freezing, and the mountains in the distance were covered with snow.

Dr. Griffin visited the scene of the Battle of San Pasqual and Mule Hill, where he found "everything just as we left it, except poor Sgt. Cox's grave, the wolves had scratched down to the body and eaten off part of the feet." A marine guard was drawn up at Bernardo Rancho and the camp of Stockton:

Excavation where sergeant may have been buried.

> The Commodore with his staff passed the night at the ranch, and report says had a fine supper. The Commodore has the most enlarged view of the hardships of a soldier's life. He has a fine tent well supplied with table furniture and bedstead, I am told, while our old General has nothing in the world but his blankets and bear skins, and a common tent, one pack mule for himself, Capt. Turner and Stewart.

On the way they passed the deserted San Luis Rey Mission and came to Santa Margarita Rancho, where they received reports of Frémont's movements from John Forster, who said his brother-in-law, Andrés Pico, really believed that the American government would never confiscate property or shoot a man though he may have violated the most sacred pledge.

To Dr. Griffin it seemed a "misfortune that our government has the reputation of exercising too much leniency. These fellows suppose that they can make war as long as it is convenient and when they get tired of it, come in and be paid high wages for little or no service."

Forster remained with them on the march to San Juan Capistrano Mission:

> Forster told us that after the Battle of San Pasqual . . . the Californians came to St. Johns, that each man told how many of our men they had killed individually, that upon computation taken of each man, they killed some 200 of our people. Of course the bragging must have been rare . . . We found here four Californians, who had been wounded in the action. Forster told us that these rascals after they had concluded to run, found some of our dead and wounded in the bushes, and actually (stuck) their lances in them so they might draw blood on their lances.

The Americans and the *Californios* finally came face to face at the upper ford of the San Gabriel River southeast of Los Angeles. Though there was some desultory artillery fire, and a few casualties, Gen. José María Flores was unable to prevent the crossing of the river. The *Californios* retreated to the Los Angeles River, but again a crossing was effected. Los Angeles surrendered on January 10. Flores turned his authority over to Andrés Pico and fled to Sonora. Pico chose to surrender to Frémont, who had reached San Fernando, and the Capitulation of Cahuenga was signed on January 13, 1847, in an atmosphere of forgiveness and goodwill.

Sometime during the closing phases of the war, Gen. Flores dispatched José del Carmen Lugo and Ramón Carrillo and fifteen men on a mission of revenge. They were joined by a band of Cahuilla Indians led by Juan Antonio. At Aguanga, between Warner's and Temecula, just north of the present San Diego-Riverside County line, they trapped many members of the small Luiseño tribe which had committed the Pauma Valley massacre. A number were killed and the rest turned over to the custody of Juan Antonio. Juan Antonio slaughtered them all. How many died is not known as the reports of the affair are fragmentary. Probably more than half of the little tribe of seventy was wiped out and the Paumas reduced to impotency.

Both Stockton and Kearny returned to San Diego, for short stays, continuing their disagreement as to their respective authorities, while Lt. Beale and Kit Carson and ten picked men were sent from San Diego to Washington with dispatches announcing the acquisition of California. They were followed by Indians for 800 miles. Beale, a slight, stoop-shouldered little man, also took with him a letter from twenty brother officers and shipmates thanking him for his success in getting through to San Diego and bringing help for the survivors of San Pasqual. The letter stated that they had ordered from England a pair of epaulettes and sword "to be presented to you . . . as a testimony of our admiration of your gallant conduct in the bold and hazardous enterprise . . ."

Kearny re-instituted regular mail service between San Diego and San Francisco, in much the same manner as that conducted by the Spaniards. Even well up into the Mexican period couriers twice a week had been dispatched in both directions, from San Diego at one end and San Francisco at the other, journeying from mission to mission. Under Kearny, each Monday two Army couriers left San Francisco and San Diego, carrying civilian as well as military mail, meeting and exchanging mail pouches half way, and then retracing their routes. Mail from San Diego arrived at San Luis Rey Monday evening; at Los Angeles, Wednesday noon; at Santa Barbara, Friday evening; at Monterey, Wednesday evening, and at San Francisco, Sunday evening.

With the establishment of the military posts on the Pacific Coast and due to the increased tension between the North and the South over the issue of slavery, it was imperative that the government mail between Washington, D.C., and the West Coast be maintained on schedule. In 1848 a military mail service was started from San Diego to Yuma. The route proceeded south from San Diego to the Tia Juana River, thence up the river for a distance and then following the low valleys where the mountains slide off below the international border, which are now traversed by the Tijuana-Mexicali highway, for about forty miles, entering California again near Campo, and continuing east down Walker Canyon, past Mountain Springs. This route long had been used by Bandini in travelling from his ranch at Tecate to Tijuana, and the rancho of Arguello, and from there along the mission road to San Diego.

SAN DIEGO'S FIRST MAIL connection with the East was a military mule route which followed the Mexican ranch road through low valleys below the border.

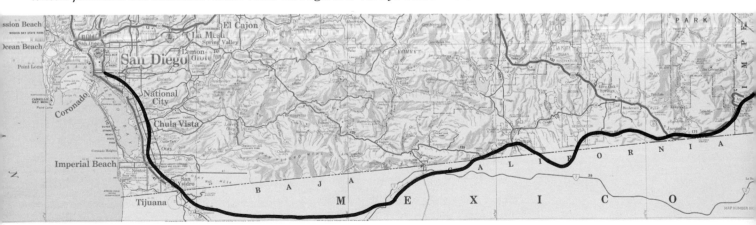

It was a natural corridor to the mountain passes. At Mountain Springs the mail route went down harsh Long Canyon to connect with the Kearny route east of Coyote Wells, and from there it went on to Yuma.

The Mormon Battalion, deviating at times from the route followed by Kearny, in carrying out instructions to open a wagon route to California, reached the Colorado River on January 8. The Battalion then was down to about 350 men, the feeblest among them long since having been sent back. With the Battalion were the wives of five officers. It had been a long and trying march by men unaccustomed to the discipline of military life and beset all the way by shortages of clothing and livestock. At the Colorado Lt. Col. Cooke accused the Mormons of indifference in getting their wagons across the mile-wide ford, a task that required three days, but in truth, their mules were worn and weak, and ahead lay the worst of the march, sixty miles of bleak, forbidding desert.

Wells in the desert ran dry, many of the wagons had to be abandoned, and the Battalion became separated from its train, and as Cooke wrote in his *Journal:*

Thus, without water for near three days (for the animals) and encamping two nights in succession without water, the battalion made, in forty-eight hours, four marches of eighteen, eight, eleven, and nineteen miles, suffering from frost and summer heat.

On the last day before reaching Carrizo Springs, their water ran out altogether and Henry Standage saw "many of the brethern

THE FAMED MORMON BATTALION under command of Capt. Cooke broke the first wagon road to California, from Ft. Leavenworth, Kansas to San Diego.

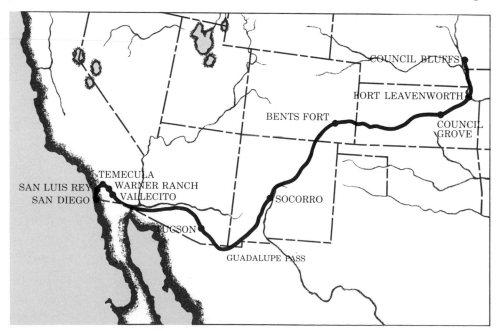

THE MORMON BATTALION is shown crossing an Arizona stream in opening a military wagon road to San Diego and the West. Painting by George W. Ottinger.

laying by the road side begging water . . . " A message for assistance had been sent to Kearny, and at this almost hopeless point some herders arrived with thirty-five mules and the sad news of Kearny's defeat at San Pasqual and the death of a number of Cooke's friends.

When they reached Carrizo Springs on January 17, to the commander's amazement, the Mormons broke out a fiddle and sang lustily all evening around their camp fires. With the disaster of San Pasqual in mind, Cooke, on January 19, ordered his men into a more military order, with scouts in front and baggage to the rear, and marched them up through Mason Valley. A guide came back with the report that it appeared as if they were coming to a dead end. At the tip of Mason Valley, the historic desert trail branched off, one an Indian road, swinging northwest up through Oriflamme Canyon to Cuyamaca and Green Valleys, high in the mountains, and the other turning slightly east through a narrow rocky chasm into Earthquake Valley and then San Felipe Valley and Warner's Pass. But the flat chasm was too narrow for the wagons and the 200-foot ridge separating the two valleys too steep for the mules and their wagons.

Cooke inspected the situation. He took off his coat, seized a pick and told his men to "fall to." By nightfall they had chipped away a foot of rock and dirt and cut a path for four and a half-miles through which the wagons could be squeezed. This was Box Canyon, and the work of Cooke and the Mormons made possible the historic Butterfield Stage Route.

The Battalion arrived at Warner's on January 21, and it rained for three days, the men seeking shelter in the timber, and the march was resumed on the 25th. They were soaked through to the skin in trying to ford a swollen creek, and finally learned they were on the wrong road. Henry Wm. Bigler, in his *Diary of a Mormon in California* writes that the whole country appeared to be alive with large bands of horses, mules and johasses, and the valleys and hills were covered with herds of cattle, and along the larger streams there was any amount of wildlife.

THE MORMON BATTALION under Capt. Cooke drove its wagons up through San Felipe Pass and then went by way of Temecula to reach San Luis Rey Mission.

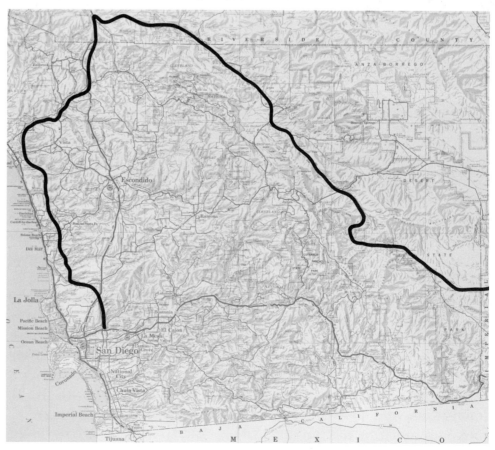

In some doubt as to their instructions, they continued on the road to Los Angeles until they reached the Temecula turn-off, where they received orders directing them to San Diego, and they went south through Rainbow and reached the broad San Luis Rey River Valley west of Pala. They followed the river west until they passed the San Luis Rey Mission on January 27th, and camped near the seashore north of what is now the city of Oceanside. From there they went south toward San Diego, in two marches, Bigler noting that "in many places there were acres and perhaps hundreds of acres of wild oats growing, looking as green as a wheat field at home in the month of May . . . I have seen some Mexicans and Indians who looked to me as if they were as old as the everlasting hills."

From Soledad Valley they crossed the Miramar Mesa and went down the padres' road through Cañada de la Soledad, or Murphy Canyon, to San Diego Mission, which had been designated as their quarters. It was January 30. Bigler writes that they found the mission rooms dirty and full of fleas as they had been occupied only by Indians for some time. The harbor was full of ships, Bigler noting the presence of two men o' war, one merchant vessel, a whaler and a schooner.

Cooke issued his "Order Number I" which follows, in part:

The lieutenant-colonel commanding congratulates the battalion on their safe arrival on the shore of the Pacific ocean, and the conclusion of the march of over two thousand miles. History may be searched in vain for an equal march of infantry. Nine-tenths of it has been through a wilderness where nothing but savages and wild beasts are found, or deserts where, for want of water, there is no living thing . . . With crowbar and pick and ax in hand we have worked our way over mountains which seemed to defy aught save the wild goat, and hewed a passage through a chasm of living rock more narrow than our wagons . . . Thus, marching half naked and half fed, and living upon wild animals, we have discovered and made a road of great value to our country . . .

The town, however, was without provisions and the Battalion was destitute of clothing. Consequently, the Battalion was ordered to move up to the San Luis Rey Mission, where it arrived February 3, and Bigler writes that "this is a handsome situation and good buildings sufficient to accommodate a thousand soldiers." A supply vessel from the Sandwich Islands arrived at San Diego, and the food situation was temporarily relieved. In mid-March the Battalion was divided, Company B under Capt. Jesse D. Hunter being ordered to San Diego to take over from the Marines the garrisoning of Fort Stockton with its seven pieces of artillery.

San Diego could never resume its old ways, but life began to flow once again, and Dr. Griffin, who had returned with Kearny's Dragoons, writes:

Philip St. George Cooke, as a brigadier general

The Commodore gave an eloquent blow out on board the *Congress*. The decorations were the flags of different nations, and the deck of the ships made decidedly the finest ballroom I ever saw. We had all the ladies from San Diego and everything went off in fine style. We had a little dance every evening at *Señor* Bandini's and . . . the whole time passes off agreeably.

Rumors of Mexican forces approaching from Sonora persisted, but nothing ever came of them, though at one time Frémont sent a force of 175 men and four pieces of artillery to Warner's. According to Dr. Griffin, Stockton upon returning to San Diego on the *Congress*, proclaimed his intention of fighting any enemy legions reported massing at San Vicente in Lower California and "Stockton made a speech to his men before sailing yesterday . . . that if pushed to the last he will make the pass of San Vicente as renowned as Thermopylae . . . Ye gods, what gas!"

The *Congress* sailed for the south with Santiago Arguello and Pedrorena but evidently saw no signs of impending danger.

The industrious Mormons brought a sense of urgency to a pueblo that had existed with only a limited feeling for time and events, and the *Californios* slowly laid aside their fears that the Mormons would run off with their women. Dr. Griffin notes:

The prejudice against the Mormons here seems to be wearing off. It is as yet among the Californians a great term of reproach to be called Mormon. Yet, as they are quiet, industrious, sober, inoffensive people they seem to be gradually working their way up. They are extremely industrious. They have been engaged while here in digging wells, plastering houses, and seem anxious and ready to work . . . they are barefooted and naked . . . Mormons building a horse mill . . . this is looked upon in San Diego as the greatest feat that has ever been undertaken in these parts.

Bigler in his diary said that masons among the Mormons built the first brick house in San Diego and "for all I know in California. The building I believe was to be used for a courthouse and school." Some fifteen or twenty wells were dug, lined with brick, pumps installed, and a kiln completed. The brick structure erected by the Mormons probably was the office and court of the *alcalde* which is shown west of the Plaza in the first sketches of Old Town made by the Americans. It appeared to be two-stories in height, with an American-type porch. The old adobe town house in the Plaza was falling into ruins.

The wife of Capt. Hunter, who had come with him with the Mormon Battalion, gave birth to a son named Diego, the first child born in Old Town of American parents. Mrs. Hunter, however, died in April, during an influenza epidemic. A census of the region

THIS MAP identifies buildings in Old Town shortly after the American conquest, as reconstructed from a map made by Cave J. Couts and old land titles.

1 Casa de Juan Lopez
2 Casa de Santiago E. Arguello
3 Casa de A. Jay Smith
4 Casa de Edward Stokes
5 Casa de Maria Machado
6 Casa de Feliciana Valdez de Reyes
7 Office of the Alcalde, Joshua Bean
8 Casa de Maria Machado de Silvas
9 Casa de A. Light & R. Freeman
10 Casa de Thomas Wrightington
11 Casa de Antonio Estudillo
12 Town Hall
13 Casa de Rosario Aguilar
14 Casa de Juan Maria Osuna
15 Casa de Henry D. Fitch
16 Casa de Joseph Snook
17 Casa de Eugenia Silvas
18 Casa de Eugenia Silvas
19 Casa de Juan Bandini
20 Casa de Francisco Alvarado
21 Casa de Juan Machado
22 Casa de Juan M. Marrón
23 Casa de Josefa Fitch (sold by Romero
   to Josefa Fitch in 1848)
24 Josefa Fitch's "New frame house"
25 Fitch's Store
26 Josefa Fitch's "Fine Garden" (Hayes)
27 Structure belonging to Bandini
28 Casa de Albert B. Smith
29 Structure belonging to F. Alvarado
30 Casa de Rafaela Serrano
31 Casa de Pío Pico
32 Casa de Juan Rocha
33 Casa de Maria de los Reyes Ybañez

NEW STRUCTURES (NOT EXISTING IN 1849):

34 Casa de Juan Alipaz
35 New Jail
36 Tents
37 Structure belonging to Fitch Estate

SAN DIEGO, just after the American conquest when it was beginning to feel the frontier pangs of the Gold Rush migration into California. The location and ownership of the original homes of the Dons, in 1848-50, has been worked out from Spanish and Mexican land grants, from deeds of the early American period, and from the first maps of the pueblo. Some of the original homes were not included in the original sketch, made by H. M. T. Powell, and in the lithograph believed to have been made from the sketch a year or so later.

130

DIEGO,

1850.

C. C. Couts del.

taken by the Mormon company listed 248 whites, three Sandwich Islanders, three Negroes, 483 "tame" Indians, and 1550 "wild" Indians. Actually, the Indian population was much larger.

During the period of the conquest José Antonio Estudillo, Pedrorena, Joaquín Ortega and Capt. Fitch served successively as justices of the peace, or *alcaldes*, as they were generally referred to, and in 1847, under American military rule, Fitch and possibly Philip Crosthwaite were elected and confirmed by military authorities. Fitch also had been appointed *receptor* or collector of customs but resigned and was succeeded by Pedro C. Carrillo, and the port was opened to foreign trade. Carrillo was succeeded, in turn, by Santiago Arguello and Miguel de Pedrorena.

In April, Fitch, as *alcalde*, reported to Kearny, as acting governor of California, that he was having difficulty enforcing his own decrees. In reply, Kearny wrote:

> I regret to learn that Mr. Warner refuses obedience to your decree. If he remain refractory, you are authorized to call upon the military officer most convenient to you for men to enforce your decree. This authority is also delegated to you in any other case in which the military may be required to give effect to your judicial acts.

Fitch resigned and was succeeded by Lt. Robert Clift of the Mormon Battalion. He, in turn, in the following year, was succeeded by Bandini and Edmund Lee Brown, as first and second *alcaldes*, respectively. Juan María Marrón succeeded Bandini. Brown had been a sergeant with the Mormon Battalion.

At the time Stockton returned from the capture of Los Angeles, he ordered the dismantling of Ft. Stockton. The cannons originally from the old Spanish fort on Ballast Point were taken out and dropped into the deepest part of the bay. According to Judge Hayes, one cannon, which had been cast in Manila in 1783, and had been hidden by Pedrorena at the outbreak of war, was left in the Plaza, on the plea of Crosthwaite, for the protection of San Diego and the firing of salutes. It was mounted on wheels and axle by the carpenter of the frigate *Congress*. However, two cannons have survived. The one cast in Manila is engraved *"El Júpiter"* and points seaward from Stockton Hill; the other, named *"El Cápitan"* and also cast in 1783, is in the Old Town Plaza.

With the war over, Santiago Arguello sought to take possession of the San Diego Mission and its lands which had been granted to him by Pío Pico but he was frustrated in this effort by José Antonio Estudillo. Estudillo exhibited a power of attorney as administrator on behalf of Fr. Vicente Oliva, thus showing that the church still claimed jurisdiction. Capt. Daniel Davis, who commanded the First Company, Mormon Volunteers, held the

Don Miguel
de Pedrorena

sale invalid though Philip Crosthwaite and E. L. Brown were placed in charge of the property. Apolinaria Lorenzana informed the president of the missions of the theft of the sacred vessels and silver candlesticks, some of which, she said, were melted down in a smithy operated by the Americans in Old Town. However, Estudillo subsequently reported finding many of the missing articles buried in the sand of the river bottom, where they must have been hidden by devout Indians.

The suspicion that missions had been fraudulently given away led Kearny to issue a proclamation halting further sale of missions and Indian lands and the United States assumed a guardianship over the properties until all claims as to ownership could be verified. As Fr. Oliva had died in January of 1847, custody of the San Diego Mission was conveyed temporarily to Padre Gonzales of the Santa Barbara Mission.

Mormon Camp in 1852

The Americanization that had begun with the arrivals of the fur ships from Boston, and then the hide ships of the days of Richard Henry Dana, proceeded swiftly. On the Fourth of July, 1847, Bigler's diary notes:

> At daylight 5 pieces of cannon were fired off in salute of the day of American independence, after which the Comp. shouldered their mustkets . . . and gave the officers of Comp. B, and the citizens of San Diego a . . . salute . . . This seemed to please the inhabitants of the town so well that they brought out their bottles of wine and (*aguardiente,* or spirits), . . . and called on the boys to help themselves to all they could drink and the day passed nicely . . .

When the time neared for the Mormons to receive their long anticipated discharges from military service, "the citizens of San Diego insisted that we enlist again . . . they seemed to be favorable to the American flag and said they knew they will ketch hell soon after we leave."

Their departure alarmed San Diego and they petitioned the military on the need of a garrison. Re-enlisted Mormons returned, but early in 1848 they were succeeded by Company I of Stevenson's Regiment of Volunteers who had been recruited in New York State and arrived by sea after the shooting was over. The company, however, remained only until September, when it, too, was mustered out, and that ended the military occupation of San Diego.

Though the fighting was long since over in California, the war with Mexico continued. The crew of the *Portsmouth* raised the American flag at San José del Cabo, at the tip of Lower California, on March 29, 1847 and at La Paz on the gulf on April 13. The American flag previously had been raised in the northern section by the Volunteers from San Diego. There was no doubt in the minds of the officers of the Navy but that Lower California would

GUAYMAS, MEXICO, was bombarded by a U.S. fleet, as depicted in this water-color sketch by Gunner Meyers. The war on the peninsula was long and bitter.

become a part of the United States as had Upper California. In July, 115 men of the New York Volunteers were landed at La Paz, while a Navy lieutenant and twenty-four men were left to hold San José. When American ships of war left these waters to block-ade mainland ports, a Mexican army, which had crossed over from Guaymas, attacked both places. The fighting raged back and forth for the rest of the year, and on into 1848, with the *USS Cyane*, whose crew had raised the first American flag over San Diego, and two whalers assisting the Americans. The *Magnolia*, under Capt. B. Simmons, which had helped in the recapture of San Diego, sent its crew, along with that of the *Edward*, of New Bed-ford, J. S. Parker, master, to the relief of an American garrison at San Jose. Finally, the Americans were reinforced and they defeated the Mexicans and captured the officers. This phase had cost many more casualties than had the actions in Upper Califor-nia. The outcome of the war, however, was decided in major battles on the mainland, and the Treaty of Guadalupe Hidalgo, signed on February 2, 1848, confirmed United States' possession of the Southwest and California, but returned Lower California to Mexico.

American whale ships had been putting into Lower California bays, particularly La Paz, for fresh provisions for some time. In a letter written in 1848, Rodman M. Price, purser of the *Cyane*, stated that:

On the Pacific Coast of the peninsula there is the great bay of Magdalena . . . a fleet of whale ships have been there during the winter months of the last two years, for a new species of whale that are found there . . . it will be a constant source of regret to this country that it was not included in the treaty of peace just made with Mexico . . . as a possession to any foreign power, I think Lower California more valuable than the group of the Sandwich Islands.

The leading figures in the conquest of California, Stockton, Kearny and Frémont, had long since left. Col. Richard B. Mason was governor. For Frémont, there was only bitterness ahead. For refusing to obey the orders of Kearny, who had brought with him authority from the President as regards civil government, the same instructions which Stockton had chosen to ignore, he was to be court-martialed in an atmosphere charged with politics, and convicted of mutiny and disobedience. Public sympathy, however, helped to make him the first Republican candidate for President in 1856. Kearny died in 1848 from fever contracted on one of his later campaigns.

THE U.S. WARSHIP DALE is sketched by Gunner Meyers off La Paz, Baja California. The American flag flies over the town after its capture in Mexican war.

135

The San Diegans returned to their ranchos, and donning the costumes of the old days that they were never really to forget, sat in their silver saddles and once again looked over their rolling empires, uncertain but hopeful in the promise of the Americans that the United States would accept them as free and equal citizens and respect their titles to their lands.

Death was removing some of the early figures of the ranch period. Juan María Osuna, a corporal of the San Diego Company under the banner of Spain, died in 1847, as did Capt. Edward Snook, who in his will left San Bernardo Rancho to relatives in England, subject to his wife's use during her natural life.

The bodies of the soldiers who had fallen at San Pasqual were removed about May 20, 1848, from their burial place under the willow tree and re-interred in Old Town by the First Dragoons. A new cemetery for Protestants was laid out in a block bounded by the present streets of Hancock, Trias, Moore and Hortensia. There the bodies remained for a number of years, and efforts were made from time to time to have a monument erected.

Pío Pico, the last Mexican governor, returned to California, entering San Diego on July 6, 1848. He failed to report to the military authorities there, and then at San Fernando declared himself still governor under the terms of the armistice that ended the war. But that was in a yesterday that was gone forever.

On the surface, all was tranquil, but Capt. Fitch reflected an undercurrent of resentment. He wrote that "the inhabitants are almost unanimously opposed to the U.S. government, and detest us from the bottom of their hearts in particular the newcomers." For the Indians, time was quickly running out.

California still was largely unknown. The map of the new territories accompanying the treaty with Mexico had to be drawn several times, as the first two had failed to include all of Southern California. The first suggested boundary line had run south of San Francisco, and the second, just south of Del Mar, about nineteen miles north of San Diego. In the end, it was set as running east from a point one marine league south of San Diego Bay.

Barely a week before the signing of the treaty that ended the war a man by the name of James W. Marshall saw some tiny glittering pebbles in the tail race of John A. Sutter's sawmill in one of the small canyons of the Sierra Nevada Mountains. Gold!

CHAPTER EIGHT

"Oh, what was your name in the States?
Was it Thompson or Johnson or Bates?
Did you murder your wife
And fly for your life?
Say, what was your name in the States?"

THE BURNING TRAIL

Some months passed before the news of gold reached the towns and settlements of California. At Monterey, on May 29, 1848, the American *alcalde,* Walter Colton, who had been the chaplain on the *USS Congress*, wrote in his diary:

Our town was startled out of its quiet dreams to-day, by the announcement that gold had been discovered on the American Fork. The men wondered and talked, and the women, too; but neither believed. The sibyls were less skeptical; they said the moon had, for several nights, appeared not more than a cable's length from the earth; that a white ram had been seen playing with an infant; and that an owl had rung the church bells.

Mexicans were the first to reach the gold fields in large numbers. Many of them had gained experience in placer mining in their own country and had begun taking gold out of the San Fernando hills north of Los Angeles as early as 1842. With the outbreak of war, they had left California but now they returned, following the Old Anza Trail across the Borrego Desert and up Coyote Canyon or the longer desert route through Coachella Valley and up San Gorgonio Pass. This became known as the Sonora Route. One of those who came over the Anza Trail in 1849 was Joaquín Murietta. He and other desperadoes from Sonora were to leave their own trails of robbery and murder.

By late June of 1848, San Francisco and Monterey were almost deserted. By December the news had reached the East Coast. By the spring of 1849 more than 35,000 persons had taken passage

THE COLORADO DESERT, with its parched distances and cruel heat, was a terrifying ordeal. Here immigrants use Signal Mountain as a guiding beacon.

139

on ships diverted to California or had crossed the Missouri River with wagon trains that soon stretched across the Western deserts. Some were to reach California in three or four months; others were to be on the trail as long as nine months.

The discovery of gold gave a sharp impetus to a westward movement already under way. The acquisition of California had heightened the dreams of new lands and new opportunities for many thousands of people in a restless age of exploration, expansion and settlement. To some, land even was more precious than gold, and they arrived to push against the vast possessions of the defiant Dons.

The sea route was by way of Cape Horn or Panama. At Panama thousands of gold seekers waited for passage north after having sailed south and crossed the isthmus on foot. Ships bound for San Francisco put into San Diego for water and provisions. One party of forty-eight left a leaky old ship about 300 miles south and walked toward San Diego, amid terrible hardships. At last they sighted the bay and the masts of two ships, as had Fr. Junipero Serra eighty years before them. One of them was their own ship, the *Dolphin*. Hundreds then thousands of adventurers and settlers followed the Gila Trail of the fur traders and transformed San Diego.

In the van of this push along the Southern trail in 1848, by chance, was Graham's Battalion. This was another unit of the United States Army, composed of two other companies of the First Dragoons and two of the Second Dragoons. With the end of the war, the battalion was marched all the way from Monterrey in north central Mexico to Tucson and California. There were 275 soldiers, 160 wagons, 205 teamsters, and a number of other workmen, or nearly 500 men in all. One of the lieutenants with the First Dragoons was Cave J. Couts.

Cave J. Couts

Couts' diary relates a story of an arduous and disorganized march because of the incompetence of the commander, Brevet Maj. Lawrence P. Graham, who had taken along a comfortable tent, an understanding mistress and a goodly supply of liquor.

After crossing the Colorado River on November 27 they began to experience the effects of the gold rush and Couts wrote that "persons, Mexicans, from Sonora, are passing us daily on their way to the *abundancia*, the gold mines! This is all we can hear, The Mines!" A few days later, after failing to receive anticipated supplies from Los Angeles, Couts wrote of the excitement there and in San Diego:

No corn, provisions scarce, men all deserting and going to the gold mines! Everybody crazy on the subject, rather hard for us to contemplate upon! Four

140

fine companies, with nearly two hundred horses, all to be now lost! Men for gold, horses for want of forage! The mania that pervades the whole country, our camp included, is beyond all description or creditibility. The whole state of Sonora is on the move, are passing us in gangs daily, and say they have not yet started. Naked and shirttailed Indians and Mexicans or Californians, go and return in 15 or 20 days with over a pound of pure gold each, per day, and say "they had bad luck and left." In Los Angeles and San Diego a man in fitting out a party of 5 or 10 men for the mines has only to go to a merchant and borrow from one to two thousand dollars and give him an "order on the gold mines." Nothing apparently sells for less than an ounce of gold. If the Government manages it properly, or luckily, it will be the richest nation on earth, if unluckily, California will prove an ulcer that will follow her to her long unhappy home. We will make our fortunes! Not a doubt of it! All is cut and dried!

The battalion trudged through one to four inches of snow in upper San Felipe Pass on the way to Los Angeles. At Warner's, where they arrived December 29, more than a month after crossing the Colorado, Couts described the trader and former trapper as "a white man, famed for his ability in telling lies, but not surpassed even in this by his notoriety as a rascal. He, Warner, stole my stallion as the horses passed. Luckily for him that it was not known to us until we had left him."

Pass Between San Felipe and Vallecito

San Diego was to hear more of Lt. Couts.

The winter saw the arrest once again of Warner, this time on an accusation of stealing government mules. He was seized by the Army, taken to Los Angeles and walked through the streets to prison, but evidently won his freedom on the contention he had obtained the mules from soldiers in exchange for fresh mounts.

The rush of business came too late for Capt. Fitch, the first American to take up residence in San Diego and who had sacrificed his United States citizenship to elope with Josefa Carrillo. He died on January 14, 1849, leaving eleven children, and his widow saw to it that he was buried in the old Spanish *campo santo*, or cemetery, on Presidio Hill. He was the last of the early settlers to be buried there, among the mounds of ruined walls and not far from the spot where Fr. Junípero Serra eighty years before had blessed the site of the first rude mission established in California. A new Catholic cemetery, near two palm trees at the foot of Presidio Hill, and enclosed with a paling fence, had been in use for some time. *Señora* Fitch and her sons continued to operate the store, a dark red adobe structure erected in 1848 on what is now Calhoun Street.

Though the fur ships had vanished from the coast, and the hide trade ships were beginning to thin out, the whalers began to appear in increasing numbers and then early in 1849 came the first passenger ships, those of the Pacific Mail Steamship Co., the side-wheelers *California*, *Oregon* and *Panama*, packed with

141

fortune-seekers from the four corners of the world. These ships forced their way up the coast from Panama, against wind and current, picking up still more adventurers at Acapulco, San Blas and San Diego.

Arriving by sea from Northern California were other military detachments, of which two companies of infantry were assigned to the San Diego area to garrison Warner's, the outlet to Lower California and Sonora, and the mouth of the Gila River, for protection of the immigrant trains rolling toward California. Companies D and H of the Second Infantry, under Maj. Samuel P. Heintzelman, arrived at Monterey April 6 and immediately were ordered to San Diego.

The journal of Lt. Thomas W. Sweeny, who had lost his right arm in the war in Mexico, records that when they arrived on the propeller ship *Edith*, it was boarded by Don Miguel de Pedrorena who said he was the recognized commandant of the Southern district but supposed he would have to resign now that the troops had arrived. The journal reads:

> As this was arrogated by himself and irresponsible, we relieved him of it at once, notwithstanding the dignity with which he maintained it and the friendly offices he had performed toward the American government.

Thomas W. Sweeny, as a brigadier general

Sweeny was disappointed in San Diego, finding that it consisted of a collection of dilapidated adobe buildings affording but scanty shelter to a population of three or four hundred Spaniards and Indians. He said the gold fever was raging and his command had been thinned by desertions. "Hidden wealth fills every mind."

Though the principal migration was over the North Platte Route from Independence, Missouri, to San Francisco, in 1849 alone more than twelve thousand persons, perhaps half of them Mexicans, forded the Colorado River in the vicinity of the Gila junction, and most of them, after crossing the desert, flowed up through the San Felipe, Coyote, San Gorgonio and Cajon Passes to Los Angeles and then directly north to the gold fields. Others, worn and destitute, drifted down the old Spanish trails and *carreta* roads to San Diego, where, after resting, they took passage on a boat, if possible, or resumed their trek up El Camino Real. However, many remained. Many others were to return.

Bayard Taylor, who was on board a vessel bound for San Francisco but which stopped at San Diego, wrote in his book, *El Dorado, or Adventures in the Path of Empire*, that he saw:

> . . . a number of men, lank and brown, "as is the ribbed sea sand" — men with long hair and beards, and faces from which the rigid expression of suffering was scarcely relaxed. They were the first of the overland immigrants by the Gila route, who had reached San Diego a few days before. Their clothes were

THE GILA RIVER country had a certain harsh beauty that was captured in this sketch which appeared in John Russell Bartlett's "Personal Narrative" in 1854.

in tatters, their boots, in many cases, replaced by moccasins, and except their rifles and small packages rolled in deerskin, they had nothing left of the abundant stores with which they left home.

To him their adventures "sounded more marvelous than anything I have heard or read since my boyish acquaintance with Robinson Crusoe, Captain Cook, and John Ledyard . . . this California crusade will more than equal the great military expeditions of the Middle Ages in magnitude, peril and adventure."

There were many variations of the Southern route though they all converged on the Gila River in central Arizona. One route led from Memphis or New Orleans to San Antonio, from where there were two different trails, both leading to El Paso, from where they diverged again, one deep into Mexico, to come together at the Gila. Another main route started at Fort Smith, Kansas, and went west to Albuquerque and then dipped southward to the Gila. El Paso then was a Mexican settlement, which is now known as Juarez, just across the Rio Grande from the present American city of El Paso.

The Gila route seemed the most practical, at first glance, having been travelled by Kearny's Army of the West and the Mormon and Graham Battalions, and with wagons, and it avoided the harsh winters of the Plains and the formidable Sierra Nevada. But it did pass the land of the dreaded Apaches and through that of the un-

El Paso

143

THE ARTIST J. GOLDSBOROUGH BRUFF graphically portrays the grim end which met the stock of many immigrant parties crossing the Western desert.

conquered Yumas. A correspondent of the *New York Tribune* who made his way to the gold fields described the various routes to California and stated:

> . . . the last and most terrible one of all is by way of Chihuahua and down the Gila across the 90-mile desert. Caution all emigrants to California to avoid this way as they would the plague. I have seen men arrive at Santa Barbara, when I was there, who were completely broken down by the fatigues attendant on this route. Across the desert thousands of skeletons of mules and horses lie.

Those coming over the Gila Trail in large proportion were Southerners and they brought with them a sympathy for slavery that was to linger in San Diego through the Civil War. So many came from Pike County, Missouri, that a certain type of Southerners, who were generally poorly educated, if at all, and inclined to wander in gypsy fashion, became known as "Pikes." Probably they were not much different from the "Okies" of later years who migrated West from the Dust Bowl.

It was a long way from New Orleans to San Diego, literally and figuratively. A port of entry for immigrants from Europe, and with more bank credit than New York, New Orleans was compared by a contemporary writer with Paris, "with lamps hanging from

144

ropes across the streets, the 'noble' old buildings such as the St. Louis Hotel which has a ballroom unequalled in the United States for size and beauty," and operas, concerts, ballets, balls and masquerades.

A tide of humanity that has never slowed surged West through New Orleans, leaving the wet malarial lands of the Mississippi Valley, where only the slave could work, and on across the rolling green lowlands of east Texas, thick with the life-saving mesquite tree, then on again, as Texas dried out into a wasteland and then gave way to the desert.

Great wagon trains were made up at New Orleans, with people who had come recently from Europe or down the Mississippi from the upper territories. Those who possessed money enough could take a boat to Panama, from where the fare to San Diego, cabin class, was $250 and steerage, $125.

The *New Orleans Daily Picayune* in March 1850 said that "large numbers of emigrants mostly from the Western states and without exception of the respectable class — the bone and sinew of the land — are almost daily arriving in our city and waiting anxiously the first opportunity to depart for the promised land."

San Antonio was the frontier. After the Mexican war it began to grow rapidly and by 1850 it had a population of more than 3000. An immigrant from Germany wrote that "women pay more attention to dress in San Antonio than they do in New York or in

THE JUMPING OFF PLACE for thousands of immigrants headed for the gold fields was San Antonio. This sketch in Lt. Emory's Report shows military plaza.

TUBAC, RAVAGED OVER THE YEARS by Apache Indians, was in ruins when immigrants passed through enroute to California. This sketch was in 1869 book.

the large cities of Europe. We have balls and revelries. Men, thank God, are not so particular; they appear on the street in shirtsleeves or woolen jackets." Beyond San Antonio was Tucson.

A few miles below lonely Tucson was the mission and village of Tubac, where Capt. Bautista de Anza seventy-seven years before had first learned from Indians of the possibility of an overland route to the Spanish settlements in Upper California. The immigrant party of Benjamin Butler Harris found Tubac deserted. Harris wrote in his narrative of the march:

> The bell and costly pictures, with other ornaments, were still in the church. Peaches and other fruits were ripening on the trees. Streets were uninvaded by weeds and the buildings still shone with new whitewash. There was not a human soul to enliven all this silence . . . When our men rang the church bell, its hollow echoes seemed a bellowing mockery of all things human. Our voices seemed unnatural and ghostly. It was a gloomy solitude—far more so than the loneliest desert.

Tubac, which served the Papago Indians, once again had been attacked by Apaches, as it had incessantly since its founding in 1752. Approaching Tucson they saw Mission San Xavier, the white dove of the desert, almost identical in appearance and style with San Luis Rey Mission in San Diego County, the church being built in the shape of a cross by a series of circular domes. Tucson, still Mexican in appearance and population, was the last town on the route to San Diego, more than 400 miles away, and Harris found

146

THE WILD, FRONTIER POST, and town of Tucson was the last town for California immigrants. This sketch appeared in Bartlett's "Personal Narrative."

it crowded with hundreds of immigrants, with *fandangos* going all the twenty-four hours of the day and night.

Etched forbiddingly against the western sky were grim conical peaks. At any moment, it seemed, they could become a line of volcanic fire shutting off all that lay beyond. From Tucson to the big bend of the Gila River there was a stretch of some 130 miles without a drop of water. At the Gila the immigrants encountered the friendly Pima Indians, who, averse to war, cultivated their lands and gave assistance to all who passed, but each man was required to keep a horse ready for war against the ever-threatening Apaches. Farther down the Gila country were the Maricopas, large and handsome Indians who engaged in wars with the Yumas as well as the Apaches. The Yumas were the most troublesome and though they could be engaged to assist in the crossing of the Colorado, they stole the mules, any goods they could lay their hands on, and in time, turned once more to killing. The immigrants had little or no knowledge of the tragedy that had taken place on the Colorado in 1781, when the Yuma Indians had wiped out two mission settlements, slaughtered more than a half hundred persons, and for many years had shut off the overland route from Sonora to California.

The country was eternally fascinating for those who could look beyond their suffering. A half day's journey above its mouth, the Gila leaves the base of a steep range of mountains and runs across the plain to meet the Colorado, which at that time was swollen with snow water from the Rocky Mountains and running five hundred yards wide. North of the river they could see peaks which to Harris resembled "a vast city with domes, steeples, minarets, roofs, house walls . . ."

Harris wrote that while they camped and rested in the grass and among the trees of the Colorado River bottom, where "several odds and ends of emigrant companies also gathered," about forty Apaches, all walking with fat, fresh horses, and well-armed and equipped for entering on a raid in Sonora, passed by:

> They must have anticipated a long and arduous campaign, else they would not have been so studiously economical of horseflesh as to lead them afoot. Considering the rapine and murder that would soon redden their track, violent intervention in our part would have been mercy and humanity. They and we being in the United States, we let them pass.

The area was strewn with wagons abandoned by Graham's Battalion, and one of them was made into a boat on which they floated their supplies across the Colorado. Once beyond the river they saw dead animals lining the road, "and being dry, had been stood on all four feet by irreverent humorists in ghastly mockery and gloomy fun."

Beyond the Colorado, John W. Audubon, son of the famed naturalist, a member of another immigrant party, reported that he saw:

> Broken wagons, dead, shrivelled-up cattle, horses and mules as well, lay baking in the sun, around the dried up wells that had been opened, in the hopes of getting water. Not a blade of grass or green thing of any kind relieved the monotony of the parched, ash-colored earth, and the most melancholy scene presented itself that I had seen since I left the Rio Grande.

The Harris party, however, encountered a miracle of the desert—a river. It was the New River, a channel which periodically carried high waters of the Colorado River, under the pressure of tidal force in the Gulf of California, back into the desert area lying below the level of the sea. In the blazing heat of August, they found the river three feet deep and thirty to forty feet wide. The re-appearance of this "river" after many years was to save the lives of many immigrants.

A physician, Dr. Oliver Meredith Wozencraft, crossed the Colorado desert by mule and observed that the sink now embracing the Imperial Valley was once the bed of an ancient lake and evidently lay below the level of the sea, and that the Colorado River seemed to flow in a channel higher than much of the surrounding area. It was Dr. Wozencraft who later conceived the plan of diverting the Colorado River water into the desert and creating one of the world's richest agricultural empires.

*Night Camp
on the Trail*

148

The rising mountains, the trees and the pleasant valleys on the western slopes appeared as a paradise to the weary travelers. On approaching the San Diego Mission, Audubon was deeply moved by the ruin and desolation:

> As the last reflection of sunlight tipped the waves of the Pacific Ocean with gold, and the sullen roar of the breakers borne in on the last of the sea breeze for that day came to my ears, tired and sad, I sat on the tiled edge of the long piazza and leaning against one of the brick pillars in a most melancholy mood, I could remain here a long time musing on what is before me, realizing in the desolation about me that all things mortal pass . . .

Mission San Diego as sketched by Lt. Williamson

To John E. Durivage, who arrived in July, it was a time for thanksgiving. He wrote to the *New Orleans Daily Picayune:*

> After much tribulation I have entered the port of San Diego—the jumping-off place against which the old Pacific beats and thumps with the same spirit as does the Atlantic . . . The comfort of having passed through all the dangers, difficulties, perplexities, and sufferings attendant upon the Gila route, and sitting down, pen in hand, once more under a roof, is indescribable . . . A man who has traveled the Gila route may throw himself upon his knees when reaching this point and thank God for preserving him through it.

Hundreds of immigrants' tents were pitched along the beach at La Playa, as were those of soldiers. The storms of winter blew them down and soaked clothes and bedding. Death from exposure was frequent.

The United States Boundary Commission arrived in San Diego on June 1, on the ship *Panama* by way of the isthmus, for the survey of the international border between the United States and Mexico, which was to begin at a point one marine league south of the Port of San Diego and run, at that time, to the junction of the Gila and Colorado Rivers. With the commission was W. H. Emory, a survivor of the Battle of San Pasqual and now a major in the Topographical Engineers. He was assigned to the commission as astronomer and commander of troops.

Emory found that San Diego as yet had not changed much from 1846:

> The news of the discovery of gold in the northern part of California produced less commotion in this quiet town than in New York or Panama. Fortunately for us, it did not feel the effect until the reaction came from the Atlantic side some months after our arrival. Had it been otherwise, all attempts to keep together the enlisted men and laborers of the survey would have been idle, and the commission would have been disorganized before doing anything.

Waiting in San Diego to accompany and protect the commission were Company A of the First Dragoons, commanded by Lt. Couts, and Company H of the Second Infantry. The Mexican commission arrived by ship on July 3, and one hundred and fifty Mexican soldiers came up from Sonora. Emory established his headquarters

at La Punta, the rancho of Santiago Arguello, at the foot of the bay, and called it Camp Riley, after Gen. Bennett Riley, now the military governor of California.

In connection with the establishment of the starting point of the boundary line, Andrew B. Gray, a civilian engineer with the commission, was assigned to measure and triangulate the shore line of the bay, the first American map other than a crude one which had been made by Capt. Fitch in trying to approximate the pueblo boundaries. Other maps of San Diego Bay had been made by Spaniards, Sebastián Viscaíno in 1603, by Vicente Vila in 1769, and by Juan Pantoja in 1782. The survey point was to be determined by the Pantoja map. Gray was to write of San Diego Bay that:

I feel satisfied that for all the ocean traffic of the Pacific, from the islands and from the Indies, it is amply capacious, being large enough to hold comfortably more than a thousand vessels at a time.

The commission, composed of civilians as well as military personnel, with conflicting instructions and antagonistic personalities, accomplished its mission under extreme difficulties. The letters of Maj. Emory tell of a fist fight in the Plaza, between a major and a lieutenant over the honor of the California sweetheart of another officer.

Lt. Amiel Weeks Whipple, accompanied by a cavalry escort under Lt. Couts, was to establish the exact point of the confluence of the Gila and Colorado Rivers, and Lt. Edmund L. F. Hardcastle was to explore the country between San Diego and the river. Disputes arose between Whipple and Couts, and Gray left his own line of survey to lead the Collier party of immigrants to San Diego, and thus never reached the Gila junction to verify Whipple's findings.

The survey also was to check out the possibility of acquiring a southeastern route for a transcontinental railroad, as had been suggested by Emory in 1847. It began on September 11, when the astronomical party left the San Diego Mission and took the road by way of El Cajon, and again Couts kept a detailed diary of the expedition. At Santa Maria Valley they found José María Ortega, whom Couts described as a "curiosity in himself":

He is 68 years of age, and cares to talk of nothing but *aguardiente* (brandy) and women. Is the oldest of 21 children, has had 21 himself, his sister (wife of old Santiago Arguello and mother of Doña Refugia) has 22.

At Santa Ysabel, also a ranch held by the Ortega family, Couts found the natives far ahead of what he called common *rancheros*:

THIS WAS THE WEST in United States maps of the Gold Rush. This one, Mitchell's, was carried by many of the immigrant parties crossing the Colorado.

They have an abundance of chickens, eggs, melons, grapes, pears, etc. They are well dressed (some even dandily) and their Captain or General (Old Tomás Chihu) is our guide, and a great old rogue he is . . .

Here they met three Americans just in from the Colorado who reported there were not less than two hundred wagons between the Pima villages and the river.

From there, instead of taking the road to Warner's, they crossed directly over the mountains on a route which he said was least known, to rejoin the wagon route at San Felipe. The distance by this pass was twelve miles; by way of Warner's, twenty-five miles. This would mark the first American crossing of the mountains by way of the Julian area, where Bill Williams, or "Cockney Bill," had his rancho on Volcan Mountain.

In the mountains the expedition shot sixteen bears to add to their supplies of food, and in the desert hills Couts noted indications of gold "and certainly metal of some kind abounds." All along the desert route they encountered immigrants, many begging for food and in all states of despair, in temperatures as high as 120 degrees. So many were from the Southern states that Couts was led to comment that "if any are left in Arks., it is more numerously populated than I had anticipated." They were whipped by sand and hail storms, threatened by a flash flood, and shaken by earthquakes which opened crevasses in the earth.

Though San Diego, as with other settlements, was filled with talk of statehood as well as gold, Congress deadlocked in session after session in an effort to establish a territorial government for California, which still was administered in large measure by Mexican laws and Spanish customs and traditions and by a succession of military governors. The issue of whether new states were to be slave or free even then was dividing the nation. Southerners were determined to maintain the equality of slave and free states.

Californians became impatient, and called for the election of delegates to a constitutional convention. Miguel de Pedrorena was chosen on August 1 to represent San Diego at the convention early in September at Monterey. Northern California had thirty-eight delegates and Southern California only ten. The convention was indicative of the change that was coming over California. Of its forty-eight members, only six had been born in California. Five others were natives of foreign countries. Pedrorena was the only native of Spain, the "mother country" of California. The convention unanimously voted to prohibit slavery in California, prepared a constitution, and adjourned on October 13 to put it before the people. It was ratified on November 13.

SANTA YSABEL was a key point on the mountain road to San Diego when this woodcut was made in 1855. It depicts the old church and snow in the mountains.

At about the same time a small Illinois company of immigrants pushed wearily along the Gila Trail. Of the original eleven members, three already had died en route of cholera. In November along the Gila they met a large train of packers on mules from Missouri who related a fearful tale of the ravages of cholera. H. M. T. Powell, an artist with the Illinois company, of whom little is known other than by the sketches he left of San Diego and other California regions, wrote in his diary:

Fires and camps all up and down the river. In fact the whole river from the Pima Villages to the Colorado is one vast camp, as far as we can learn.

At Carrizo Creek, this company left the regular trail and embarked on "Colonel Collier's" route over the mountains more directly to the west, and on the way, before entering the high country, they met a government train from San Diego bringing relief rations to immigrants reported in near-starving conditions

153

in the desert. Powell says they struck the foot of rugged peaks and then climbed gorges and ravines for four miles, which "beat anything I ever saw." This is in the rugged Carrizo Gorge country. They emerged into a pretty valley with plenty of grass and a spring, and then swinging south by west went by way of Tecate and along the border, meeting several other immigrant trains, and finally arrived at La Punta, Emory's headquarters, on December 3. Thus were marked out the routes which were to become the roads and highways of the future.

CHAPTER NINE

"All night long in this sweet little village
You hear the soft note of the pistol
With the pleasant screak of the victim
Whose been shot prehaps in his glzzard."

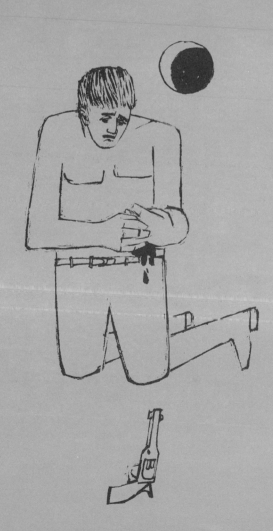

91

Road to Mission

Ford   River San Diego

Old Fort Stockton
SAN DIEGO

Beach

Grass Flats

NEW SAN DIEGO

Main Road from Upper to Lower California

True Meridian
Mag. Var. 12° 55' Easterly

N

Sweet Water Falls

SKETCH
of the
PORT OF SAN DIEGO
1850.
Compiled from recent Surveys.

Average rise and fall of the tide Six feet.   Soundings
are in fathoms at low water — Those on the bar outside
were taken by Officers of U.S. Steamship Massachusetts,
and those inside of Port by A.B. Gray.

U.S. Military Depot, Established at New San Diego.

Santiago
Ha

Scale of Sea Miles
¾ ½ ¼

Scale of Statute Miles.
¾ ½ ¼ 0

Initial Point of Boundary

UNITED ST

MEXICO

LIFE ON A FRONTIER

San Diego, crowded with gold seekers, Mexican and American gamblers, destitute settlers, the discontented soldiers of two nations, and burly teamsters of the government mule trains, was a frontier town. The Indian wars were about to begin, and the deserts and mountains were to be stained with blood. The executioners would return to the Spanish Plaza.

The artist Powell, in his terse and illuminating notes, tells us a little of the San Diego of the gold rush during two months of his stay:

The public square is boarded in for a bullfight. Miserable affair . . . Got the blues terribly . . . Bullfight again . . . miserable bullfights continue. Thin ice this morning. Snow in mountains all around back of foot hills . . . Very cold. Bullfights still. Pigs here are very good . . . Monte banks; drinking, etc., their manners here are detestable. Dreadful lumbago last night . . . bed of river dry when we came in; today the water came rolling down a foot deep. Strange sight . . . Very sick . . . Many immigrants in same condition. River falling. Beautiful weather. Changing silver for gold . . . Hard work to get it. Singular in this gold country. California sports in Plaza . . . Gamblers and gambling rife here Sunday or no Sunday . . . Everybody gets drunk here. The gambling and drinking of the officers here and their exceedingly supercilious manners to the immigrants is very reprehensible . . . A party came in from Mexico City today . . . they set up a Monte Bank in the evening; piles of doubloons . . . Large lumps of gold. In better spirits now . . . Owens (Dragoon) died a/c for cutting and maiming another Dragoon . . . a Mexican soldier . . . murdered another right here in town last night . . . so little notice taken of it that I did not hear it until evening.

THIS SKETCH OF 1850 shows the plan for New San Diego and the route of El Camino Real, which connected the missions of Upper and Lower California.

157

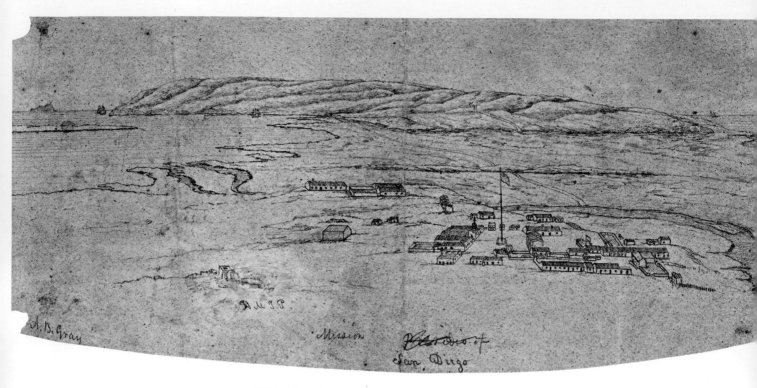

THE ARTIST H.M.T. POWELL, who came over the Gila Trail, sketched San Diego in 1850. He sold a number of similar sketches to residents of Old Town.

Powell slept in wagons and sold sketches and maps of San Diego to keep himself alive, and tried to interest Miguel de Pedrorena and a "Mr. Fitch," presumably one of Capt. Fitch's sons, in starting a school, but nothing came of it. He sketched San Diego and the Mission for Lt. Couts for $8. The sketch of the Mission has survived, as has another Powell sketch of San Diego. The arrival of so many settlers set off a land boom, especially at La Playa, the site of the old hide houses and ship anchorage, and Powell was kept busy preparing maps and site sketches. By March 9 he had earned enough money to depart for the gold fields and left San Diego, "I hope for ever."

Provisions were scarce, flour from Valparaiso selling at a price of four to six dollars for a fifty-pound sack. Nearly all of the ranchos had been depopulated. Wages of common laborers rose to $150 a month, and of carpenters to $10 a day. By the spring of 1850 American settlers and immigrants were dominating the affairs of the little pueblo, though the *Californios* remained active, both in business and in ranching. The Dons clung to their old ways and their costumes, and the gold rush created a demand for meat which they were to supply from their ranchos. For a brief time, at least, the silver on their saddles would grow richer and heavier. Powell referred to several wedding processions in the Spanish tra-

158

dition, including one for the daughter of *Alcalde* Marrón, with their rich and colorful costumes and bedecked horses. To Powell, being a stern Protestant, it was all a "miserable mummery."

The process of setting up a formal government continued through the winter. Peter H. Burnett had been installed as governor in December. Symbolic of the change with the years was San Diego's designation of E. Kirby Chamberlain to serve as senator, and Oliver S. Witherby, who had come to San Diego with the Boundary Commission, as assemblyman, to the first Legislature in California, which was described as the "legislature of a thousand drinks." It doesn't seem to have been any different from modern legislative assemblies, though it did successfully launch the great state of California, and under an act of February 18, 1850, created San Diego as the first county. It contained at first 37,400 square miles, an empire in itself, from the Pacific coastline 200 miles east to the Colorado River, and included the present counties of San Diego, Riverside, Imperial and San Bernardino, and the easterly portion of Inyo. It was to be governed by a Court of Sessions.

While the residents of Old Town were preparing to organize governments for the county and the city, and at last break away from the laws and customs of Spain and Mexico, the bark *Hortensia* was lying at anchor off La Playa, in ballast, with the owner, William Heath Davis, who had first seen San Diego as a boy in 1831, ready, as he wrote in his memoirs, "for any adventure that might offer a profitable voyage." Instead, he listened to a different proposition. Gray, the engineer with the Boundary Commission,

Peter H. Burnett

LA PLAYA was a rowdy settlement in the early days of San Diego, with hotels, stores and bars. It was a port of entry during the Gold Rush steamship days.

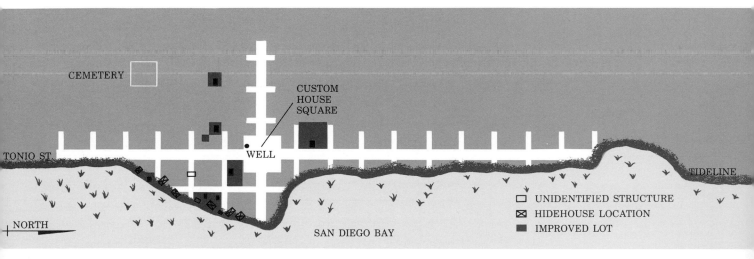

159

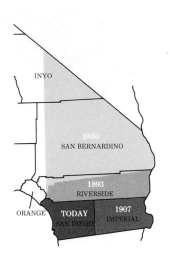

San Diego County 1850

suggested that he join a number of other San Diegans in building a new port and laying out an entirely new town, on the broad, flat land on the bay south of the old pueblo and directly on *Punta de los Muertos*, or the Point of the Dead, where the Spanish Expedition of 1782 buried those who had died of scurvy. The old point lies under filled land at the intersection of Pacific Highway and Market Street.

Davis, known as "Kanaka Bill," perhaps because he used so many Hawaiians, or Sandwich Islanders, as crewmen, assented. The other partners were José Antonio Aguirre, Miguel de Pedrorena, and William C. Ferrell, who became San Diego's first district attorney. However, they soon acquired a new partner. A vessel arrived at La Playa with lumber for enlarging an Army depot at La Playa. The Army also planned to erect a barracks and other installations, as supplies for military posts were to be brought in by sea and transshipped by mule train to posts in Southern California and Arizona. The promoters quickly realized the advantages that would accrue to them if the Army could be induced to move its operations across the bay to New San Diego. Second Lt. Thomas D. Johns, of the 2nd Infantry, in charge of supplies, was given one of the eighteen shares in the project and he agreed to re-ship the lumber to the new site. On March 18, 1850, the town attorney, Thomas W. Sutherland, the first American attorney to arrive in San Diego, transferred 160 acres of land to the promoters for $2304 but it was stipulated that a wharf and warehouse should be built within eighteen months. The area included all the land lying between the bay and Front Street on the east and Broadway on the north. In return for his share of the realty, Davis agreed to build the wharf and warehouse, and the new town eventually became known as "Davis' Folly."

Davis and the other investors counted heavily on the Army's plans, but they hadn't counted on the Army running out of money. Davis laid out a subdivision of fifty-six blocks, thirty-one of which were on dry land and the rest of which were on tide flats. The mean high tide line ran parallel with the west side of Pacific Highway to Market Street, then angled southeast to Front and J Streets.

The Army had two full blocks, one for the depot and barracks and the other for stables and stock. The depot was on the block northwest of Kettner and Market Streets, the stables were on the block which in 1963 was the site of the Federal Building. A park block laid out between F and G, India and Columbia Streets, is still known by its original name, Plaza Pantoja.

The land was low, gently sloping back from the bay and covered with low, stunted brush, a little cactus, and the streets, other than

160

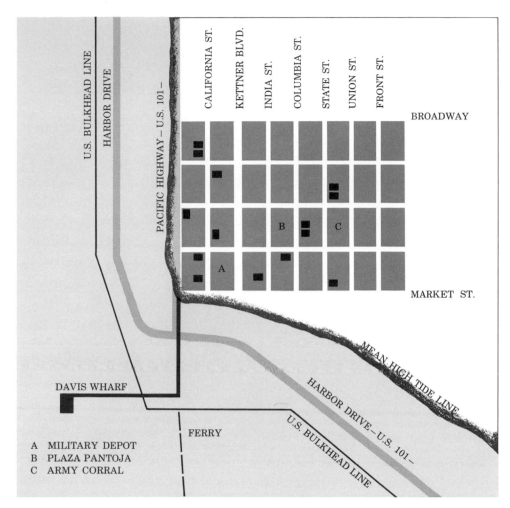

NEW TOWN, the site of modern San Diego, laid out by William Heath Davis syndicate, had few buildings and faded with the end of the Gold Rush period.

those on Davis' subdivision maps, consisted of a wagon track from Old Town that came down Pacific Highway to Market Street, turned eastward and connected with the main wagon road that followed south along the bay to La Punta and Tijuana. The site for the wharf was a sandbar that extended from the corner of Market Street and Pacific Highway about 750 feet due south to the present Coronado Ferry landing. There, the bar dropped off sharply into the channel, where there were six fathoms of water, sufficient for even large ships.

From March to December 1850, there was a flurry of activity in New Town. The Army brought in its shipload of lumber and Davis purchased lumber, bricks and some prefabricated houses which had been brought from the East Coast by the brig *Cybele*, and work began on his warehouse and wharf. The latter was an L-shaped structure that probably was about six hundred feet long, though the original bid had specified 1100 feet. The new settle-

161

ment experienced some embarrassment by the failure to locate a supply of fresh water, and a water train had to be sent each day to the San Diego River in the vicinity of Old Town. Eventually two successful wells were sunk, one near Front and B Streets and another near State and F Streets.

One of the partners, Pedrorena, died on March 29, of apoplexy. In a letter to Davis, who had returned to San Francisco, Lt. Johns wrote that "not only his family but the whole town has been thrown into deep gloom at this melancholy announcement." He was only forty-one years of age, and though he possessed large tracts of land, his widow, son and two daughters were left in strained financial circumstances.

The first county election was conducted on April 1, with votes cast at two precincts, Old Town and La Playa, for the election of judges and county officials. John Hays was elected county judge though Witherby had been designated by the Legislature as district judge. Juan Bandini and José Antonio Estudillo were the only *Californios* elected to office, Bandini as treasurer, though he never served and was replaced with Philip Crosthwaite, and Estudillo as assessor. Agoston Haraszthy, a native of Hungary, was elected sheriff.

O. S. Witherby

For seven hundred years the family of Haraszthy had been prominent in Hungary. Haraszthy, often identified as a count, became involved in rebellions, encouraged Hungarians to migrate to America, and came himself in 1840, settling in Wisconsin and laying out what is now Sauk City. He visited Hungary to find his estates had been confiscated, and returned to the United States with his father, known as the "old general," and his wife and three children. In the spring of 1849, seeking relief from financial difficulties, he packed his wife, six children and his father in an ox-drawn wagon and came to San Diego. Father and son planted acres of grapes in Mission and San Luis Rey Valleys, as the padres had done before them. Politics and trouble came naturally to this son of Central Europe.

The Legislature also had incorporated San Diego as a city, and the first election was held on June 16. Joshua H. Bean, who had been serving as *alcalde*, was chosen as the first mayor. José Antonio Estudillo was elected as treasurer and Bandini as assessor, though he again failed to serve. Sheriff Haraszthy also was designated as city marshall, and his father, Charles Haraszthy, was elected as one of the five councilmen. Bean, who had fought with Gen. Zachary Taylor in Mexico, served as mayor less than a year, and removed to San Gabriel where he opened a grog shop and became a general in the State Militia.

The first official acts of the Council were to approve maps of San Diego and its tidelands as made by Lt. Couts and Mayor Bean, and to certify the legality of certain grants of land made while Bean was still serving as *alcalde*. They soon voted to provide themselves with salaries, despite pre-election assurances they were anxious to serve only for the honor of it; set up license fees for games of chance; provided that Indians jailed on one pretext or another could be let out for private labor, at the discretion of the mayor; organized a committee to determine the best possible means of diverting the flow of the San Diego River into False, or Mission Bay, and awarded a $5000 contract for building a new jail to Councilman Haraszthy's son, the sheriff. It was constructed so poorly that there has been some suspicion through the years that this was San Diego's first example of official graft.

The lands of the pueblo were being divided among eager buyers, mostly friends and relatives, for speculation. A syndicate which included Agoston Haraszthy, Couts and Emory obtained 687 acres to form still another town to be known as Middletown, a narrow strip of land running along the bay from Old Town to New Town. The promoters grandiosely offered to donate land around a projected central plaza for the grouping of all public buildings, which was the first mention of a civic ambition that was to go unfilled for more than a century. Emory invested heavily in San Diego, because he believed implicitly that the railroad to the West would follow the 32nd parallel and terminate at San Diego, which then would become the metropolis of the Pacific Coast.

Land prices set by the Council ranged from $25 for a lot to $80 for twenty acres, all to be paid for by installments expected to be extracted from a stream of immigrants. The prices of some lots at La Playa were to reach as high as $500. But already the stream was beginning to slow, though the indications were not clearly visible as yet in a town which in a few years would be cut off from the main stream of the Westward movement. The bright hopes of the early 1850's for a great metropolis would have to wait for a new generation.

The frontier conditions were disturbing to some of the Dons, and if they were not to be overwhelmed by the Protestant invasion, and if sin was to be held at bay, a church would have to be built. The Catholic chapel in the Estudillo home no longer was large enough for religious services and weddings and festivals. On August 24, 1850, the Council granted land for church purposes to Fr. J. Chrisostom Holbein, who had come to San Diego as a successor to Fr. Oliva, and José Antonio Aguirre, Juan Bandini and Pedro J. de Pedrorena. This land was on the other side of the

Pueblo of San Diego in 1769, as claimed by President and Trustees of City of San Diego

163

river near where the padres' road to Mission San Diego intersected with El Camino Real. The cornerstone of the new church, however, was not laid until October 9, 1851.

The national census of 1850 gave San Diego County a population of 798 and the city, including La Playa, 650. Indians weren't counted. There were 157 registered voters, eighty-eight in Old Town and sixty-nine at La Playa, of whom 136 had arrived during or since the conquest.

In the mountains the wily Warner built a new trading store three miles farther down the immigrant trail coming up through the Carrizo Corridor and San Felipe Valley. Here the trail forked off, one branch leading directly west over a low hill to meet the regular trail from Agua Caliente to Santa Ysabel, and the other leading north in the direction of Los Angeles. Sections of the old trace were visible in 1963 on the hill above the old ranch house which is now an historical monument.

Out in the desert, along the Colorado River at the edge of San Diego County, the Yuma Indians became more apprehensive and more aggressive as thousands of immigrants invaded their territory. They exacted tribute for the crossing of the river, in return for assistance that sometimes was more costly than helpful, in the loss of horses, mules and goods. Early in 1850 a native of Illinois, Dr. A. L. Lincoln, returned from the gold fields and established a ferry at the junction of the Gila and the Colorado. It proved to be immensely profitable. He had six employees, and he kept them heavily armed.

Riding out of Chihuahua and Sonora with a band of desperadoes came John Glanton, a native of Tennessee. After service in the Mexican war, Glanton became a bounty hunter, collecting the scalps of ravaging Apaches and selling them to a grateful Mexican government. Soon, however, the Glanton gang turned to murdering Mexicans and selling their scalps as those of Apaches. When finally driven out of Mexico, they came to the Colorado and imposed themselves on Dr. Lincoln and his profitable ferry business.

The Yumas sought to divide the river business with Lincoln but Glanton became abusive and struck their chief. When Glanton went to San Diego to purchase provisions and more whiskey, the Indians sent spies into the ferry camp and at the same time gathered 500 warriors. On the night of April 23, when Glanton and his men had returned, and had gorged themselves on food and drink and fallen asleep, the Indians, upon signal from their spies, attacked. Glanton, Lincoln and four men were hammered or axed to death before a shot could be fired in resistance. Five men operating the ferry were surprised and killed. Three others who had gone to cut willow poles managed to escape, jumping into a skiff and floating down river, shooting and possibly killing ten of their pursuers. They drifted as far as fourteen miles below Algodones, a little Mexican town on the border below Yuma, and then worked their way back toward the camp on foot.

All of the structures had been burned, along with the bodies which had not been thrown into the river. There were reports that three bags of silver and a bag of gold, had disappeared. In a deposition taken in Los Angeles, Jeremiah Hill testified that he was one of fourteen immigrants arriving at the crossing just after the massacre and that the Indians had held another council of war and were determined to kill all Americans coming to the river. Hill's party, however, was allowed to cross, but were told they were to be the last, and Hill warned that there were between seventy-five and a hundred men, women and children approaching the Colorado.

One of the men who had escaped, William Carr, gave a deposition at San Diego as well as at Los Angeles, and said he had asked the commanding officer of United States troops to send a force to the river but that none had been sent, and "there are forty U.S. soldiers, infantry, at said town of San Diego." When the reports reached the state capital, Governor Burnett ordered the sheriff of Los Angeles to raise forty men and the sheriff of San Diego, twenty, and place them under the command of Joshua Bean, the former mayor and a general of the State Militia. Bean, however, remained at his grog shop and sent Joseph C. Morehead, the state's quartermaster general and a former member of Stevenson's Volunteers, marching against the Indians. By the time they reached the river his force of twenty men had grown to more than one hundred but the Indians proved illusive, fading into the tangled thickets of the broad Colorado River bed. So, the story goes, Morehead and his Indian fighters, after indecisive brushes with the enemy, vigorously attacked their rations, liquid and solid, harrassed the immigrants and robbed passing Sonorans of their gold, for three months, before being ordered to disband and return, with many guns and much ammunition missing and the new-born state in debt $120,000 for supplies and salaries.

Reading in a San Francisco newspaper of the massacre of the Glanton company, and of the huge sums which had been earned, George Alonzo Johnson, an unemployed seaman, decided to go into the ferry business himself. He arrived in San Diego with a number of partners, including Louis J. F. Jaeger, or Iaeger, as it was sometimes spelled, who was to become the best known of the Colorado River ferry men. They purchased mules from Couts and

Bandini and reached the river in July. In October, three companies of soldiers under Maj. Heintzelman left San Diego Mission to establish a fort at the river for the protection of the immigrants. They went by way of San Pasqual, driving their loaded wagons up the hilly *carreta* road with great difficulty, and reached the river on December 1. They soon established a camp on the ridge opposite the mouth of the Gila, where the Yuma Indians had attacked and burned the mission settlement in 1781.

A large proportion of the immigrants now entering California were seeking land and opportunity more than gold, but conditions in California continued to be turbulent, with titles to land in dispute and with government largely ineffective. The question of the admission of California to the Union as a state, which had become embroiled in the controversy over the extension of slavery, finally was resolved, with California admitted under a compromise as a free state. The news of the signing of the law on September 9, 1850, by President Fillmore, did not reach California until six weeks later, but it set off a wild celebration, from San Diego to the gold fields.

The ranches of the Spanish and Mexican periods were slowly passing into new hands through death or marriage. Lt. Couts, the young West Point officer and nephew of a Secretary of the Treasury under President Polk, married Ysidora Bandini, a daughter of Don Juan, on April 5, 1851, and in October he resigned from the Army. He later made his home on Guajome Rancho which had been a wedding present to his wife from her brother-in-law, Abel Stearns, of Los Angeles. A brother, William Blounts Couts, also came to San Diego and married a daughter of Santiago E. Arguello. Henry Clayton, a surveyor with the Boundary Commission, who was elected county surveyor in 1850, in time married the widow of Capt. Snook and owner of Rancho San Bernardo.

Among the many immigrant trains arriving in 1850 over the Gila Trail was the Robinson party, led by James W. Robinson, who had been lieutenant governor and governor of Texas during its days of independence, and had been seized and held captive by the Mexican general, Santa Anna. With him came Louis Rose, a native of Germany and former resident of New Orleans, who was to engrave his name on the geography of San Diego. Old San Diego was reaching its height.

For more than a half-century efforts to establish and maintain schools in San Diego had never borne fruit. In 1845, before the arrival of the Americans, only eleven of twenty-five voters were able to write. Now the Council voted to hire a Miss Dillon as a teacher, and was able to induce the sheriff to rent two rooms in

Louis Rose

166

his residence for use as classrooms. These were in the adjoining homes of the dead sea captains, Fitch and Snook. Sessions were conducted intermittently, and again soon were abandoned.

In San Francisco, a young newspaperman who also wrote under the name of "Boston," learned of the prospects of New Town and the desire of its promoters to establish San Diego's first newspaper. He was John Judson Ames, born in Maine. On his sixteenth birthday, his father, a shipbuilder, had called his son before him. Ames later told this story:

> On the day on which we completed our sixteenth year, a wise father turned us out into the world with the parting words: "Jud, you are now old enough to take care of yourself, and I think there is enough of the Yankee in you to insure your success. If you make a good beginning, I will render you any assistance you may require—if you must try again. Be industrious—practice economy—shun wine and women—and I'll insure you for ten per cent on your original cost."

John Judson Ames

After some years at sea, he got a job helping to build the pioneer telegraph line from Memphis to New Orleans, in 1847, and then turned to newspaper work, founding *The Dime Catcher* in Baton Rouge, the new capital of Louisiana. The gold fever seized him and in 1849 he closed his little newspaper and went to San Francisco by way of Panama. A visit to San Diego late in 1850 convinced him of its future, and in December he issued a prospectus on his projected newspaper. He returned to New Orleans by boat and packed up his old press and printing equipment and shipped them to Panama. While crossing the lakes of the isthmus, his boat sank, though he managed to salvage the press and boxes of type. Upon reaching the Pacific Coast side with his equipment strapped to mules, he fell ill of fever and missed his ship to San Diego. He finally obtained passage on another boat which promptly sprang a leak, almost sank, and had to be laid up at Acapulco for a week for repairs. He finally made it to San Diego, and the first four-page issue of the weekly *San Diego Herald* came off the press on Thursday, May 29, 1851, just twelve days after the first newspaper had appeared in Los Angeles. He was thirty years of age, and six feet, six inches tall.

His opening editorial promised that the *Herald* would be independent but not neutral. It was neither independent nor neutral, as far as politics were concerned. He did, however, have an aversion for unhappy news and probably many of the more exciting local events of those days never reached print even though he had no source of national or international news except the newspaper exchanges which arrived weeks and months late.

In a period of ten days in May, eleven ships from ports in many parts of the world, from Liverpool to Valparaiso and San Fran-

167

SAN DIEGO HERALD.

VOL. 1. SAN DIEGO, CAL., THURSDAY, MAY 29, 1851. NO. 1.

THE SAN DIEGO HERALD.

J. JUDSON AMES,
Editor and Publisher.

OFFICE—OVER HOOPER & CO.'S STORE.

The HERALD will be published every Thursday, at 10$ per annum—half in advance.

TERMS OF ADVERTISING.—One square of eight lines, or less, first insertion, 4$; each subsequent insertion 2$. Business and address cards inserted monthly at reasonable rates.

A liberal discount made to yearly advertisers.

THE HERALD.

We make the following extract from a sweet little poem, written by our talented young friend M. F. Bigny, which we find in a recent number of the *New Orleans Delta*.

It is entitled *The Clouded Star, the Hidden Flower, and the Broken Vow.* We regret that we have not room for the whole poem.

By a river I sat in a musing mood,
And autumnal leaves were around me strewed,
And mournful and blighted with wasting grief,
Which mocked at the thought that would ask relief,
A man appeared,—and the lines of care,
And the deeper traces of dull despair,
Which darkened his youthful brow, gave me
A look of pitying sympathy.

I asked of the stranger his cause of grief—
If his sorrow were such as disdained relief—
And he told me the tale of his trustful life—
Of the maid who had promised to be his wife—
Of the damning curse of a broken vow,
Which had written distress on his youthful brow.

" But Hope," he said, and aloud he grieved,
"Is not for the heart that has been deceived;
No future trust can again unshroud
The star that is covered with falsehood's cloud;
And the flow'r which joys in its faithless plight,
Can never emerge from its cheerless night;
And the heart, which has worshiped a worthless thing,
Is a winter of storms which can know no spring."

Extensive Farming Operations.

The most extensive farming operation probably ever entered into in any country, has been successfully carried through in California during the past autumn and winter. We allude to the speculation of Horner & Co.

Mr. Horner's Rancho is situated in the San Jose valley. It contains 1000 acres of land and is enclosed by an iron fence which alone cost $10,000. Last autumn three hundred acres only were under cultivation, two hundred and fifty of which were planted in potatoes, the rest in turnips, tomatoes, onions &c.

Day before yesterday the last sack of the potato crop was sold, and the gross proceeds of this crop have amounted to $178,000. There have been eighty hands employed on the Rancho, and the total expense of carrying it on during the season has been $80,000. The sacks in which the potatoes have been shipped cost over $8,000, while the gross receipts for the total crop of the rancho have amounted to $223,000.

This season the entire 100 acres are under cultivation, six hundred and fifty being planted in potatoes and the remainder in other vegetables.

Mr. Horner will doubtless be enabled to monopolize the potato trade for the next twelve months. We have seen in one of the eastern papers, an estimate made of the probable sale of this potato crop when it was first planted. This writer judged that they would amount to $175,000; and to show how close the calculation was, had it not been for the recent fire and the rise of potatoes, the extra $3,000 making $178,000 the actual receipts, would not have been made.—*Sacramento Trans.*

Mr. Stillman lately brought into our office a piece of wood taken from a cayota hole on Lawson's hill, sixty-two feet below the surface. It is beautifully encrusted in places with sulphate of iron, and is a great curiosity.—*Nevada Gazette.*

We were yesterday shown a lump of gold weighing 8 lbs. 8oz., taken out of Poor Man's Creek a few days since by Mr. T. Turner, brother of Mr. Turner of the Nevada House in this city. It was taken from the bed of the creek.—*Ib.*

THE HANGING OF McCAULEY.—McCauley was hung in his cell during Thursday night, we announced yesterday. Gov. McDougal concluded to commute his sentence to imprisonment cisco, put into San Diego harbor with their cargoes of gold seekers and settlers. As significant, perhaps, were reports in the *Herald* that in June 3000 sheep from the states of Durango and Chihuahua, in Mexico, had arrived in San Diego, after being driven over the Anza route from Sonora up through San Felipe Pass on their way to the gold fields, where the demand for meat was jumping the price of cattle higher and higher. Cattle once killed for their hides which sold for $2, brought as much for awhile as $500 a head.

In the following month 6000 more sheep from Mexico reached the Colorado ferry crossing, and they were to be driven through San Diego over the new route by way of Jacumba. Behind them were reported 4000 sheep being driven West by Americans. The trailing of these sheep opened the way for cattle drives over the Gila Trail from Texas that were longer and far more difficult than those of the famed Chisholm Trail of the Western Plains two decades later.

The soaring cattle market in the North did not at first affect the three communities around the bay of San Diego. With most of the soldiers away at the Colorado, and with the tide of immigration slowing up, a temporary depression brought a halt to much of the building and land speculation.

Old Town still huddled around the barren, dirty Plaza, but the old adobe houses were being converted into commercial establishments. Only a few trees along the river's edge offered a touch of greenery. At high tide, the bay was three blocks west of the Plaza; at low tide, a mile and a-half. Merchants, landowners and cattlemen were the hard core of officialdom. They executed the laws and spoke for stability and sanitation. In practice, their efforts ranged from mild success to total failure. The frontier had overwhelmed the remote pueblo which once stood on the rim of empire.

On the south side of the Plaza the home of José Antonio Estudillo was still considered one of the finest in California. On the west was the small brick courthouse and office of the *alcalde*. Next door Cave Couts had converted a store into a hotel and saloon known as the Colorado House. With his marriage to Ysidora Bandini, Couts was well on his way to becoming one of the wealthiest men in the county. His hotel was a wood and adobe structure with a high false front, and besides food, liquor and lodging, it offered such pleasures as billiards and monte bank. George Teb-

THIS IS THE FIRST PAGE of the first edition of the San Diego Herald. *It lasted nine years and died with the decline of San Diego in the late 1850's.*

169

C.P. Noell

Thomas Whaley

betts had his Exchange Hotel next to Couts' hotel. It was a one-story adobe. On up the street Judge John Hays and Councilman Charles P. Noell were partners in a mercantile store. Two recent arrivals, James Marks and Charles Fletcher, also had opened a store. Two blocks away, across the river, William Leamy, the local butcher and a city councilman, took on a partner named M. M. Sexton in the operation of a slaughter house and small store.

The local physician, Dr. Fred Painter, also served as county assessor and deputy postmaster. His medical practice was on the Plaza, and his official offices over Hooper's Store in New Town. Sheriff Haraszthy's office was a few doors off the northeast corner of the Plaza on Calhoun Street, probably in the old Carrillo-Fitch adobe. Josefa Fitch still owned the family store across the street.

Other merchants were A. J. Matsell, a farmer and Army forage contractor who was to sell out before the end of the year; Francis Hinton, a wagon master turned merchant, and his new partner, R. E. Raimond, a well-respected businessman who later would move to San Francisco. Louis Rose, a man of many ventures, was just beginning his business career in his first store near the corner of present Juan and Wallace Streets, next to Pío Pico's old house. San Diego would remember him for Rose's Store, Rose's Tannery, Rose Canyon, Roseville, Rose's Hotel and Rose's Wharf. Two other newcomers to San Diego that year were two San Francisco associates of William Heath Davis. They were Lewis Franklin and Thomas Whaley, who opened their *Tienda California*. Both were to play major roles in San Diego's future as businessmen and civic leaders. P. A. Goldman, a San Francisco merchant and an associate of Louis Strauss, opened a store in San Diego that year destined to become one of the city's largest.

On the southeast side of the Plaza, the main room of the famed Bandini house, where the social life of San Diego had once held sway and Commodore Stockton had danced while the Battle of San Pasqual moved to its tragic finale, had been converted into a store to fill the needs of the travellers and hopeful settlers.

Near the edge of the bay, two blocks south of the Plaza, was the largest structure in Old Town, the Gila House. A frame building with an adobe kitchen, it was built by Bandini and was more than 250 feet in length and two stories high. It proved to be a monument to bad judgment. Before the year was out, Bandini was in financial troubles and he turned the management of his property over to a son-in-law, Charles R. Johnson, a former San Francisco cattle auctioneer who had married Dolores Bandini, and retired to his Guadalupe Ranch, fifty miles southeast of San Diego and resumed Mexican citizenship. Adolph Savine, a wealthy businessman who had come West seeking new opportunities, held a $10,000 mortgage on the hotel at four per cent per month. Another son-in-law, wealthy Abel Stearns, of Los Angeles, took over the mortgage to save Bandini in mid-1851.

Despite the bitter disappointment of having the Army establish its depot at New Town, La Playa held its own and even had expanded a little by the end of the year, as there still were considerable numbers of ships in and out of the harbor. The little cluster of rough wood and adobe buildings five miles west of Old Town included the four dilapidated hide houses, four stores, a ramshackle customhouse, a hotel of sorts and a few scattered dwellings. Commercial buildings were all near the water's edge where the shoreline bulged out into the stream and the land lifted gently back to the base of Point Loma's highland backbone. The area is now the site of the U.S. Navy's Refueling Depot. Stores were operated by Holden Almy, Frank Ames and Eugene Pendleton, John Cooke, and David Gardiner and John R. Bleecker. Charles Johnson, Mrs. Fitch and José Aguirre owned three of the hide houses. William E. Ferrell was port collector at the customhouse. The name of the owner of the New Orleans Hotel is not known. By October, Abel Watkinson had opened the Playa House Hotel and James Donohue the Ocean House Hotel in a combined store and residence building purchased from John Cooke. The hide house owners were going into their second year of boring an artesian well that was to prove a dry hole at six hundred feet seven months later. The Army had two companies of troops living in tents near the business center, and the Pacific Mail Steamship Co. had its freight and passenger depot there.

Frank Ames was not related to the editor of the *Herald* but was a cousin of Julian Ames, the otter hunter, though he was employed as a compositor on the paper and wrote articles under the by-line of "Puff." His partner in the mercantile business at La Playa, Eugene Pendleton, was a brother of George Pendleton.

New Town virtually was a Davis enterprise. He established a store operated by George H. Hooper across from the Army depot, and a saloon and billiard parlor known as the Pantoja House on the east side of Pantoja Plaza. It was operated by Charles J. Lanning and William P. Toler. The *Herald* had its offices on the second floor of Hooper's store. Ames and Pendleton crossed the bay and founded a lumber and mercantile business two lots south of Hooper's store on California Street; Levi Slack and Ephraim W. Morse, partners from San Francisco, opened the Boston House, an eating and lodging establishment on the south side of the Pantoja House. Capt. Nathaniel Lyon, Lt. Col. J. Bankhead

Ephraim W. Morse

171

Magruder, Lt. D. M. Beltzhouver, and Andrew B. Gray were among those who built houses in New Town.

New Town did not prosper and Hooper reported to Davis at San Francisco in September that "with respect to the Pantoja House, everything goes on very quietly — indeed too quietly, for there is no business doing here or anywhere." A month later he wrote that New Town "appears to be perfectly deserted." In November he was selling off the goods as fast as he could, some at cost and some at a loss, and there is "no use auctioning goods as hardly a week passes without an auction at Old Town or the Playa . . . there is no money here, and the Lord only knows when there will be any."

At the year's end, Hooper had left. He later operated a store on the Colorado River with Francis Hinton, the Old Town merchant. Lanning and Toler faded from the scene. All that remained were Ames & Pendleton's Store, the Boston House, the Pantoja House and the *Herald*. Business had come to a standstill. Old Town had entered the year with eight stores, two hotels and three low groggeries, or small saloons. At the year's end, there were twelve stores, three hotels and three small saloons. La Playa started the year with four stores, four hide houses, a custom house and one hotel, and by year's end had lost one store and gained two hotels.

The first stages began to creak over El Camino Real in 1852 with the establishment of irregular service between San Diego and Los Angeles. Phineas Banning and D. W. Alexander started a stage line which followed the regular trail up Rose Canyon, across the mesa and down through Soledad Valley, with an overnight stop at San Juan Capistrano, and gradually replaced the *carretas* and mule trains which had been seen in New Spain for more than three hundred years. The next year a rival service was begun by J. L. Tomlinson. Others soon appeared, and by the end of 1853 Northern and Southern California were linked by stage service through connections at San Luis Obispo, Santa Barbara and Buenaventura. It was to the East though that San Diego always turned its eyes.

In the spring of 1851 Capt. Nathaniel Lyon, looking east from San Diego on a clear day, saw two mountains, one covered with vegetation, which he believed was named San Miguel, and the other, higher and appearing white with granite boulders piled in huge masses, and noticed "the inviting appearance" of a depression on the north side which "determined me to attempt a passage." Thus a new route east to the desert was discovered.

This route would have taken him through Chollas Valley, Lemon Grove, Spring Valley and across the Sweetwater Lake basin through Jamul Rancho and to the base of Lyons Peak. In

172

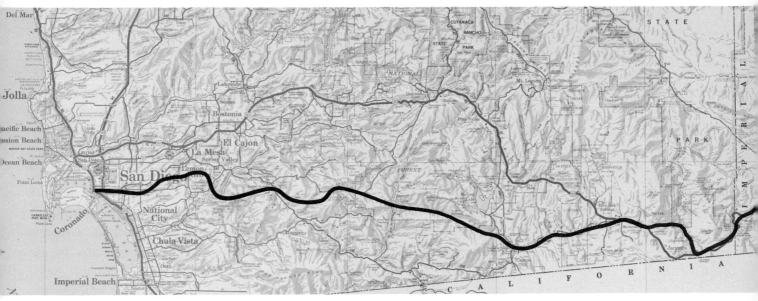

THE ARMY, struggling to supply Fort Yuma from San Diego, for a time used a new route discovered by Capt. Nathaniel Lyon, too steep and rocky for wagons.

a small depression on the north base of the second peak he discovered an Indian trail which he followed slightly south of east into "one of the most remarkable mountain gorges in nature, having on either side, high, steep mountains, covered with huge granite blocks. Though the rocks appeared impassable from a distance, the trail opened onto a "fine valley, having grass and water and beautiful oak groves," and extending along the foot of the mountains most of the distance to the high country. Lyon traveled eight miles along the water course, gradually climbing to its source. Then he noted a slight rise beyond which the water flowed eastward: "High, undulating country stretches far in every direction, oak groves, valleys, grass and water extending north and south."

Lyon's description probably was of a route across the Barrett Lake Basin and up the great natural declivity of Cottonwood Creek and Hauser Creek, which would have brought him out on the high woodlands north of Campo. From there, he travelled a little north of east for twelve miles, crossing a low ridge and descending its steep and rocky east side by an old Indian trail to Jacumba Basin. "East out of the valley are mountains bordering the desert," and the trail followed a northerly direction with a slight ascent, then began descending gradually in the same direction to a steep, rocky declivity, "which everywhere presents an obstacle to a direct route." Here again, the Indians from Jacumba showed Lyon a gradual descent which "with little work, it could

173

be the best pack mule trail of all, short of the long wagon road" by way of Warner's. From the foot of the trail, where there was water, but little grass, Lyon said he wound a northerly route for five miles along a dry creek bed.

This route would have taken him down Boulder Creek through In-ko-Pah Gorge. It did not become a wagon road, but it was a pack trail eighty miles shorter than the wagon route by way of Warner's and San Felipe. This trail was used by sheepmen and cattle drovers coming west and by Army pack trains going east to supply Fort Yuma. Interstate Highway 8 would twist its way through In-ko-Pah Gorge in later years, but the struggle to fulfill the dream of a practical low-level route over the mountain barrier, to end the geographical isolation of San Diego, would have to go on.

The new city, which had been lavish in salaries for its officials, soon went bankrupt and issued scrip in an attempt to meet its current bills. The legislature revoked the city charter, and in 1852 a Board of Trustees was organized to administer public affairs. Pueblo lots were ordered sold off to raise money. One of the lots contained a "fine brick building" which was identified as the courthouse.

But prosperity would come again to the ranchos, as it had done in the days when they belonged to the Franciscan missions. Hooper, in one of his last letters to Davis, had written "it is expected that San Diego will be quite gay this winter. Forster of San Juan, Don Joaquín Ortega and several other Spanish families are expected to pass the winter here. If so, San Diego will look up a little."

The *rancheros* of San Diego County, their cattle multiplying on the grassy hills and wet valleys, began putting together great herds which were driven up the old mission route 600 miles to Stockton, Sacramento and San Francisco, the Mexican and *Californio vaqueros* taking the trail with riatas and *chaparerras* that had come down from Spanish days and which gave the cowboys of America the traditional costumes of the Western Frontier.

CHAPTER TEN

"Slack your rope, hangsman,
O slack it for a while;
I think I see my mother coming,
Riding many a mile."

THE GARRA UPRISING

The county of San Diego, in need of tax money, sent Sheriff Haraszthy among the Indians in 1850 and he collected $600 in taxes on cattle and other property held by the Diegueño and Luiseño Indians and the small Cupeño tribe living in the vicinity of Warner's ranch. The next year the county again levied tax assessments on the Indian property but Gen. Joshua Bean, arriving in San Diego in the summer, advised the Cupeño Indians not to pay. In the dispute that followed the state Attorney General ruled that the assessments were proper and the taxes must be collected. The sheriff visited many of the Indian villages and notified their chiefs that unless the taxes were paid he would return with a large force and seize and sell their cattle. A few tribes responded. To some of the chiefs a time of decision had come. Their best lands were being taken away from them, the missionaries who had protected them, and the missions which had sheltered them, were gone from their lives, and thousands more white men were streaming over the mountain passes. The Indians had no vote and no voice in what was to happen to them.

San Diego had been well-protected up into early 1850. Lt. Col. J. B. Magruder and Company I, 1st Artillery, were stationed at the San Diego Mission, and Maj. Samuel P. Heintzelman and Companies D, H, and L, 2nd Infantry, were at the Yuma post.

Supplying of the men at Fort Yuma by wagon trains across the mountains proved to be impracticable, Maj. Heintzelman recom-

FORT YUMA was built at the junction of the Colorado and Gila Rivers, to protect immigrants to California and to control and subdue the Yuma Indians.

177

THIS SCENE AT AN INDIAN VILLAGE at Temecula was sketched by the artist Vischer in 1865, and drawn in 1871. It was a scene common to San Diego.

mending that it be done by boat up the Colorado River from the Gulf of California, and in June the troops, with the exceptions of Lt. Sweeny, a corporal and nine enlisted men, were instructed to fall back to Santa Ysabel. From there they were ordered back to San Diego, where they were divided between New Town and La Playa. In August, the *Herald* complained that four companies were living in tents and no precautions had been taken to shelter them from the "inclemencies of the approaching winter, nor is there a cent of money available to secure the means for these preparations." The hoped for barracks at New Town had not materialized, though the depot was in use.

The troops were ordered withdrawn from San Diego, and on November 14, Capt. John W. Davidson's company of sixteen men, the last at La Playa, left for the Gila River for the relief of Lt. Sweeny's guard. San Diego virtually was left defenseless, and the people talked of organizing a new militia in event of Indian troubles which always had to be considered as imminent.

Living at Warner's ranch was Antonio Garra and his son, who went under the same name. The elder Garra had been educated at San Luis Rey Mission and was a willing listener to the whispered suggestions of Bill Marshall, the white renegade who had encouraged the Pauma Valley Indians in the murder of the eleven *Californios*. Marshall assured Garra that the *Californios* and Mexicans, once a revolt had begun, would come to their assistance against the Americans. Garra dispatched runners to all of the Indian tribes between the coast and the Colorado River, and from the San Joaquin Valley south into the upper country of Baja California. One message went to Juan Antonio, a leader of the Mountain Cahuilla, one of three branches of the Cahuilla Indians who roamed the eastern mountain and desert area of Southern California and who never came under the direct influence of the missions. Juan Antonio, it will be remembered, had helped the *Californios* in the capture of the Indians who had participated in the Pauma massacre and, on his own initiative, had slaughtered the captives, men, women and children.

In his letter to Juan Antonio, Garra wrote:

> This is an explanation you already know who we are going to do, secure each point of rancherias since this thing is not with their *capitanes*. My will is for all, Indians and whites, since by the wrongs and damages they have done, it is better to end us at once. Now those of Lower California and of the River are invited; but those of the River will not come soon. They move slow. If we lose this war, all will be lost — the world if we gain this war; then it is forever; never will it stop; this war is for a whole life. Then so advise the white people, that they may take care.

Wild reports raced through the hills. It was believed that the Cahuillas were to descend on Los Angeles, and the Yuma and other Colorado River Indians were to cross the mountains and join the Diegueños and Luiseños in wiping out San Diego. Gen. Bean, who had urged the Indians not to pay taxes, now was faced with a major Indian war. As they had done many times in the past, the Dons fled their ranchos for the safety of San Diego. Friendly Indians left their valley and mountain homes and sought the protection of the Whites. Juan Bandini came up from Lower California and reported the Indians far down the peninsula were in a state of rebellion. Because of the shortage of guns and ammunition, all blacksmiths were put to work making lances, as had been done before the Battle of San Pasqual.

THE DIEGUENO INDIANS *threatened to attack San Diego. This Diegueño Village in San Felipe Valley was drawn by John Audubon, son of the naturalist.*

Warner's ranch was attacked on the night of November 27. Warner had sent his family away, and he had remained behind with a hired man and an Indian boy who had been placed with him in exchange for a bushel of corn. One hundred Indians surrounded the trading post, and Warner and his hired man held them off until their ammunition ran out. They then fled from the ranch house toward horses that had been kept saddled for just such an emergency. Warner and the Indian boy escaped but the hired man was killed. The Indians burned the house, drove off the stock, and then proceeded to the Hot Springs three miles away where they murdered four Americans who had gone there from San Diego to rest. One of them was Levi Slack, merchant partner of E. W. Morse. Four American sheepherders were killed near the Colorado River crossing.

San Diegans prepared to defend the town and a volunteer company was organized under Maj. E. F. Fitzgerald, of the U.S. Army, as commander. Cave J. Couts was named captain and Sheriff Haraszthy, first lieutenant. In a letter to his mother and sister, dated December 2, 1851, Thomas Whaley wrote:

. . . The tocsin of war Sounds. We momentarily expect to be attacked by the Indians who under their great chief Antonio Garra are swarming by thousands into the South. The town of San Diego is proclaimed under martial law. Every man is enrolled a Soldier. We are but a handful of men numbering not quite a hundred. Already several parties have gone out to fight and this morning thirteen more leave all of whom will be under the command of Maj. Fitzgerald U.S.A. The party is supplied with ammunitions and rations for thirty days. They are to act only on the defensive till reinforcements arrive from the north. There are only thirty five of us left to protect the town . . . my turn to Stand guard comes rather frequently . . . I have contributed fifty dollars in cash and Some few things towards getting up the expedition.

. . . The first attack the Indians made was upon the rancho of J. J. Warner, member of our State Legislature, burning his house, Stealing everything belonging to him and murdering a man in his employ. Four men have been murdered upon the Gila and four more Americans from this place at the Springs of the Agua Caliente who had gone there for their health . . . the rancheros are sending their families to town for better protection . . . I am well armed with a brace of Six Shooters and have a horse ready to Saddle at any moment.

Lt. Sweeny, who had been left with a small body of soldiers at Fort Yuma, was joined by Capt. John W. Davidson and sixteen additional men who had been sent from San Diego as a relief party, and by the parties of Maj. Henry L. Kendrick and Capt. L. Sitgreaves, who had been engaged in exploring the Colorado River. Though they now had thirty men it was decided to abandon the fort on December 6 because of a lack of supplies, and take the road to San Diego. Cave Couts, in a letter to Abel Stearns, reported that Kendrick had found the whole desert frontier ablaze. The mountains were covered with signal fires from Carrizo Creek to

Santa Ysabel. An American by the name of Whitley, living at Cockney Bill's ranch on Volcan Mountain, told Davidson and Sweeny that Indians had collected from Vallecito, San Felipe, San Jose and neighboring mountains to attack the military train but upon seeing the number of soldiers, because of the presence of Capt. Davidson's men, had given up and now professed only friendship to the Whites.

At San Pasqual they received orders to return to Santa Ysabel, where their forces were joined with those of Majs. Heintzelman and Magruder and about one hundred soldiers who had been quartered at Mission San Luis Rey. Sweeny and his men were ordered to protect San Diego, and he took the mountain trail toward El Cajon and arrived on December 21. The populace, especially the women, welcomed them with cheers, Sweeny writing that "they looked upon me as their deliverer from the tender mercies of savages," who, they said, would have attacked the town if his men had been cut off in the mountains. This was later confirmed. During the absence of the Army regulars, a force of recruits had arrived by sea and they also had kept San Diego in a state of unrest with their drinking and rioting. Their ringleaders had been placed in irons. Sweeny ordered all 250 recruits to line up and he reviewed them without a sidearm of any kind. The soldiers were silent and respectful. A virtual state of mutiny ended.

John B. Magruder, as major-general

Fitzgerald's Volunteers left San Diego on December 27 reached Agua Caliente and burned the village of the Cupeño Indians, and proceeding to the site of Warner's store, found nothing but ruins and the bodies of two Indians. Haraszthy went out with a small party and took Marshall and two Indian companions into custody and delivered them to San Diego for a court martial headed by himself. The principal evidence against Marshall came from Indians but it was decided that their testimony could not be accepted before a legal tribunal. Justice was pre-ordained. Gallows were erected before the trial began.

The court martial made quick work of Marshall and one of the two Indians captured with him, whose name has been variously given as Juan Verdugo, or Juan Verde or Gerde. The *San Diego Herald* reported on December 18:

The trial of these men was concluded on Friday evening last; on Saturday morning, it was announced on the Plaza they were to be executed at 2 o'clock the same day. The Fitzgerald Volunteers were ordered to be on duty at that time to conduct the prisoners to the scaffold, which had been erected a short distance out of town, near the Catholic burying grounds. The graves were dug, and all the preparations made, during the forenoon, for carrying out the sentence of the court martial. About 2:00 o'clock the Volunteers were under arms, the people began to gather in considerable numbers about the Plaza and Court

House. A Priest (Fr. Juan Holbein) was with the prisoners most of the forenoon and accompanied the men to the gallows, where they received final absolution. They were then informed that a short time would be allowed them, if they wished to make any remarks. Marshall was the first to speak . . . He said he was prepared to die and he hoped that his friends, and the people around him, would forgive him, that he trusted in God's mercy, and hoped to be pardoned for his many transgressions. He still insisted that he is innocent of the crime by which he was about to die . . .

Verdugo spoke in Spanish. He acknowledged his guilt and admitted the justice of the sentence passed upon him; said he was ready and willing to yield up his life for forfeit for his crimes and wickedness. The ropes were then adjusted, the priest approached them for the last time . . . repeated the final prayer, extended the crucifix, which each kissed several times, when he descended from the wagon, which immediately moved on, leaving the poor unfortunate wretches suspended about five feet from the ground.

The hanging took place on December 13, 1851. The site of the executions may have been near the new Catholic church being erected on a site across the river, and burial was in an adjoining cemetery. Warner's Indian servant boy was found guilty of giving false testimony and sentenced to receive twenty-five lashes.

The United States Army forces, which had established headquarters at Santa Ysabel, divided into two divisions to take separate routes through the mountains toward the village of Los Coyotes where the Indians had been holding their councils of war, and the one under command of Heintzelman was attacked by Indians led by a chief named Chapuli. The soldiers concentrated their fire on Chapuli. He was killed, and as the Indians fled up the sides of a mountain, a second chief was shot dead.

The encounter led to the capture of a number of prisoners in the vicinity of Los Coyotes, among them a number known to have taken part in the attack on Warner's, and after a military trial on the spot, four chieftains were condemned to die, and were executed on Christmas Day while kneeling before their graves. Some eighty Indians witnessed the executions which took place at the site of the village near the creek bed. All traces of the village on the desert route into the mountains first explored by Anza, have disappeared.

At San Diego Fitzgerald's Volunteers were reinforced by volunteers brought by boat from San Francisco, who were dubbed "The Hounds," in memory of the hoodlums who had so terrorized the northern city. Organized as the Rangers, at the call of the governor to assist if needed at San Diego, they had been ordered disbanded with news of the success of the military. But they came anyway. They wrought more harm and misery on San Diego than did the Indians. With no enemy to fight, they camped in Mission Valley and ranged through Old Town on drunken sprees and

Philip Crosthwaite

THE GOLD RUSH BOOM was under way when this scene of San Francisco in 1849 was sketched by Henry Firks. The great bay was beginning to fill with ships.

threatened to sack the town. The authorities sent an appeal to Lt. Sweeny, at the old barracks at La Playa, and he led a sergeant and eighteen men into Old Town. That same afternoon, Philip Crosthwaite, a sergeant of Fitzgerald's Volunteers, engaged in a row with one of the Hounds identified as a Lt. Watkins. Both were wounded in an exchange of gunfire on the street, and Crosthwaite barely escaped death, retreating under a heavy fire from other members of the Hounds. Sweeny ordered his soldiers to form in the Plaza, and he writes "it was the general opinion that if my men had not been present that day the streets of San Diego would have been drenched in blood." Watkins' leg had to be amputated, and it was presented to Crosthwaite as a trophy of war. The soldiers remained on guard in Old Town until the Indian war had ended, and the Hounds had been loaded up and shipped back to San Francisco.

The general uprising did not materialize, however, because of the failure of the Cahuilla Indians as a whole to follow the lead of the men from Los Coyotes, and because of a change of heart on the part of the Yumas who had pledged their cooperation to Garra. The Yumas and Cocopas had halted their own inter-tribal wars long enough to unite for the intended attack on San Diego, but soon fell out, the Yumas even turning on each other in a fight over the division of the abandoned sheep of the four American herders murdered on the desert. Fortunately for the Whites, the Indians lacked the ability to pursue an objective.

At Los Angeles, Joshua Bean led thirty-five men who were to combine forces with a group of Mormons from San Bernardino and some *Californios* under Andrés Pico. Meanwhile, Juan Antonio, upon the urging of a mountain man, and after serious reflection as to the future of the Indians, decided to again cast his lot with the Whites. He laid an ambush for Garra, invited him to a conference, and took him prisoner. Garra was turned over to the military. Garra's son and ten followers soon also surrendered themselves to Juan Antonio.

Garra's son and four other Indians were hastily executed at Chino, San Bernardino County, but the elder Garra was taken to San Diego, where he was tried before a militia court martial, headed by Gen. Bean, on charges of treason, murder and robbery. He acknowledged guilt only in the murders of the American sheepherders, and testified that the raid on Warner's was made by a small band of Cahuilla Indians, that he was not with them, and that he had not taken part in, or ordered, the murders of the four San Diegans at the Hot Springs. Indian witnesses, accepted in this court, gave conflicting testimony, but the burden of evidence seemed to show that Garra had ordered the attacks, but, in a sudden seizure of fear, had feigned illness and had not taken part in them.

Though Indian witnesses had testified that Marshall and the Indian hanged with him had consulted with Garra just before the murders, Garra denied they had been involved in any way. Instead, he insisted that two *Californios,* Joaquín Ortega and José Antonio Estudillo, had encouraged the Indian uprisings in the hope of getting rid of the Americans. These accusations were denied, and according to memoirs of participants, which included the leading people of San Diego, were conclusively refuted.

Garra was found guilty of murder and theft on January 17, 1852, and sentenced to be shot. Before the execution Lt. Sweeny talked with Garra in his cell. He wrote that Garra acknowledged that he had induced the Yumas, Cocopas and Cuchanos to unite against the Americans, and that he had urged that a party of 400 be sent against Sweeny's camp at Fort Yuma, to cut him off, and then they were to join in a general descent on the settlements.

Though Sweeny had refused to sit on the court martial, ruling that it was a state matter, and would not let his soldiers carry out the execution, he did provide arms and ammunition for the citizens' militia. On the same day that the verdict was returned, Garra was marched from his cell at the head of an execution squad of ten men, to a freshly dug grave in the Catholic cemetery. A large crowd was on hand. He was asked if he had anything to confess. He answered: "Gentlemen, I ask your pardon for all my offenses, and expect yours in return." He was blindfolded, told to kneel, and the order to fire was given.

Three months later, according to the *Alta California*, a San Luis Rey Indian named Cosmos was led into Los Angeles, with a *riata* around his neck, by a group of Indians eager to collect the rewards offered for the capture of those who had taken part in the Garra uprising. Cosmos reputedly confessed to taking part in the killing of the four Americans at Agua Caliente and gave authorities the names of seven San Luiseño and four Cahuilla Indians who also had participated. That night he hanged himself in his cell, using a peg driven high in the adobe wall. His captors, led by one named John the Baptist, collect their rewards of cloth and trinkets, ate four beeves, and celebrated with a dance.

The executions broke the rebellious spirit of the Indians, and though many incidents were yet to occur, especially along the Colorado, they no longer were to present a major threat, and the Diegueños and Luiseños, probably numbering about 5000, and the Yumas, about 3000, were hastily driven down a path toward near-extinction. Edward F. Beale, who had taken part in the Battle of San Pasqual, was appointed Indian agent for Southern California in 1852, and Cave Couts as sub-agent for San Diego. A report on the Indians, compiled by B. D. Wilson, agent for California, reported that the value of the missions and their property, exclusive of land, had been five million dollars in 1834, and "that so much property should have passed from the mission Indians in the short space of six months, without any known agency of theirs, is an event calculated to leave an impression upon the minds of reflecting men, long after the actors in such a wholesale confiscation shall be forgotten." An appropriation for the protection of the California Indians was reduced in Congress from $120,000 to $20,000 and Sen. William M. Gwin of California warned that "if this is to be the policy of the government towards this people, it will form a dark page in our history, if it does not bring vengeance from heaven upon us as a nation."

California entered a period of lawlessness that exceeded that of the settlement of the Western Plains two decades later. Historian Bancroft is authority for a statement that 4200 murders were committed in California between 1849 and 1854. Bandits wandered the countryside. Gen. Bean, the first American mayor of San Diego and a commander of the state militia, himself did not live long. He was fatally shot under mysterious circumstances while riding to his home at San Gabriel from a tight-rope walking exhibition. A poor shoemaker of San Gabriel, who was identified as a member of Solomon Pico's gang of bandits, was hanged for the crime. Years later, according to Bancroft, someone else confessed to the murder.

The general's brother, Roy, fled from some escapade at San Gabriel and in San Diego engaged in another quarrel in which he wounded a man named John Collins. Bean and Collins had challenged each other with pistols, but Collins was shot while fleeing on his horse. Both were indicted by the grand jury on charges of sending and accepting challenges and of assault with intent to commit murder. Bean escaped by digging his way out of the jail and fled to Texas, where he nominated himself a judge and became known as the "Law West of the Pecos." Two others also were indicted for sending challenges to duels, and one of them, George H. Davis, was also accused of refusing to fight.

The grand jury despaired of enforcing law and order. A report issued on April 13, 1852, and signed by Lewis A. Franklin, as foreman, deplored the prevalence of drunkenness, even among public officials who they said "oftentimes rend the air with their wild shouts of drunkenness, or, mounted on some fiery steed, bound here and there in mad disorder, while another pertinaciously clings to your button-hole, to resist which freedom, a violent and abusive tongue would spit its venom upon you." The jury could not refrain from "naming the proprietors of those dens of iniquity who slyly vend poison to the half-savage Indian and his depraved mistress" and said they were Don Juan María Marrón, Don José Jesús Moreno, and Mrs. Snook, "who all have low groggeries, where at any hour of day or night, the lazy and indolent Indians congregate."

The streets of the town were described as being filled with rubbish and garbage, and cattle roaming through them at will, and the surrounding countryside disfigured with native huts which were eyesores and the hiding places of idle, pilfering Indians. The bane of the community, however, was the practice of a transient element going about armed with pistols and bowie knives.

The patience of the people was at an end, when a luckless derelict and troublemaker by the name of James Robinson, known generally as "Yankee Jim," and two companions had the misfortune of climaxing a series of misdemeanors by stealing a rowboat belonging to Joseph C. Stewart and Enos Wall. Though it was found abandoned a short time later, Yankee Jim was taken into custody, a grand jury, with Cave Couts as foreman, met and pronounced the theft a capital crime, and the Court of Sessions, after a trial returned a verdict on August 18, 1852, sentenced him to death by hanging. Yankee Jim was described as a French Canadian, six feet and three inches tall, and perhaps to justify the sentence, a legend grew in later years that he had committed many murders upon hapless victims in the gold fields. On September 18 Yankee Jim was taken in a wagon to the present site of the Whaley House, where a scaffold had been erected from two beams and an iron crossbar. He was ordered to stand, the rope was fastened about his neck, and the wagon driven off. His companions were sentenced to the state prison. Other lawbreakers were taken out and flogged.

Adventurous Americans embarked on filibustering expeditions into Lower California. They ostensibly had as their objective the annexation of Lower California to the United States, and in this they were encouraged by Juan Bandini, who had moved his operations from San Diego into Mexican territory, and was interested in copper mining. Though gold had been found in a creek emptying into Mission Valley in 1851, the reports of gold in Lower California started a stampede of idlers and adventurers from San Diego.

Two of them, identified only as Vanness and McDonald, spent several weeks in San Diego trying to organize a looting party, and Cave Couts, in a letter dated March 10, said he intervened to save Vanness from being hanged, which "the following day I regretted." Vanness and McDonald were slain in Lower California. San Diego had its own Vigilante Committees and in the same letter Couts reported that a horse thief had been taken from the jail and given fifty lashes on his bare back, and that a few days before, Franklin, who had been foreman on the grand jury, and Col. Magruder, had had a fist fight in the Plaza. "Fought some 15 min. & no damage; next day, the Col. whaled him all over the Plaza with a stick; and since that, F. has been running about trying to find a civil officer to sue him — not one is to be found."

A large military force was sent back to the Colorado River and a number of engagements were fought with the Yuma and Cocopa Indians. In one engagement, forty soldiers were ambushed, fought all night against two hundred Indians, had a sergeant and eight men killed. The villages of the Indians were burned and their crops destroyed. A stubborn, difficult war in the tangled growth of the river channels continued for months, but, in the end, the resistance and power of the Yumas were broken. Their long rule of the lower Colorado River, which had defied the authority of Spain and Mexico, was at an end. The heat and the months of lonely guard duty at the dreary post at Fort Yuma, wore down the soldiers, and many deserted, some to die in the desert and others to be slain by wandering Indians. Lt. Col. Louis S. Craig, in charge of a military escort for a new boundary survey party, was murdered by two deserters near Sackett's Wells east of Carrizo Springs, after he had laid down his weapons and offered to intercede on their behalf. The killers were captured near Temecula by Indians who had been alerted by military couriers. Bound hand and foot, they were packed off to San Diego and handed over to Maj. Magruder at the Mission, where they were hanged.

Wagons from San Diego, pushed and tugged over the difficult mountain trails, continued to supply the little fort until the day when a steamer finally would make its way up the Colorado from the Gulf of California. In November a series of earthquake shocks opened the earth in many directions, sent steam gushers into the sky, hurled chunks of Chimney Rock to the ground with clouds of dust, jumped the level of the river a foot in some places, in others left fish to die in dry channels. But even before the shocks had fully subsided, a column of smoke was seen in the distance. It heralded the approach of the steamboat *Uncle Sam*, which docked below Fort Yuma on December 3, 1852. She had been fourteen days puffing up from the gulf and her arrival, according to a letter in the *San Francisco Herald* from a correspondent at Yuma, created as much excitement as had Fulton's steamboat on the Hudson. River boats would supply Fort Yuma and Arizona points for many years.

CHAPTER ELEVEN

"Feet in the stirrups and seat in the saddle,
I hung and rattled with them long-horn cattle."

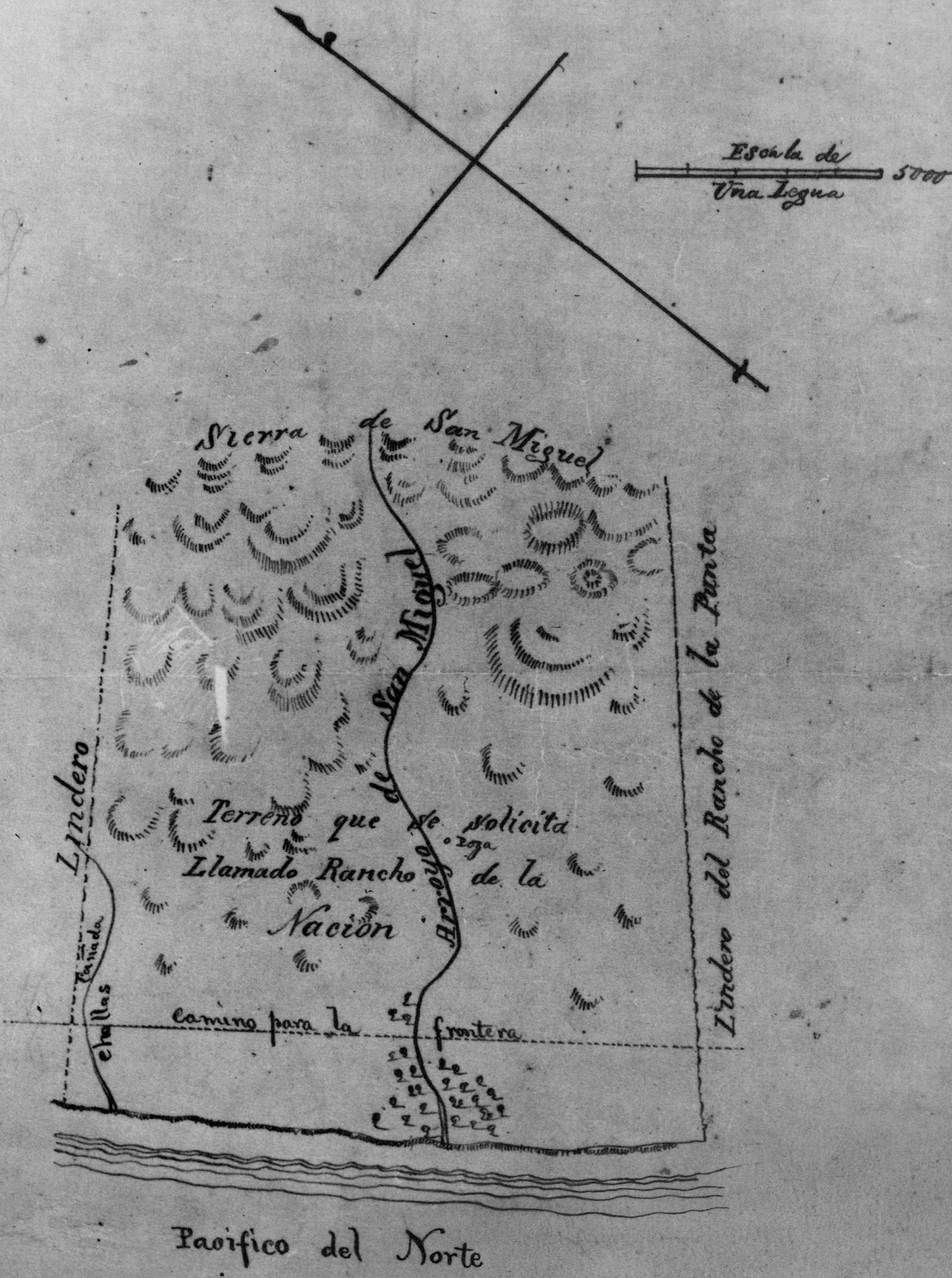

Escala de
5000
Una Legua
Sierra de San Miguel
Arroyo de San Miguel
Lindero
Lindero del Rancho de la Punta
Terreno que se solicita
Llamado Rancho de la
Nacion
Cañada
ehallas
camino para la frontera
Pacifico del Norte

EMPIRES OF CATTLE

The crack of the cattle whip echoed along worn El Camino Real as the *rancheros* and their *vaqueros* drove their herds north to the gold country. Cattle were reported bringing $75 a head in San Francisco, and in May of 1852 Cave Couts wrote to his brother-in-law, Abel Stearns, that he was leaving the Soledad with 800 head of cattle, large and small, and using one hundred mares, and Bandini was preparing a corral in which he hoped to gather a thousand head, mostly from Lower California.

The long drives were handled by the *majordomo* and four or five *vaqueros*. They started from San Diego when the winter grass reached maturity, and moved from ten to fifteen miles a day along the mission road through Soledad Valley, back of Del Mar, and across Rancho Santa Fe and through to Mission San Luis Rey, and then to San Gabriel. There, they left the mission trail and were taken across Tehachapi Mountains into the San Joaquin Valley. At San Jose and at Sacramento, or along the shores of San Francisco Bay, the cattle were fattened and then sold to supply the demands of the gold market.

With the Indian problem at least temporarily relieved, all of the rancheros had their stock on the trail that spring, through a countryside so heavy in yellow mustard weed that they often lost sight of the cattle. Stampedes and thieves plagued their steps. Couts tells of outwitting a nest of thieves at Santa Clara, but

THIS CRUDE MAP, or diseño, was submitted to the U.S. Land Commission to establish John Forster's original grant of entire area of National City, Chula Vista.

191

others were not so fortunate, John Forster, José Antonio Estudillo, the Machados and others losing large numbers.

The market was not as good as had been reported that summer, though Couts sold 943 cattle at $20 a head at San Joaquin City. Buyers reported that at least 50,000 loose cattle were roaming the interior valleys and it was feared they would depress the market, and more cattle were reported on the trail to California from Texas. It was the California gold trail which established the cattle industry in the Southwest. Although some cattle had been driven from the Texas ranges northward to Missouri and eastward to New Orleans for a number of years, 1500-mile treks to California were the first major American drives, though they have received little place in the literature of the Great West.

Large herds began to appear on the Gila Trail as early as 1849, though generally they were part of the many immigrant trains. By 1853, with the cattle market still strong in San Francisco and Stockton, thousands upon thousands of cattle bought for as low as $5 a head in Texas were driven across the blazing deserts, their progress marked by the bones of lost or parched animals.

The *Herald* on November 11, 1854, reported:

A man recently in from the Colorado informs us that there are large parties of emigrants on the road—most of them will go up the country by the way of the Monte and San Gabriel. They have a large amount of stock and they are generally better fitted-out than the emigration of any previous year. There is a large amount of stock being driven over this year—mostly from Texas—amounting during the past eight weeks to something like 6000 head of cattle across the Colorado. Among the others, Mr. Dunlap has crossed 500 head; Erskine, 800 and a Mr. Ryne, who lost so many cattles last year by the Apaches, has over a 1000.

The diary of Michael Erskine tells of crossing the desert in October with 800 to 900 cattle, and coming upon a place where a drive just ahead of them had lost 100 to 125 cattle from poisoned feed or water, and that their own cattle had stampeded time and again. Four of the animals were so worn they fell dead while the herders were trying to force them up over Box Canyon. The cattle often were rested and fattened in the mountain valleys of the Lagunas and Cuyamaca, before being taken back on the trail.

In December, Couts was able to report to Stearns from San Francisco that "cattle are the highest & in greater demand than ever before. Good beef cattle. If you can, at this season, part with from five hundred to a thousand head of fat cattle, and turn them over to me on shares, I will defer my trip to the states for the present and drive them up." If they could be brought up fat, "my word for it they will pay handsomely."

Ranchero's California saddle

Lady's Mexican sidesaddle

192

Prosperity rushed upon the ranchos and the future of Southern California was determined for many years to come. Horace Bell, in his *"Reminiscences of a Ranger,"* says that *rancheros* paid as much as $2000 for silver trappings for their horses and $1000 for their costumes. While the population of Northern California grew swiftly, and industrialization followed upon the gold mining, the South remained largely a pastoral country and its counties became known as the "cow counties." Statehood had not solved political problems and the Southerners were resentful of domination by the North. Taxation without representation became an issue that led to repeated movements to divide California into two states. New Town experienced a temporary revival of activity because of the arrival during the year of several hundred more persons, with all of the houses occupied, but in Old Town the Colorado House and several stores had been closed down, and signs of decay were beginning to creep over old adobe walls. John Russell Bartlett, with the second United States Boundary Commission, wrote in his *"Personal Narrative"* that San Diego, like Monterey, was noted for its excellent society:

Dancing on the Veranda

There remain many of the old Castillian families here, who have preserved their blood from all mixture with the Indians. In this circle all Americans and foreigners visiting the place have experienced much pleasure, for such is its refined and social character, that one almost imagines himself once again enjoying the delights of home. The California ladies are said to possess all the fine qualities of their sex, whether of the head or heart, and make the most excellent wives. Such have been the attractions of these fair *señoritas* for the young American officers, that many have been induced to relinquish their commissions in the U.S. Army, and become planters and stock raisers in California.

Old San Diego reached the height of its civic and social life. A grand ball, typical of ones being held in Old Town despite the roughness of the times, was given in April of 1852 by the newly-organized Pacific Pioneer Yacht Club. The *Herald* describes the event at the Gila House as follows:

At half past eight P.M. a brilliant band, in their full uniform, marched through the public plaza and entered the salon to the tune *"Come Haste to the Wedding."* At 9 the salon began to fill with the fashion and beauty of San Diego and vicinity; all the ranchos not further than a hundred miles, poured out their gay and graceful *doñas*, who with lidded eyes, bounding feet and palpitating hearts, might compare favorably for beauty, grace, symmetry and *je ne sais quoi* female attraction, with any other community on record. The officers of the United States Army and Navy made their appearance in large numbers, in full dress, while the brilliancy of their uniforms was admirably sustained by the courteous ease and their vanity of polished gentlemen.

Doña Mariana Coronel grinding corn

Next Page, RANCHO LIFE dominated Southern California's "cow counties." This famous painting shows Silver Dons, grown wealthy, roping bear for sport.

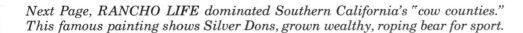

193

At 12:00, supper was announced, the long and glittering line of *Señoritas* and *Caballeros* marched in to the stirring strains of the well-appointed band playing *"The Campbells are Coming."* The table presented a spectacle rarely seen in any country, never before in California. A large *paté* graced the center of the board and was composed of peacocks, whose gaudy plumage was artistically arranged with the most striking effect. Bears, hams, green turtles stewed in the shell, haunches of elk, antelope and deer, wild turkey and wild geese, canvas backed ducks and mallards, snipe, plover and curlews, grouse, partridges and . . . fish of the lakes, rivers and the ocean, oysters, clams, rozar fish, crayfish, pastry, fruits and flowers—in fine, everything that could be obtained or thought of, decked the festive board and insistent and merry popping of Champagne corks, french liqueurs, aromatic coffee and refreshing tea, gave proof of the abundance of good things in the liquid line.

José Guadalupe Estudillo

The grand Don of San Diego, José Antonio Estudillo, died in 1852 at the age of 47. With him passed much of the Spanish flavor that had lingered ever since the revolution in Mexico. The grace and ease of the pastoral days were gone. His home had been a fortress in time of trouble and its chapel had kept flickering the flame of Catholic faith.

He and his family held the adjoining ranchos of Janal and Otay, and his son, José G. Estudillo, went before the United States Land Commission, as did all of the Dons, to fight for the lands which had been granted to them which they thought had been guaranteed by the American invaders. The Land Act of 1851 made it necessary for all claimants to present their petitions for verification within two years or forfeit their rights, and as the burden of proof was placed on the Dons, they often were hard-pressed to locate the carelessly drawn titles and maps of by-gone days. Friends testified for each other as to boundaries that were both vague and altered by use and claims of squatters. The Land Commission hearings went on for ten years, and court hearings followed upon them, until lawyer fees and court costs had eaten up much of the wealth that the land had represented.

The right of the widow of Juan María Osuna to possession of San Dieguito Rancho, or Rancho Santa Fe, was challenged by the U.S. Attorney because she was unable to produce a map and could not prove she had built and occupied a home within one year of receiving the property. She produced her own sketch of the location of the home she said the family had built, and Santiago Arguello came to her defense, testifying that he knew of his own knowledge that a house had been built, and that he personally had defined the boundaries of the rancho in settlement of a boundary dispute.

Estudillo adobe baking oven

Jesús Moreno was a witness for the widow of Capt. Snook on her claim for Rancho San Bernardo, and he testified that he was

196

an Marcos, as claimed by Lorenzo Soto

Peninsula de San Diego, as claimed by Frederick Billings

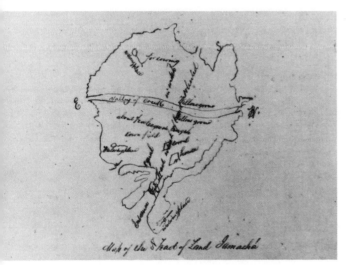

amacha, as claimed by Apolinaria Lorenzana

Monserrate, as claimed by Ysidro Alvarado

uejito y Cañada de Palomía, as claimed by G. W. Hamley

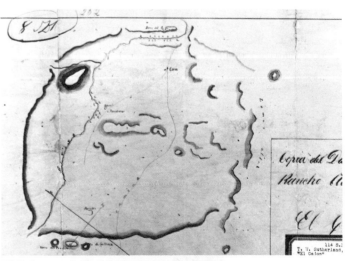

El Cajon, as claimed by Pedrorena Family

The restored Chapel at Rancho Santa Margarita

The restored Chapel of the Estudillo House where Old San Diego worshipped for many years

well acquainted with the boundaries as he had lived in the neighborhood for twenty-four years and that in passing by he had seen the servants of Capt. Snook piling up stones and was told these were the marks of Snook's boundaries.

The children of Miguel and María Antonia Estudillo de Pedrorena were aided in their fight for possession of El Cajon Rancho by Santiago Arguello who said he knew that *Señora* Pedrorena had settled upon the rancho with her husband in the year 1845 and that they had built houses and corrals for their stock and occupied it with their family and cattle until the time of the death of Miguel Pedrorena, and harvested large crops from the land. Apolinaria Lorenzana, the orphan friend and benefactor of the Indians, had lived on her Jamacha Rancho but had removed her cattle and possessions as a consequence of the war. Her claim was challenged by the government on the contention she had no map outlining the boundaries and had failed to comply with the conditions of building a house and living in it.

And so they went. The Land Act had been written to aid the new settlers more than the old families, and squatters had torn down fences, moved known boundary markers, and occupied remote valleys, and the *rancheros* were finding it more difficult month after month to dislodge them. Though he was a successful petitioner before the Land Commission, Warner never returned to his trading post on the immigrant trail. After serving out his term as a state senator, and as a member of the first county Board of Supervisors which convened on January 1, 1853, he removed to Los Angeles in 1855. Sections of the ranch were sold off to satisfy creditors. In the *Southern Californian* of April 11, 1855, Bandini commented bitterly on decisions of the Commission:

Of the lands mentioned, some have been in the quiet possession of the proprietors and their families for forty and fifty years. On them they have reared themselves homes—they have enclosed and cultivated fields—there they and their children were born—and there they lived in peace and comparative plenty. But now—"Our inheritance is turned to strangers—our houses to aliens. We have drunken our water for money—our wood is sold unto us. Our necks are under persecution—we labor and have no rest."

The first County Board of Supervisors was created in 1853 by the old San Diego Court of Sessions which had governed affairs of the county since 1850, and the seven elected members reported they found the books and accounts a "botch of botches," incomplete and incomprehensible. One of the Board's first acts was to order diversion of three-fifths of the poll tax levied on every able-bodied man to the support of roads and highways, and those not paying were required to work it off.

The sport of bullfighting continued in the Plaza for a number of years, and Ames, an editor from New England, looked upon the events with some distaste, reporting on occasion that "several . . . bulls were bothered or tortured to different degrees of insanity, but nobody suffered damage in the conflict." If there wasn't a bull-fight, there was a horse race and betting. He was distressed by the lack of interest in establishing public or private schools, and deplored seeing "daily running in our streets ragged little urchins who have neither the modesty of youth nor the decency of shame."

The deterioration of New Town, despite a temporary demand for its houses, continued, and in July of 1853 the *Herald* moved into the Colorado House in Old Town and Ames re-named it "The Herald Building." The growing Protestant population made the Masons a strong factor in San Diego, and Fr. Holbein, who had administered the last rites to the Garra insurrectionists, forbade his flock to look upon their ceremonies, or even to go out into the streets during a Masonic procession. The *Herald* in September 1853 noted with great relief that Fr. Holbein was leaving Old Town. Because of the strong feelings which had been aroused, gifts to complete the Catholic Church had dwindled, and it was never finished. High water in the San Diego River in January of 1855 undermined the foundations and the building collapsed.

There was considerable worry about the future of San Diego because of the silting up of the bay. Frequent attempts by local residents to force the river back into its old channel, by erection of barriers of sand and brush, had failed. The U.S. Coast Survey warned in 1851 that the bay might be destroyed entirely "and this is an excellent harbour and its loss would be severely felt."

On January 8, 1853, Lt. George Derby, of the U.S. Topographical Engineers, came to San Diego to report on what should be done. He had made a number of reconnaissances in the West for the Army and had explored the lower Colorado River in search of a suitable supply route to Fort Yuma. But Derby was known in later years, not for his contributions as an engineer and explorer, but as a humorist, writing under the name of John Phoenix. He contributed many articles to the *San Diego Herald*, even serving for a while as its editor while Ames was on one of his many unexplained trips to San Francisco, and reversing its political complexion from Democrat to Whig. Ames gave no indication of being outraged, continued to use Derby's writings and took a collection of them to New York, where they were published in book form under the title, "*Phoenixiana.*"

As Derby's ship pulled into San Diego Bay he saw "two crazy old hulks riding at anchor" and a bark he identified as the *Clar-*

Lt. George H. Derby

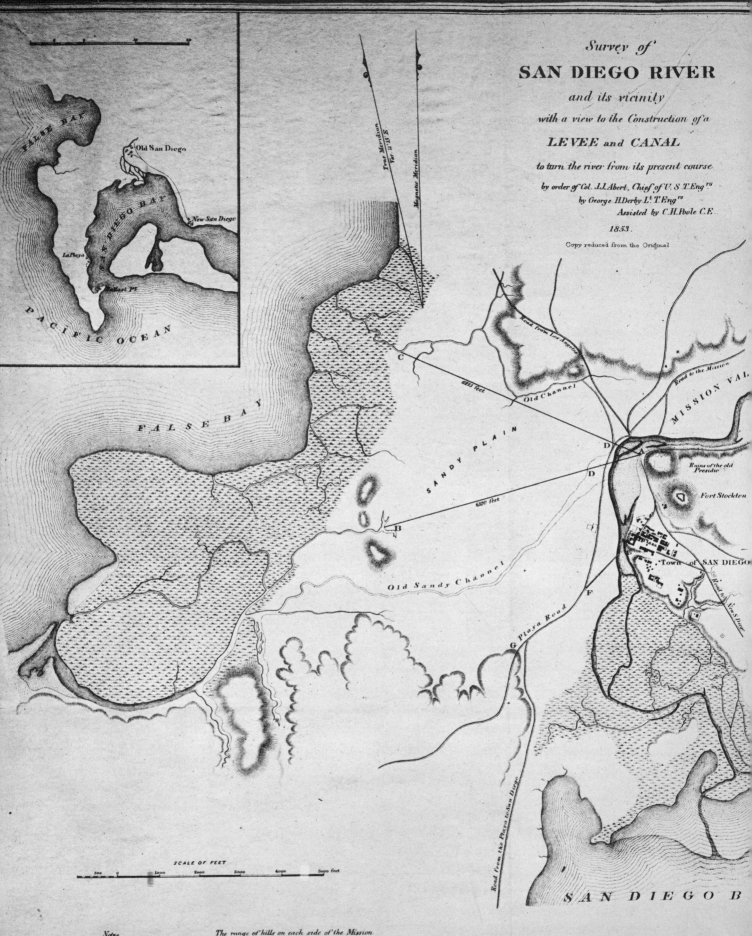

Survey of
SAN DIEGO RIVER
and its vicinity
with a view to the Construction of a
LEVEE and CANAL
to turn the river from its present course
by order of Col. J.J.Abert, Chief of U.S.T.Eng^{rs}
by George H.Derby Lt T.Eng^{rs}
Assisted by C.H.Poole C.E.
1853.
Copy reduced from the Original

FALSE BAY

Old San Diego

SAN DIEGO BAY

New San Diego

La Playa

Ballast P^t

PACIFIC OCEAN

True Meridian Var 11° 15' E

Magnetic Meridian

Road from Los Angeles

Old Channel

Road to the Mission

MISSION VAL.

SANDY PLAIN

C

6843 feet

D

D

6320 feet

B

A

Ruins of the old Presidio

Fort Stockton

Old Sandy Channel

F

Playa Road

Town of SAN DIEGO

Road to Nem Dingo

G

Road from the Playa to San Diego

SAN DIEGO B

FALSE BAY

SCALE OF FEET

500   0   1000   2000   3000   4000   5000 feet

Notes
During the Freshets of the Rainy Season, the Marsh
south of the Town is entirely inundated as well as
that part of the Valley and Plain bordering on the
River.

The River is here represented at its average height
as observed during the months of January, February &
March of the present year.

The range of hills on each side of the Mission
Valley, extends back to the Coast Range of
Mountains

The Channels marked upon this plan with
a shaded line, contain water at high tide, those
not so marked are dry at all times

The difference of level of the bed of the
River and the site of the town is about 15 feet

J. Ackerman Lith. 377 & 379

issa Andrews, filled with coal for the Pacific Mail Steamship Co., "wherein dwells Captain Bogart, like a second Robinson Crusoe." Capt. J. C. Bogart, once on the whaler *Black Warrior*, became the steamship agent at La Playa and later was active in politics.

A study of the river showed that while its bed usually was dry between May 1 to November 1, freshets occurred during the rainy season; the ordinary rapidity of the current was two to three miles an hour, and its greatest ordinary depth two to three feet, but during the freshets, its velocity would rise to five miles an hour, its depth five to six feet and its width from 100 to 400 feet. At times much of the entire plain between Old Town and Point Loma was covered with flood water, presenting the appearance of a lake.

The plan recommended by Derby, for a new and straight channel two miles in length leading directly to Mission Bay with the south or harbor side to be buttressed with an embankment of heavy construction, was not approved by the Board of Engineers. He was instructed to deepen the old twisting channel to Mission Bay. Sand excavated from the river bed was thrown southward to form a levee. Where his line crossed the existing river bed he erected a bulkhead of dirt and timber, which had the effect of turning the river into False Bay. In his report Derby warned that the whole plain had a substratum of quicksand and that any barrier on such a soil would be quickly undermined.

The work was begun in late September and Derby commented that he had come to San Diego to dam the river and he had damned it ever since. The job, done with Indian labor, was finished in November. The dike began to give way within two years, with the exceptionally heavy rains of 1855, and the river returned to its old channel into San Diego Bay. Flood water perhaps scoured out the burial grounds across the river, at the site of the ruined church, and at the foot of Presidio Hill near the aged palm trees, as it was about this time that a new cemetery south of town came into use.

The Old Town of Derby's day had about 100 houses, some of wood but mostly yet of adobe, and contained about 700 inhabitants, "two thirds whom are 'native and to the manor born,' the remainder a mixture of American, English, German, Hebrew, and Pike County . . ." He stopped at the Exchange Hotel, which he noted was maintained "by Hoof (familiarly known as Johnny, but whom I have christened 'Cloven') and Tibbets, who also is called Two-bitts, in honorable distinction from an unworthy partner he once had, who obtained unenviable notoriety as 'Picayune Smith.'"

LT. GEORGE DERBY made a detailed survey of the San Diego River, before trying to divert its flow, and accurately located all early buildings in Old Town.

He referred to George P. Tebbetts, whose name sometimes appears in the record as "Tibbitts," and P. H. Hooff.

As acting editor of the *Herald* he reported:

Very little news will be found in the Herald this week: the fact is, there never is much news in it, and it is well that it is so; the climate here is so delightful, that residents, in the enjoyment of the *dolce far niente*, care very little about what is going on elsewhere, and residents of other places care very little about what is going on in San Diego.

When he brought his bride from San Francisco, he resided in a two-story frame house owned by Juan Bandini which a son-in-law, Charles Johnson, had been occupying. It later became the property of the Pendleton brothers, George A. and Eugene. George Pendleton married Concepción Estudillo, daughter of José Antonio Estudillo. Derby visited the Gardiner and Bleecker Store at La Playa, "than the inside of which nothing could be bleaker, for there's nothing in it," and saw the ruins of two of the hide houses immortalized by Dana and commented that "from present appearances one would be little disposed to imagine that the Playa in five or six years might become a city of the size of Louisville, with

HOTELS AND TWO-STORY homes were sprouting in San Diego within a few years after the American conquest. Letters identify ones built from 1851 to 1855. (A) Gila House Hotel; (B) Pendleton house; (C) Miguel Alvarez house; (D) Cota house; (E) Gaskill house; (F) and (G) Miguel de Pedrorena houses (later sold to Ysabel Pedrorena de Altamirano); (H) Colorado House Hotel; (I) Franklin House Hotel; (J) Robinson house; (K) José Serrano house; (L) Lorenzo Soto house. Improvements prior to 1850 appearing here but not shown in preceding picture of San Diego, 1850, on Page 130 are: (34) María Soto house, later Rose's Store; (35) Juan Marrón house; (36) Soto's pear garden; (37) Soto's Corral.

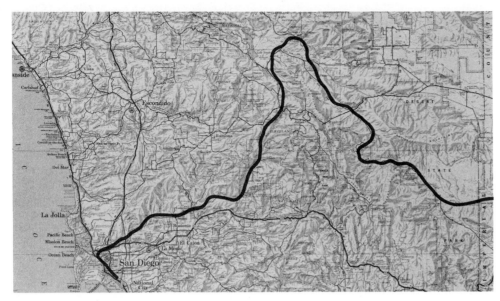

SAN DIEGO FOUGHT STRENUOUSLY to become the Western terminus of a transcontinental railroad and made its own survey. But the route was too steep.

brick buildings, paved streets, gas lights, theaters, gambling houses, and so forth. It is not all improbable, however, should the great Pacific Railroad terminate at San Diego . . ."

The political battle over the selection of a route for a transcontinental railroad kept the Congress busy for many years. At one point Sen. Thomas Hart Benton of Missouri quoted Kit Carson as saying the Southwest was so desolate a wolf could not make a living in it, and ridiculed the idea of a railroad running along and at times below the international border as had been recommended by Emory, stating that "it takes a grand national school like West Point to put national roads outside of a country and leave the interior without one."

Waving aloft a map of San Diego which had been termed a "paper city," and referring to investments there of Maj. Emory and other military officers, he said:

It is said to belong to the military — to the scientific corps — and to be divided into many shares, and expected to make fortunes of the shareholders or lot holders as soon as Congress sends the Pacific Railroad to it.

In a letter to his mother, Thomas Whaley wrote:

. . . I have a Rockaway waggon which will hold four or six persons comfortably and a fine span of sorrels with silver mounted harness, so that we enjoy ourselves to the envy of a great many. We all talk about the great railroad and believe that it must terminate here. And if it does I have enough land to make me as rich as any man can wish to be. For this alone, I am induced to remain in this dreary place, the inhabitants of which (many of them) are from the rough-scruff of creation. But when things take a change and we have more people here, the villains who trample upon honest men now will sink into insignificance and become the inmates of a prison or poor house. Let this suffice for the present dear mother . . .

All the hopes of San Diego now rested on the topographical surveys to locate suitable passes through the Sierra Nevada and Coast Range for a railroad route to connect California with the East. The expedition of Lt. R. S. Williamson first explored five passes in the Sierras, of which only two were found practicable, and then examined the passes into Los Angeles and San Diego. Three passes were found, New Pass connecting the desert with Santa Clara River valley north of Los Angeles, Cajon Pass, which led to Los Angeles, and San Gorgonio Pass, which was pronounced the best.

The report was a blow to San Diego. It found that there was no feasible route between the Gila River and San Diego, that both Warner's Pass and Jacumba Pass were impracticable. Enroute to San Diego, with his only barometer broken, Williamson reported that "the wagon road on which we travelled is so utterly impractical that it would have been wasting time to have attempted more than a survey with the eye." As for Jacumba, or Jacum pass, as it was known, he reported that Lt. J. G. Parke had made a rapid reconnaisance and "the mountains were high and rugged and it was almost impossible to travel by muleback off the trail." Parke also followed the San Luis Rey River west from Warner's ranch to the mission, and passed through rocky canyons which he said were impassable even for mules.

But early in November of 1854 as a result of Southern agitation for a railroad route along the 32nd parallel, San Diegans organized the San Diego & Gila, Southern Pacific & Atlantic Railroad Company, for the purpose of building a railroad to Yuma, where it could connect with any line coming West along a southern route, the dream of the old South.

LT. R. S. WILLIAMSON, while on a U.S. railroad survey, sketched Old Town and the hide houses at La Playa as they appeared from the entrance to the bay.

An engineer, Charles H. Poole, was hired and he surveyed a 200-mile railroad route to Yuma that followed the bed of the San Diego River, climbing 1087 feet gradually in thirty-nine miles through Mission Gorge, Santee, Lakeside, and Capitan Gorge and northeast through the steep-walled canyon to the base of Eagle Peak. From there the grade became increasingly steep for the next seven and a half miles, climbing 1255 feet out of the canyon to the floor of Santa Ysabel Valley, near where Coleman Creek flows into the San Diego River. The last mile and a half from the canyon to the southern edge of the valley floor was to be a climb of 452.7 feet per mile through what Poole called Santa Ysabel Gulch. But the grade was more than 8.5 per cent, virtually impassable. From Santa Ysabel, the route was to follow the wagon route to Warner's and down San Felipe Pass. Other surveys were to be made and many arguments advanced, and the hopes of San Diego lingered on until buried by the Civil War.

In the next few years three routes were used to climb up into the mountain valleys, but they remained largely horse and mule trails, over which supplies sometimes could be moved by wagon. But no wagon train was to make its way over the mountain barrier except through Warner's pass, a route far more favorable to Los Angeles than to San Diego.

In 1853 the Board of Supervisors was making every effort possible to open an easier way to Temecula, by which San Diego could tap into the main wagon route to Los Angeles and San Bernardino, and also make San Diego the port for the products of an inland empire that slowly was developing. This effort also was to go on for a century.

Sometime shortly after 1854 two former Army teamsters, Joe Swycaffer and Sam Warnock, received a contract to carry Army mail between San Diego and Yuma, and it is believed their first runs were made over the old military route discovered by Capt. Nathaniel Lyon in the spring of 1851, through Spring Valley, around the north side of Lyons Peak and southeast into the high country near Campo, and down by way of Jacumba, where the Army had established a small pack train base in 1853.

A trail over which lumber and some milled products moved to San Diego followed the general route of Interstate Highway 8 from El Cajon to Alpine, through Viejas Valley, Guatay, and then into Green Valley and Cuyamaca Valley. In a civil suit years later Swycaffer testified that he delivered government mail by way of Green Valley, from where he followed an old Indian trail down the mountains to join the regular road from Vallecito to Warner's. Returning, he indicated, he came up Oriflamme Canyon, a route first discovered by the Spanish, into Cuyamaca Valley. In 1856 the Supervisors were to appropriate money to try and improve the main wagon route that led up San Pasqual hill to Ramona, Santa Ysabel and Warner's. A new route, selected to eliminate San Pasqual hill, turned east about a mile north of Lakeside and went up the hill into the San Vicente grant and connected with the Kearny route near Ramona.

The years passed more slowly and uneventfully. Long lists of delinquent taxes in the *Herald* indicated that the boom was over. By the spring of 1853 there was little left of New Town but empty buildings, a deserted wharf and the few Army buildings at the depot and the corral block. George Hooper had sold out in 1851, as had E. W. Morse after the Indians killed his partner, Slack. Ames and Pendleton were the last to go. Eugene Pendleton took over management of Davis' wharf and he and Ames moved their business to Old Town. As were many American towns, San Diego was a melting pot. A native of Prussia, Joseph S. Mannasse, found his way to Old Town in 1853, opened another small store, and was to take on a partner four years later, another native of Prussia, Marcus Schiller.

J. S. Mannasse

The first Protestant services, Episcopalian, were conducted in 1853 in the little brick courthouse on the Plaza, by an Army chaplain, though they lasted for less than a year, and from then on there were only intermittent services by occasional visiting ministers.

The steamer *Golden Gate*, working up the coast from Panama with a broken propeller shaft, put into the bay on January 18, 1854, for supplies. She headed out into a heavy storm that same evening, and was driven back onto Zuñiga Shoal at the harbor entrance. Her passengers remained on the stricken vessel all night, and were taken off in the morning and distributed among San Diego residences, until they were able to continue their journeys on other vessels. The *Golden Gate* was pulled off the shoal and a week later made her way to San Francisco. One of the passengers was the Right Rev. William Ingraham Kip, the first Episcopal Bishop of California, who became the guest of Juan Bandini, and he held services for those who had died on the voyage. On Sunday, January 22, he conducted a public service in the courthouse, with Lt. Derby assisting.

Marcus Schiller

The first regular school was established in 1854, and by early the next year it had thirty pupils, with a Miss Fanny Stevens as teacher.

Louis Rose built a tannery in Rose Canyon and prospected for gold and copper without too much success. The gold that would stir new life into a fading town was still hidden in the high mountains. The federal government began erecting a lighthouse high on Point Loma, overlooking the entrance to the harbor through which Juan Rodríguez Cabrillo had first sailed more than 300 years before. But the lanterns and lenses from Paris cast their beams above the overcast which so often clings to the coast.

In San Diego in 1855 there was only one unmarried American girl, and Thomas Rylan Darnall, who owned a store and later became a County Supervisor, wrote that "she can neither read nor write. Scarcely any of the native Californians can read or write." Though they might not be able to read, the California girls were great dancers, and Darnall commented that on this "they excel any girls I ever saw. They likewise beat all creation in eating. A party of 20 California girls will eat more than 100 American girls." In the summer the weather was so humid that Darnall wrote "I go bathing almost every evening in the ocean, and every Sunday certain, for the girls go along and Oh! what a luscious time! 'we does has.' That is a luxury I never enjoyed in the States."

The San Diego Guards was organized as a militia company in August of 1856, with George A. Pendleton as captain, and the state sent forty percussion muskets, and while no battles were in immediate sight, the Guard was available to fire the necessary salutes at all formal ceremonies and dedications. Judge Hayes describes a series of severe storms in 1856, with lightning and thunder as never heard before in San Diego, and on September 20, a heavy earthquake was felt throughout the county. "We are informed that at Santa Ysabel the shock was so severe as to shake down the plastering of rooms of some of the buildings. The cattle on the farms stampeded . . . and havoc was created among all the Indians in the vicinity."

A company of Mormons, remnants of the old Mormon Battalion, began digging on Point Loma for coal that had been discovered in 1855. San Diego had long figured in the Mormon dream of a corridor from their Deseret Empire to the coast, through which the Mormons of the world could come by sea and reach the inland haven. The Mormons had methodically been extending their settlements westward, with the most distant outpost at San Bernardino. San Diego as a port of entry for Mormons did not prove out, as few ships then were arriving here from distant lands. But the industrious Mormon colony in San Diego in 1856 began boring a prospect hole from the surf line on the ocean side of Point Loma, and passed through five veins of coal less than a foot in thickness and struck a vein four and a half feet thick at eighty-six feet. The prospect hole is still visible in the surf line at the foot of the bluff 7400 feet north of the Point Loma Light, though the cliff has receded at least ten feet through erosion. The entrance to the main shaft, perhaps 150 feet deep, lies about 100 feet east of the shoreline and at an elevation of 150 feet. Its entrance has been closed. Laterals extended from the main shaft, one perhaps 300 feet, the second seventy-five feet ending at a vein of coal ten feet thick. No significant amounts of coal were removed, and as the mine had to be continually pumped out, it was abandoned.

When the Catholic church across the river had been washed away, the people resumed holding services in the Estudillo house, but in 1856 Don José Antonio Aguirre promised them that if he won a court case against Abel Stearns involving $20,000, he would build a new church. Benjamin Hayes, who was riding circuit as the district judge for Southern California, was skeptical of the vow: "These two old men, each tottering on the edge of the grave, will fight over this sum, until they sink beneath the turf, and leave the controversy to their heirs—in all probability." But Aguirre evidently won some kind of a settlement, as the adobe home of John Brown was purchased for $350 and remodeled into a church and dedicated on November 27, 1858, as the Church of the Immaculate Conception, with Fr. Juan Molinier in charge. It still stands.

The large brick, two-story residence and store now known as the Whaley House was completed by Thomas Whaley on San Diego Avenue in the spring of 1857, and with the passing of so many of the old Dons, who so long had dominated affairs, it became the center of a new social life.

Adventurers, disillusioned when the quick returns in the gold fields ended with the fading of placer mining, or still burning with the expansionist fever of "Manifest Destiny," organized filibustering expeditions. The first was that of Gen. Joseph C. Morehead, who had failed to subdue the Yuma Indians. In 1851 his vessel stopped at San Diego and it was searched for guns, but none were found. He planned to capture Lower California with arms evidently sent overland, but most of his men deserted and he was forced to return to the United States. Three expeditions from California, led by French immigrants, one with as many as 500 men, were directed against Lower California and Sonora. They too failed, and two of the three Frenchmen were slain. The most famous filibusterer was William Walker, a journalist and lawyer, who in 1854 announced his intention of organizing an expedition to seize Lower California and Sonora and declare them independent republics. Eventually they were to be annexed to the United States as slave states. This plan, too, came to nothing and the remnants of his men finally surrendered to American author-

William Walker

208

ities at Tijuana in May. Many of Walker's proclamations and decrees were published in the *Herald*, which he employed more or less as his official "voice." Walker was tried in San Francisco for violating the neutrality laws, was found not guilty, and then he undertook two expeditions to Nicaragua. He was shot in Honduras in 1860.

The last and most tragic California filibustering figure was Henry A. Crabb, a prominent politician in Northern California whose wife claimed that she was a descendant of Juan Bautista de Anza. He hatched a plot to colonize Sonora in cooperation with a Mexican political leader, with the intention of having it annexed to the United States. In 1857 he organized a company of more than 100, including a half dozen prominent persons, and they went through San Gorgonio Pass and down the Colorado River to Fort Yuma, and eventually into Sonora. He was betrayed by the Mexican who had induced him to undertake the venture, and after a brief encounter with Mexican forces at Sonoita, he surrendered himself and his men. They were taken out in squads of five and ten and executed. Crabb himself was shot more than 100 times, and his body decapitated. That ended all the enthusiasm for filibustering.

The backwash of the Gold Rush also brought a rise in crime in the late 1850's, with desperadoes on both sides of the border ranging freely and little effective enforcement of laws even within communities.

Disaffected elements banished from Baja California by the governor assembled in the vicinity of San Diego under a leader named Juan Mendoza and, aided by some Americans, slipped across the border and started a war of their own. From reports in the *Alta California* a number of skirmishes were fought with Mexican troops along the Tijuana River bed. The newspaper's local correspondent bewailed the lack of fortifications along the border and contended that the governor of Baja California had afforded San Diego more protection for ten years than had the United States.

Tiburcio Vásquez

While Joaquín Murietta was the most notorious of the California bandits, Tiburcio Vásquez and Juan Flores were active throughout Southern California. A band led by Juan Flores raided San Juan Capistrano in 1857, murdered a German shopkeeper, sacked several stores, and fled, threatening to strike at Couts' ranch and even at San Diego. A search party from San Gabriel captured three of them. Two were hanged, and the other shot. Three others were captured by Andrés Pico.

A party of horse thieves in 1856 raided Jamacha Rancho, which had come into the possession of Robert Kelly, a native of the Isle of Man, and Asher R. Eddy, a former Army lieutenant, through some process which Apolinaria Lorenzana never understood. Kelly was shot three times but escaped with his life. The *majordomo* of San Vicente Rancho was identified as a cattle thief and given one hundred lashes, with a physician standing by to make sure he was left with a spark of life. A sheriff's posse, with a burst of unusual concern, arrived at Pala in the nick of time to prevent the hanging of three Indians, a mother and her crippled son and her Spanish-speaking daughter. They had been accused of bewitching Manuelito, the respected chief of the Luiseños, and causing him to become ill. They had been duly tried and convicted as witches, and a large crowd had gathered to witness their execution.

The streets of Old Town also reflected some of the atmosphere that in later years would mark Western towns from Arizona to Montana. A man identified as William Leroy walked into Lewis Franklin's store and slashed the arm of Henry Whaley, a brother of the merchant, so severely it had to be amputated. Leroy was

THIS SKETCH by W. H. Hilton depicts a recogida, or roundup, of wild horses in the pastoral days of the open ranges during the California rancho period.

THE LANCE which took so many lives at the Battle of San Pasqual was still in use in California rodeos in 1880 as shown in this painting by an unknown artist.

captured but escaped from jail. A rowdy walked into a home in Old Town and shot a youth to death, and the *Herald* commented that he continued to walk around the town, armed and unmolested. An Indian strode up to another Indian and ripped him open with a knife, as quietly, the *Herald* said, "as if he were cutting a watermelon."

Indians, naturally indolent and degraded by liquor and servitude, often were harshly treated, but did have their defenders. Cave Couts was indicted by the grand jury twice in 1855, on charges of beating two Indians with a rawhide riata. One of them was a boy, and in his case Couts was acquitted of a charge of assault. In the other case, an Indian named Halbani died as a result of the beating and Couts was tried on a charge of manslaughter brought by the Grand Jury of which Charles H. Poole was foreman, and the district attorney, J. R. Gitchell. Couts' attorney, O. S. Witherby, won a dismissal on the contention one of the grand jurors was an alien.

With cattle by the thousands roaming the unfenced hills, and with subsequent disputes as to ownership, judges of the plains, surviving from Spanish days, were the most important officials in the county. Rules describing their duties were defined in 1857. There were to be three judges of the plains at large and each township was to have at least one. It was required that they be advised of all killings of cattle, that hides be kept at least two days for inspection as to brands, which were required for all ranches, and

211

that all persons buying hides were to maintain records of them, and that cattle pens were to be inspected to be sure that "cows and calfs corresponded." Roundups, or rodeos, were conducted at all of the ranchos, and neighbor *rancheros* were notified, so they could come and separate their own stock. Judges of the plains settled all disputes.

The cattle market had been depressed in 1855, prices falling as low as five dollars a head, and the winter of 1856-57 was a terribly dry one, and parched lands and dying cattle foretold a still greater tragedy of nature that in a few years would bring the last of the Dons on their knees.

In April the *Herald* said that the absence of rain had completely destroyed all the crops in the county:

> Not one solitary blade of barley, wheat or other cereal is left. Every blade of grass this side of San Bernardino is parched up and withered and our ranchos are selling off their cattle at any price that is offered. But for the money realized from the sale of stock, which will enable our farmers to purchase from abroad what, under other circumstances, they would produce at home, two-thirds of the rancheros in the county would be obliged to abandon their farms and seek a home in some more favorable part of the state. For the few cattle that are left remaining here will have to be driven back into the mountains where there is grass and it will be a miracle if any escape the starving Indians . . .

On one day in March a hot wind blowing in from the east increased to a gale in twenty minutes. At dawn the hillsides had been covered with verdure and wildflowers. At dusk, they were a withered waste.

The cattle market was further depressed by the arrival of tremendous flocks of sheep. In 1858 one flock alone of 35,000 sheep went through San Diego bound for Los Angeles. More than 100,000 sheep crossed the Colorado River at Yuma by late winter and 46,000 more were reported strung back along the Gila Trail.

The *Herald* deplored the announcement that the Army post at the mission would be abandoned, and the troops withdrawn from Southern California, and warned that "the Cahuilla Indians alone could muster enough warriors to accomplish the destruction of all the American population of Los Angeles, San Bernardino and San Diego in eight and forty hours."

San Diegans working copper and silver deposits in Lower California were threatened with death in the aftermath of a lynching perpetrated by William Cole and two other San Diegans. They captured an American named Bill Elkins and a Mexican in Lower California and put them to death as horse thieves. This deed greatly excited the people there, and Cole and his companions were seized for trial. Thomas R. Darnall went to Santo Tomás to see what he could do to obtain their release, and he, too, was imprisoned. San Diegans threatened to go to their rescue and all Mexican citizens below the frontier were summoned to arms and guards were posted on all roads. San Diego sent to Los Angeles for additional volunteers. Darnall soon was freed, and presumably the others also, though the records are not at all clear.

The following year San Diego was swept with reports of bands of outlaws from Lower California intending to attack San Diego, and at a public meeting it was decided to place a guard of twelve persons around the town each night. Cattle thefts became so numerous that desperate measures were proposed. The *Herald* said that whipping "has gotten to be of small account in deterring the Indians and we have come to the conclusion that the delectable and efficious remedy of hanging is about the best remedy of all. One fellow whom they whipped out near Santa Ysabel the other day got so mad about it that he just walked off about 100 yards and lay down and died." The *Herald* commented that "how long this state of things is to continue, God only knows."

The following fall San Diego experienced one of the worst gales in its history. At 11 o'clock on the morning of October 2, a terrific gale sprang up from the south southeast and continued with fury until 5 p.m. when rain commenced to fall. The *Herald* said it blew with such violence and the air was filled with such dense clouds of dust that it was impossible to see across the Plaza, and it was with the greatest difficulty the pedestrians could walk the streets. Damage to property was considerable; houses were unroofed and blown down; trees uprooted and fences destroyed. The cottage of Ames, editor of the *Herald*, situated on the flat across the river, was lifted from its foundations, thrown over and completely demolished. The roof of the house of Matías Moreno was blown off and carried some distance into a neighboring corral. The south portico of the Gila House was torn down, the roof stripped of its zinc covering and the house otherwise materially damaged. The house of Andrew Kriss on the flat was completely destroyed. The portico of Col. Ferrell's house was blown down. The schooners *Plutus* and *Lovely Flora* were driven on the beach. The schooner *X.L.*, on the ways being repaired, was blown over. The *Clarissa Andrews* and *Teresa* rode out the gale without damage. At Point Loma, the lighthouse keeper was obliged to leave at noon fearing the tower would fall.

The absences of Ames from the *Herald* became more frequent and conditions in San Diego grew more listless. One company of soldiers, Company G, 6th Infantry, under Capt. W. S. Ketchum, returned to San Diego in December of 1858, providing some stimulus to the community, and they took up quarters at the old

New Town depot in buildings which the *Herald* said "had been the homes and dwelling places of owls and Indians." That ended a decade of use of the mission as a military post, and its buildings, left to the hazards of weather, slid faster into decay. On April 3 Leandro Osuna, who had shot to death a captain of the U.S. Dragoons in the Battle of San Pasqual, committed suicide in the Osuna family home on San Dieguito rancho. He shot himself with a borrowed gun while lying in bed. He was 37 years of age. Receiving much less attention was the death of Juan Bandini in Los Angeles on November 12, 1859, after a brief illness. Bandini had sought to recuperate his fortunes in Lower California, but once again had been forced to flee revolutionary troubles in which he had chosen the wrong side. The *Herald* reminded San Diegans that Juan Bandini had been a prominent citizen and left a large circle of friends "who sincerely mourn his demise." Thus passed, with only casual mention, one of the stormy figures of California politics, who had been an instrument of both agitation and progress under the flags of three nations, Spain, Mexico, and the United States.

CHAPTER TWELVE

"What shall be said of the sun-born Pueblo
This town sudden born in the path of the sun?
This town of St. James, of the calm San Diego,
As suddenly born as if shot from a gun?"

THE WEST IS LINKED

The linking of the East and West by transcontinental stage was at hand and the question of the route to be selected emerged as a heated political struggle between the North and the South. In California there was a division, too, between the politically dominant North and the "cow counties" of the South. The North favored the proposed Central Route from Salt Lake across the plains and over the Sierra Nevada. The South favored a route over the Southern Immigrant Trail.

In Texas a group of citizens conducted a public meeting in El Paso to discuss the establishment of a mail coach line from San Antonio to San Diego by way of El Paso, and a resolution pointed out that its success would be a great factor in eventually determining the route for a Southern Pacific railroad. The report of the meeting, as published in part in the *Herald*, in October of 1856, read:

This route is imminently the best and most practical, free from the snows of winter and the withering heat of summer; passing through a climate salubrious and delightful; tracking fertile and beautiful valleys and not endless treeless prairies and scorching deserts of sand; encountering abundance of wood, water and grass and not thirsty desert plains and bleak barren mountains, burning as a furnace in summer and frozen and ice-clad in winter; open and passable at all seasons, with everything to cheer the immigrant and traveler, in rich soil and varied landscape, with no mountain barriers—no natural wall to cross the pathway, the route contemplated is superior for a great mail route and immi-

A WARM SUN, the "firing" of anvils and shooting of guns welcomed arrival of the first transcontinental mail. San Diego's hopes for greatness were high.

217

grant road across the continent, to any other north of it, and there can be none south, passing through our own territory.

The many immigrants who had traversed the Gila route with such sufferings might have wondered if they had dreamed it all. During 1856, four overland mail bills were submitted to Congress, and President Franklin Pierce signed another bill authorizing $300,000 for building a wagon road over the Southern Trail. On August 18, Congress passed an amendment to the Post Office bill authorizing the establishment of Route 12,578, the Great Overland Route, from the Mississippi River to San Francisco. The selection of the eastern terminal, the contractor and the actual route was left up to the Postmaster General. It also authorized him to set up an immediate interim service that would provide adequate mail connections between the East and West until the Great Overland Route 12,578 could get into service. The Post Office Department called for bids, which were to be opened July 2, 1857, and the power struggle between Northern and Southern factions was on.

Two principal companies emerged, one an Eastern giant, the other, a Western giant, both capable, both financially sound. The Eastern group was a combine headed by John Butterfield of New York, which collectively controlled the most powerful express companies on the Eastern Seaboard. Leading contender from the West was an ambitious young empire-builder with an idea, initiative and money. He was James Birch, 28. In three years in the Northern California gold fields, Birch had built his own stage line, merged it with four other operators, and in January, 1854 was president of the California Stage Company, the largest and most efficient stage line in the West.

The election of James Buchanan as President in 1856 offered little encouragement to Birch, since Buchanan and Butterfield were intimate friends. But Buchanan's Postmaster General, Aaron V. Brown, was a Southerner. Birch resigned as president of the California Stage Company and went to Washington to see Brown. On June 14, 1857, Brown awarded to Birch a four-year contract to carry the mail over Route 8076 from San Antonio to San Diego. It was an extension of a contract previously held by G. H. Giddings, for Route 8076 from San Antonio to El Paso. Birch had seventeen days to get his 1478-mile line into operation. His contract specified a two-way service, twice a month, with coaches and passenger service both ways, for a subsidy of $149,800 a year, or averaging $3120 a trip each way, beginning on July 1, the day before the Postmaster General was to open bids on the Great Overland Route 12,578.

James E. Birch

John Butterfield

218

At San Diego, under Birch's plan, mail and passengers could continue to Los Angeles and San Francisco by steamship. It was promptly derided as the line that ran from "nowhere to nowhere."

Birch hired Isaiah C. Woods, a well-known stageman, to ramrod the line as superintendent. George Giddings was named division superintendent at San Antonio and R. E. Doyle at San Diego. Giddings got the line moving before Woods arrived at San Antonio. He dispatched the first mail by mule train from San Antonio on July 9 under the charge of James E. Mason as conductor. The first 650 miles from San Antonio to El Paso was over well-beaten wagon roads through Comanche and Apache country frequently travelled by Army supply trains. From El Paso and up to Maricopa Wells, now Phoenix, the route of 454 miles was one of mesquite, sagebrush, cactus, sand, rocks, unbroken trail through heat and dust that led one traveller to write, "if God ever pronounced this part of the earth good, it's more than man ever did."

From Maricopa Wells, the trail turned west again, following the Gila River 190 miles to its junction with the Colorado at Fort Yuma. From there, it dropped south into Mexico for fifty miles around the sand dunes of Imperial Valley, then went northwest across the forty-eight miles of desert to Carrizo Creek, climbing into the Cuyamaca Mountains from Vallecito, then turning southwest downhill to San Diego.

The original plan was to stock way stations with fresh animals and supplies as the first mail trains passed through the country. Giddings sent out one advance group under William Alexander Anderson Wallace, 40, Indian fighter and frontiersman better known as "Big Foot" Wallace. About 123 miles west of San Antonio by Fort Clark, they were attacked by Apaches who killed one driver, wounded two others, routed eighteen soldiers with the party and made off with twenty-four head of stock. But the mail went on.

San Diego had yet no inkling that the first mail was on the way. And in San Antonio the news had not reached there that, two days before the first mule train left San Diego, Birch already had lost his chance at the Great Overland Mail contract. The *New York Times* on July 7 reported that Postmaster General Brown had decided to give the Great Overland contract to Birch, but was overruled by President Buchanan, who gave it to Butterfield and the powerful combine. But it was specified that San Francisco—not San Diego—was to be the terminus.

Thus, the first transcontinental mail, operated by James Birch, a man who was never to see it in operation, was obsolete before the first letter left the depot. And the second mail train was on the trail before San Diego found out for sure that the mail was coming to San Diego at all. Capt. Henry Skillman left San Antonio with the second mail in a light ambulance wagon on July 24, as scheduled. Skillman was a full day out of San Antonio when the *San Diego Herald* of July 25 carried the announcement that the contract had been signed and that scheduled mail would leave on the 9th and the 24th of each month. The *Herald* declared:

> We deem this a more important measure for the immediate prosperity of San Diego than would the passage of a railroad bill to connect us with the Atlantic States—for that probably would not go into operation for ten or twelve years while this is of present benefit and insures a railroad by the Southern route and by opening up the rich country by which the stage route passes.

In anticipation of the business expected over the new line, Wells Fargo & Co. reopened its forwarding office in San Diego, with Eugene Pendleton in charge. The *Herald* in August of 1857 also indicated that a stage line was operating between San Diego and the Jesús María Mines in Lower California. Two new hotels were opened, the Colorado and the Franklin, both on the west side of the Plaza. The old Exchange house had been rebuilt into a three-story structure and renamed the Franklin by Lewis and Maurice Franklin.

By the first of August, the *Herald* was happily advising its readers to send by steamer to San Francisco for stamps and envelopes, since none were available in San Diego. On the same day Birch arrived by steamer in San Francisco, already aware that Butterfield had edged him out of the Great Overland contract.

Woods had ordered Doyle to dispatch the first east-bound mail from San Diego on July 24, the same day on which the second west-bound mail was to leave San Antonio, but as Doyle could not find enough good mules in San Diego, it didn't leave until August 9. Even then R. W. Laine, the conductor, had to buy ten more mules at Warner's Ranch because the ones he brought from San Diego were not strong enough to make the entire trip. Laine followed the wagon road through Ramona, Santa Ysabel, Warner's and San Felipe, the same route taken by the first west-bound mail.

At 11 a.m. August 31, 1857, Conductor Mason's arrival at San Diego set off the wildest celebration the little village could muster. The first dispatch was fifty-three days out of San Antonio, but the trip had been made in good time. The *San Diego Herald* said: "Today arrived the first mail from San Antonio, Texas, making the journey in thirty-four travelling days. San Diego is rejoicing." And indeed, it was. Since *El Jupiter*, the old bronze cannon, had been cracked some years earlier by an over-enthusiastic charge for another celebration, Ames, the *Herald's* editor, and an old sea

Pioneer woman's dress (linsey-woolsey)

captain named Stevens, borrowed two anvils and commenced firing in a manner befitting the first scheduled linking of the Atlantic and Pacific by overland carrier. They turned one anvil upside down and set the other one on it so they were base-to-base. In the hollow pocket between the two bases they poured a charge of gunpowder, or blasting powder, with a fuse to be touched off with a red-hot iron rod. What it lacked in ballistics, the anvil salute more than made up with a cloud of smoke and an ear-splitting roar. While Ames and Stevens fired a 100-anvil salute, the rest of the celebrants greeted the first mail with a fusillade from shotguns, pistols and rifles, and exploding firecrackers.

Old Anvil

San Diego celebrated not knowing that already politics had dealt a death blow to the San Diego and San Antonio Mail. Birch, himself, had only a short time to live. On September 12, Birch, returning to New York from San Francisco, in the hope of saving his line, was one of 400 persons lost when the steamer *Central America* sank in a storm off Cape Hatteras. Two days later, the Great Overland contract was awarded to the Butterfield combine, allowing them a full year to get into service.

Conductor Laine and the first east-bound mail were twenty days on the trail from San Diego when they met Woods forty miles east of Tucson. The mail went on, but Laine turned around to guide Woods back to San Diego. They found the water holes west of Yuma dry and were forced to cross ninety-four miles of desert without stopping. They arrived at Carrizo with spent animals and the mail already six days overdue. Leaving the coach at Vallecito, to follow on the regular immigrant route by way of the narrow twisting gap cut through Box Canyon by Capt. Cooke and the Mormon Volunteers and up through Warner's, Woods took a short cut over the Cuyamacas, following for eighteen miles an old Indian trail up into Green Valley. Obtaining fresh horses at Lassitor's place, he took the mail into San Diego on September 9, thirty-eight days out of San Antonio.

Lassitor's place was owned by James R. Lassitor, who had operated a store and hay station for military trains and immigrants at Vallecito, then married the widow of John Mulkins, who resided in Green Valley. He cut wild oats in Cuyamaca Valley, which he hauled down Oriflamme Canyon along the old "hay road".

For the next seven weeks, Woods was busy in San Diego acquiring or equipping men, coaches and animals and dispatching them to take up stations along the Western division from San Diego to the Pimos Villages turn-around east of Tucson. He announced passenger service on October 3. Woods sent two coaches from San Diego heavily loaded on October 6; two more on October 22, and

221

by October 27, when he started over the mountains with the mail, a mule train and a herd of mules, he had three more coaches being built in San Diego. A month later he noted in his journal that the line had more than 200 mules west of the Rio Grande, seven coaches on the line and three being built in San Diego, "so we can already take passengers thru from ocean to ocean by stage coaches."

The coaches probably were built by John Van Alst, a carpenter and wagonmaker, and Robert D. Israel, a blacksmith. Van Alst and Israel formed a partnership which they announced in the *San Diego Herald* on September 26, 1857. They continued as partners until January, after which Van Alst carried on the business alone.

The evidence indicates that the only San Diego passengers who travelled the full distance east by coach were the few who went with the new coaches being sent around the long northern wagon road by way of Warner's to join the line east of the mountain barrier. At the same time, other passengers on the line were being sent from San Diego to Yuma by mule train. Later, the service was improved so that passengers went by stage to Lassitor's, in Green Valley, then went by mule down a mountain trail to Vallecito, where they transferred to stages again and continued their trip. This system continued as long as the line ran.

From San Antonio the fare was $100 to El Paso, $150 to Tucson and $200 to San Diego. Between intermediate stations the fare was fifteen cents a mile. Passengers were provided with food except where the coach stopped at public houses. They were allowed to carry thirty pounds of personal baggage, exclusive of blankets and arms. The carrying of pistols and rifles was recommended. Extra baggage cost forty cents a pound from San Antonio to El Paso and $1 a pound to San Diego. Postal rates were three cents a half-ounce.

By January, the line was advertising "the entire distance except eighteen miles, is by coach." But the mail apparently moved considerably faster than passengers. Service was being constantly improved, although passenger travel was always uncomfortable, dirty, dangerous and uncertain. By March, the mail was going through in as little as twenty-three and a half days, and in June it made its record speed of twenty-one days from San Antonio to San Diego. When Birch's creditors learned that he was dead, the line almost collapsed, but G. H. Giddings and R. E. Doyle took it over and the name was changed to Giddings & Doyle, with Woods as superintendent.

Woods, having completed his full circuit of the route from San Antonio to San Diego and back between August and January,

Robert Decatur Israel

Coach rides were guaranteed, except on the desert, where it was "mules only."

filed his report with the Postmaster General. He stated that the 1476-mile route included 1300 miles of road "superior to any other" and that the rest of it was "fair," except for twenty-two miles of sand from Cooke's Wells to Alamo Mocho, but that it was a good road in all seasons. Of the desert in Arizona in August, he said that "the air is pure and clear and the heat produces a copious perspiration, so that it gives no feeling of oppression in breathing." In winter, when it turned so cold the water froze in the canteens, the people sleeping on the ground didn't suffer from it, according to Woods, and the only people who got sick were those who ate too much fruit along the way in the Rio Grande Valley.

The stories told by the passengers were somewhat different. A correspondent for the *San Francisco Herald*, who signed his dispatches with the initials "B.H.M." wrote from Tucson on November 25:

The next day after writing you from San Diego, I made arrangements for my passage to Tucson by depositing $50, and after some days' delay, took my place in the coach and away we started for San Antonio and intermediate

JACKASS MAIL arrived in San Diego by mules using Oriflamme Canyon, or along the dotted line. The few stages had to go around by way of Warner's Ranch.

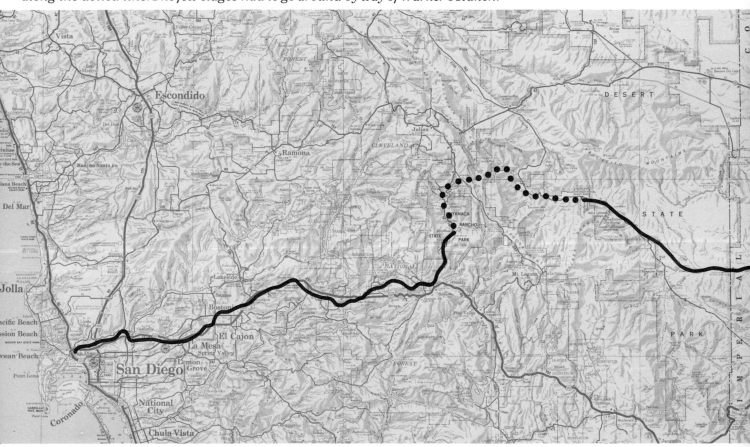

places. After rolling over a very good road for twenty miles we stopped for dinner near a house where dwelt a fair maiden, of whose beauty I had heard even at Sacramento. We went to the house, as some of our party were acquainted there, and saw the fair Stephana, and were regaled with a bottle of native wine, a dish of olives, etc. There is a little vineyard and a few fruit trees; the first, and in fact, the only fruit trees I saw growing in San Diego County, except at the town and the Mission . . .

At night we reached San Pasqual, a battle ground where a few Americans were killed in 1845 . . . Our coaches were heavily laden, each having about 1500 pounds of freight for the Pimo Village to be used in trade for corn and wheat with the Indians there . . . We remained three days at San Pasqual, waiting for mules from a neighboring rancho. The mules were all *muy broncos*, and the drivers had an exciting time breaking them to harness. In crossing the mountain, when in front of San Pasqual, one of the stages broke down and had to return to San Diego for repairs. With the other we moved on . . . to Santa Ysabel Rancho . . .

The weather at Santa Ysabel is cool, frosts nearly every month in the year. There was a vineyard there but when we passed along (October) the grape season was over. We purchased barley at our stopping place sufficient to reach Cariso Creek, a place some seventy miles farther on, paying four cents per pound . . .

The next day we passed Warner's Rancho, reaching in the evening San Felipe which is neither a town nor a rancho, but an adobe house, brackish water and poor grass, like that usually growing on salt land. The population of San Felipe consists of a German who occupies the aforesaid adobe house and supports himself by selling necessities to travelers. We next arrived at Vallecitos, a city very much like San Felipe, but one grade inferior, as the water and grass are not quite so good. The proprietor was away, courting an emigrant girl, and had a young man employed at a dollar a day to attend the business of the "hotel."

Another passenger, Charles F. Runing, correspondent for the *San Francisco Chronicle,* rode the stage by the alternate route to Green Valley, and at Lassitor's place, climbed aboard a horse for the hard ride down Oriflamme Canyon. His report reads:

We had four passengers . . . We made twenty-one miles that afternoon and stopped at Ames' Ranch . . . For supper we had jerked beef, tea and *algunas tortillas mal hechas* (some poorly made tortillas). Our landlady was an Indian woman. Next day—twenty-seven miles to Lassitors . . . arrived there late at night, slept in low hut with fire in the middle, Indian fashion. Had a good supper and breakfast—fresh butter, bread, mutton, coffee.

We started next day with part fresh animals, and part former ones. We had only eighteen miles to travel that day, three of which were over snow, and we had a very steep hill to go down. The country is very hilly and almost destitute of vegetation . . . We rode on horseback that day, and slept in a house on a hard dirt floor. Here we met passengers coming from the other end of the route, five in number; they complained very much, and had had a very hard time of it; one was a newly married lady, and I thought it must have been a rather dangerous honeymoon; however, she was fat and hearty and had got along better than any of the men. The place is called Vallecitos, and from the name one would expect to see a few houses, but we found only one solitary habitation . . .

As Giddings & Doyle, the line continued operation through 1858, while Butterfield was stocking and building 139 stations between

George H. Giddings

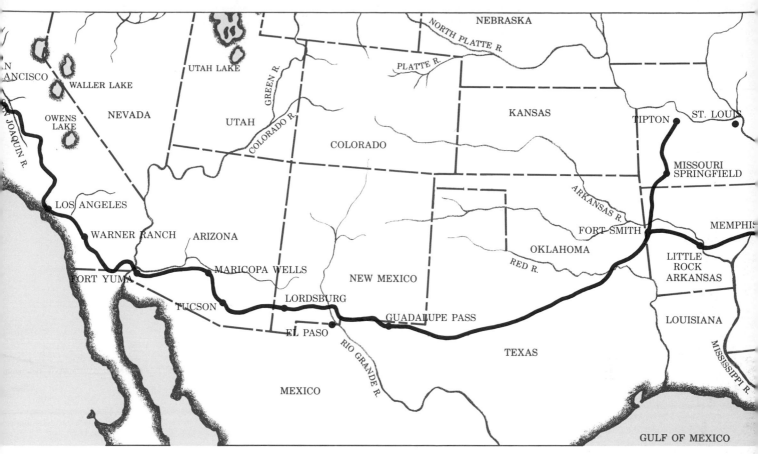

THE BUTTERFIELD STAGES by-passed San Diego, though going through Warner's Ranch, ending the city's hope of being a transcontinental terminus.

Tipton, Missouri, and San Francisco. Butterfield's route was to overlap the Giddings & Doyle route for 750 miles between El Paso and Vallecito. Butterfield had to construct corrals, dig wells and cisterns, and assemble 1200 horses, 600 mules and 100 coaches. There were wagon shops and blacksmith shops to set up, fords over rivers to prepare, and 750 to be hired to staff the way stations.

He went into operation on schedule, the first stage leaving Tipton on September 16, opening the Great Overland Mail Route 12,576, a total of 2800 miles on a twenty-five-day schedule, terminal to terminal. San Diego was by-passed, the main route now passing through Warner's Ranch and Temecula to Los Angeles. There were five stations in the present limits of San Diego County, at Carrizo Springs, Vallecito, San Felipe Valley, near Scissors Crossing; Warner's, in the ranch house and store that were rebuilt after being burned down in the Garra uprising, and at Oak Grove.

Next page, THE BUTTERFIELD STAGE swings toward the Warner Ranch station in gloom of evening in this striking oil painting by Marjorie Reed Creese.

But the San Diego line did not die quickly. A month after Butterfield started running, his line took over the mail transport between El Paso and Yuma, thus cutting route 8076 into two sections, San Diego to Yuma and El Paso to San Antonio. Then, strangely enough, the Post Office department increased the subsidy on the San Diego and San Antonio Line to provide weekly delivery. But it was a dying gesture, for its passengers still had to ride mules over the mountains from San Diego to Vallecito. On October 1, a year later, Giddings & Doyle announced that the line was discontinuing passenger service. Political opposition to the line persisted in the North. The *San Francisco Call* stated:

The editorial friends of I. C. Woods in this city are working hard to create a diversion in favor of the San Antonio and San Diego Jackass Overland Mail route. We hope that the Congress will not hesitate to lop off this useless mail . . . and apply the money now spent for the comfort of I. C. Woods to the Central Overland route, a mail which is of the first importance to California and the contiguous territories.

In its last days, the line was branded the "Jackass Mail," and as such it has been known ever since. It continued to haul "Jackass Mail" for two more years until the outbreak of the Civil War in 1861 caused its discontinuance. So ended San Diego's hope that was dying even as it was being born, when the *San Diego Herald* said: "It was looked upon as the most important event which had ever occurred in the annals of San Diego."

The advent of stage transportation to the Pacific Coast also brought to an end an experiment in the use of camels for which the Congress appropriated $30,000 in 1855. The idea of using camels had swept the country as a result of the published reports of the long and dry marches across the deserts which were necessary to reach California. Lt. Beale, who as Indian agent for California and Nevada had explored much of the Southwest, and himself had been interested in the use of camels, was placed in charge of the project, and the public mind envisioned "fast camel passenger trains" running from the Missouri River to the Pacific Coast. On May 14, 1856, the United States' vessel, *Supply*, arrived at Indianola, Texas, with twenty-three camels, nine dromedaries, and one calf, or thirty-three in all. With them were six Orientals. One of them was a camel doctor. Another load of forty-four camels arrived the following February.

Embarkation of Camels for Southwest Desert

Left, top, ROLLING DOWN SAN FELIPE VALLEY, the Butterfield Stage pulls ahead to reach the desert crossing. Middle, VALLECITO was a stop known to all desert travelers. Here the Butterfield Stage heads out toward the parched desert floor. Bottom, AGUA CALIENTE was a lonely spot on the way to Carrizo Springs. Here the worn Butterfield Stages meet. All paintings by Marjorie Reed Creese.

Lt. Beale put them through severe and successful tests and finally, on October 14, the "ships of the desert" reached the Colorado River on the road to Bakersfield, and Beale managed to coax them across. But the experiment was a failure. Soldiers never took to the camels, treating them as harshly as they did their mules, with stubborn results. And the San Diego and San Antonio Mail Line, and then the Butterfield stages, had overtaken them. The camels were sold, those stationed at Fort Yuma being driven up to Benicia and auctioned off. Others were turned loose in the desert and the Apaches hunted them down and found camel meat to their liking. For many years reports of the sighting of camels in the desert persisted. One of the last confirmed reports was in 1881, when a Prescott, Arizona, newspaper reported that nine had been captured by Indians near Gila Bend and sold to a circus at Kansas City.

By-passed by the transcontinental stages, discouraged by the results of the railroad surveys, and with the prospect of even a camel caravan now gone, San Diego, possessing a fine natural harbor, an unmatched climate, and a land inviting to settlers, had no means by which to divert the river of west-bound immigrants who were turning north as they reached the jagged mountain barrier at the southern tip of the Coast Range. In a day of plodding oxen, sweating mules and wagon wheels, San Diego was virtually walled off from a commercial world whose routes followed the natural valleys and watersheds.

CHAPTER THIRTEEN

"So be cheery, my lads, let your hearts never fail,
While the bold harpooner is striking the whale!

CHASING THE WHALE

The fur ships which had opened the sea routes to California, and which had played such important roles in the Americanization of San Diego, long ago had ceased putting out from Boston. Though hides still made up part of the coastal commerce, the vivid days of the regular visits of the Boston hide ships had ended and the large barns at La Playa made famous by Dana had virtually disappeared. But in their wake the whaling ships turned to hunting the California gray whales and once again the names of New England and the old colonial ports, New Bedford, Nantucket, Sag Harbor, and New London were heard in San Diego. The rising prosperity of the United States in the 1800's had created more demands for oil and for spermacetic candles, and for whalebone for stays, corsets and umbrella ribs.

The California gray whale is medium-sized, thirty-five to forty feet long, and it was discovered that each winter they migrated from the western Bering Sea and the Arctic Ocean to the warm water bays and lagoons of Upper and Lower California, passing near the shore, and upon occasion they put into San Diego Bay in such numbers that they were menaces to small boats.

At first San Diego saw itself as a chief supply port for the Pacific whaling fleet, and for a time there was a considerable traffic in and out of the harbor of whalers whose cruises to the Pacific lasted as long as three years. As had the fur and hide ships, the whalers brought the goods of New York and New England to barter for

THE WHALESHIP CHARLES W. MORGAN, *shown slipping through the fog, was a familiar sight on the coast. It is still in existence, at Mystic Seaport, Conn.*

233

food and repairs. However, the practice of shore whaling was developed in 1851, and a few years later whaling stations were established along the coast, including two in San Diego Bay.

It will be recalled that in 1848 the purser of the sloop USS *Cyane*, operating with United States forces in attacks on Lower California, had sighted a large fleet of whaling ships wintering in Magdalena Bay, which is 660 miles south of San Diego, and that the captains had reported finding a new species of whale, which, though rather small, yielded a fine quality of oil.

Terrifying tales of killing whales in shallow and narrow waters circulated throughout the whaling fleet, and a few years passed before coastal whaling was taken up seriously. C. M. Scammon, as captain of whaling barks which frequently put into San Diego, later wrote *"The Marine Mammals of the North-Western Coast of North America,"* and in this he tells:

> But with all the warnings and direful tales, Magdalena Bay whaling was resumed with ardor about the years 1855 and 1856, and was continued and extended along the whole coast of both Upper and Lower California. Every navigable lagoon of the region was discovered and explored, and the animals were hunted in every winding and intricate estuary which were their resorting or breeding places. In the seasons of 1858 and 1859, not only the bays and lagoons were teeming with all the varied incidents of the fishery, but the outside coast was lined with ships, from San Diego southward to Cape St. Lucas. A few vessels of this fleet cruised near the shore by day, standing a little way off at night; but by far the largest number anchored about the islands, points, and capes, wherever the animals could be most successfully pursued.

Page from whale ship's log book

The whaling ships too often were virtual prisons for crewmen who had longed for adventure or unfortunately had awakened one morning and found themselves lashed to a strange bunk. Charges levied against them for food, clothing and supplies usually ate up any earnings of years of danger and bone-tiring work. But the sight of sails has never failed to lift the hearts of men, and from the shores of San Diego and other whaling ports could be seen the gaily decorated sails of the small boats which were used to pursue the giant and formidable devil fish of the sea.

Scammon writes:

> It was a novel sight to view a single ship, or a small squadron, anchored off some exposed headland or island, rolling and surging at their cables in the ugly ground-swell, and the fleet of boats lying along the line of kelp just without the surf-bound shore, or, with their sails spread to the breeze, skimming over the waves in the various directions the gigantic game led them. At such times, a feature was observed in this fishery which is not often witnessed, namely: the peculiar marks or devices pictured upon the sails of the boats belonging to the different vessels. Some had a large cross covering the mainsail, while others would have the whole sail of blue, with a white jib or gaff-topsail. On another boat's canvas would be figured one, two, or three balls; or stars, or crescents; or a large letter or number designated the ship to which they belonged. The

diversity of colors, and the different tastes displayed in painting the boats, added another pleasing feature: some were pure white, others black, still others of a lead color; or fancifully striped with tri-colors, or with the bow red, blue, or green, while the rest of the craft would be of a contrasting shade. Sometimes a huge eye on either side of the stem, or a large circle, would be the designating mark; all these combined making up an extended group of dashing water-craft, especially pertaining to the California coast and fishery.

Capt. Scammon is credited with discovering one of the principal breeding grounds of the California gray whales. This was Scammon's Lagoon, an arm of Vizcaino Bay more than 300 miles south of San Diego. Another inlet is named after the whaling ship *Black Warrior*, a familiar sight of old San Diego, which was lost trying to force an entrance. An article printed in the *Boston Journal of Commerce*, and preserved in the Whaling Museum on Johnnycake Hill, in New Bedford, relates Scammon's experiences:

Capt. C. M. Scammon, whose name the lagoon has since borne, was in 1857 in command of the brig *Boston* owned by Tubbs & Co., of San Francisco. He had fitted out in the Spring for a cruise along the lower coast in search of whales, seals, and sea elephants. The pursuit in the open sea was unsuccessful. He had heard that a lagoon, as yet unknown to whalers, branched off inside the coast somewhere opposite to Cedros Island. If unknown, there was reason to believe that devil fish might be abundant, and he determined to explore it. The entrance was made after not much more than the usual difficulty, and after a few days of preparation in wooding, etc., they were ready for work, and no better explanation of the peculiarities, the dangers and the successes of lagoon whaling can be given than to make a simple statement of what befell the crew and what they accomplished.

The brig was taken as far up toward the head of the lagoon as the water would allow, and there anchored "for the season." The sight about them was a remarkable one; the oldest whaleman of them all had never seen anything approaching it. The water in the channels was not over eighteen to twenty feet, and over most of the lagoon not six. But the whales! Whales to the right of them; whales to the left of them. One here close to the brig; one out there beyond the channel, where he cannot get his back under water any way, lying flapping his flukes and ready to shove himself off when he gets ready. It is no exaggeration to say that there were whales enough within sight at one time to load the ship with oil to her full capacity. But the oil, swimming through the lagoon, was not the same thing as though already in the casks, and that they speedily learned.

The excitement of the first day almost turned to tragedy on the second. The crew took to their boats and two large cow whales were quickly killed:

Their first experience was favorable. Two large cow whales were killed without difficulty, and every one was in high spirits accordingly. But the next day told a different story. Before the first whale was even struck, a whirl of his flukes sent the boat into splinters, broke one man's leg, another man's arm, and seriously injured three other men. As a relief boat hurried up to rescue the wounded, another devil fish passing along gave it a little tip by way of divertisement and boat number two was smashed. This was bad enough, five of the crew disabled, but this was not the worst of it. After waiting two days to allow the men time to recover from their excitement, a boat was again sent out, but

Inside of bomb lance

Bomb lance gun used in whaling

235

WHALING SCENE IN THE CALIFORNIA LAGOONS.

though the crew pulled off as usual from the ship, yet no sooner did they approach a whale then every man dropped his oar and jumped overboard, utterly overcome with fear.

The crew was demoralized. A way out of their difficulties was found by ambushing the whales in the narrow channels through which they passed to and from the lagoons. They were "bombed" from safe positions where the water was too shallow for the whales to attack. Every cask on the ship was filled. Every effort was made to retain the secret of the lagoon, but when they arrived the next season a whole fleet of whaleships appeared, and in a few years the lagoon had been "fished" out.

The first mention of a whaling station in San Diego appeared in the *Herald* in February of 1859:

The company of whalemen at the Playa, in this bay, have killed about a dozen whales in the few weeks since they commenced operations, only five of which they have been able to get into port. These five yielded 150 barrels of oil, worth about $2000. If some means could be devised to prevent the whales from sinking, three or four parties could do a good business during the season, by catching whales within ten miles of the entrance to the harbor.

The following month proved a profitable one, and five whales were taken in five days, and the *Herald* commented that "one hundred men might find profitable employment at whaling

THE LAGOONS of Lower California were breeding grounds for the gray whale and exciting tales are told of mass killings and many brushes with sudden death.

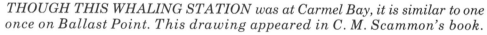

THOUGH THIS WHALING STATION was at Carmel Bay, it is similar to one once on Ballast Point. This drawing appeared in C. M. Scammon's book.

in our bay . . ." A week later the *Herald* announced that whaling already had become a profitable business with fifteen whales taken in a few weeks, and a fine quality of oil was being shipped directly to the Atlantic states, instead of to San Francisco dealers, and was bringing sixty to sixty-five cents a gallon in Boston and New York markets.

Two companies were in business on Ballast Point. Benjamin Hayes tells of visiting San Diego during the whaling season and though the populace seemed to be "without business, money or any visible prospect for the future, I have yet to see the first 'sad' man, woman or child. Withall a happy spirit of contentment presides over their feelings."

The whaling season lasted from December until April, and Hayes reported:

> The ship *Ocean*, Capt. Clark, is here; he has been here five weeks; has made 500 barrels of oil, from twelve whales. Capt. Alpheus Packard, who operates from Ballast Point, has taken 13 whales, yielding 450 barrels. Capt. Henry Johnson, also on Ballast Point, has made 200 barrels, from seven whales. Through last season, Capt. P. made 900 barrels. He thinks, the business will soon be destroyed, in consequence of the large number of ships that will come in, hearing of the success of the *Ocean*.

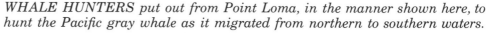

WHALE HUNTERS put out from Point Loma, in the manner shown here, to hunt the Pacific gray whale as it migrated from northern to southern waters.

238

THE CALIFORNIA GRAY WHALE was chased from the ice of the Bering Sea to the lagoons of Baja California, as shown in this sketch of whale hunting.

Small boats put out from the shore stations and drew up alongside the migrating whales, much as the sightseeing boats from San Diego were to do a hundred years later, and Scammon describes the process of killing:

When the gunner fires, if he hits his game, the next effort made is to haul up near enough to shoot a bomb-lance into a vital part, which, if it explodes, completes the capture; but, if the first bomb fails, the second or third one does the fatal work. The prize is then towed to the station; and if it be night, it is secured to one of the buoys placed for the purpose, a little way from the surf, where it remains until daylight, or until such time as it is wanted, to be stripped of its blubber. The whales generally taken by the shore parties are Humpbacks, and California Grays; but occasionally a Right Whale, a Finback, or a sulphur-bottom is captured.

When captured and towed ashore they were flensed, or stripped, much in the same manner, Scammon suggests, as was done by the New England whalers of more than a century and half before:

At the point where the enormous carcass was stripped of its fat, arose the "whaling station," where try-pots were set in rude furnaces, formed of rocks and clay, and capacious vats were made of planks, to receive the blubber. Large mincing-tubs, with mincing-horses and mincing-knives, cutting-spades, ladles, bailers, skimmers, pikes, and gaffs, with other whaling implements, surrounded the try-works; and nearby, a low structure covered with brush-wood, constituted the store-house for the oil. A light shanty, with four apartments, served the purpose of wash-room, drying-room, store-room, and cooper's shop; and a sort of capstans, termed "crabs," were used in lieu of the ship's windlass, . . . which served to roll the massive forms of the captured animals on the beach during the process of flensing.

Scammon had estimated that a thousand whales a day were passing along the coast, and while the hunting was to continue into the 70's, their numbers were being swiftly reduced. For many years oily smoke drifted over San Diego from Ballast Point stations but it blew away, along with the hopes for a new prosperity.

CHAPTER FOURTEEN

"I had a dream the other night,
When Everything was still;
I thought I saw Susanna
A-coming down the hill."

Jornada del Muerto

JOURNEY OF DEATH

Old San Diego was entering its final phase. Nature and war added their blows to the mistakes and the poor foresight of the ranchers. The Franklin House, now in possession of George Tebbetts, the Colorado House and two boarding houses were open but the Gila House had been dismantled. Louis Strauss and Hyman Mannasse, a nephew of Joseph Mannasse, sold off the goods in their large stores and closed up. Bad debt suits filled the court calendar and the Grand Jury noted that the town was filled with idlers and vagrants.

The *Herald* published complaints that the town had no tailor, no watchmaker, no gunsmith, and was in need of mechanics of every description. It said:

San Diego is now the largest and thinnest populated county in the state, yet it could be made the richest, most populous. A little wise statesmanship and masterly activity is all that is necessary to make everybody rich, happy and contented.

The *Herald* ceased publication on April 7, 1860, and Editor Ames removed to San Bernardino to start another newspaper. In a year, with the admonishments of his father that he should "shun wine and women" long forgotten, Ames was dead of over-drinking.

Though the population of the county increased from 798 to 4324 in the decade from 1850 to 1860, most of the people did not reside in town but had taken up farming or ranching in the public

THIS DRAMATIC SKETCH by W. H. Hilton symbolizes the disaster that came to California and the great cattle ranchos with the cruel drought of the 1860's.

domain, the open lands that had not been granted away in the Spanish and Mexican days, or operated mills or stores of one kind or another in the hills and mountain valleys. Trade was concentrated in Old Town but the bustling frontier days were over. The vibrant tide that had swirled across the continent had been slowed or diverted, and the Civil War was to cut it off completely. The war also would see the seizure of a large part of the whaling fleet.

Buena Vista Rancho retained flavor into modern times.

The national census of 1860 indicated that the number of cattle in California had risen to more than a million, far above the needs of the state, and there were no alternative markets. The cattle drives over the Gila Trail had dropped away. Once again, as in days gone by, cattle would be killed for the money that could be realized by selling the hides for leather and the tallow for soap and candles. The wool of thousands of sheep would go uncut. Many of the *rancheros* still enjoyed a life of ease and plenty. Others had lost their land and lived in the past. The Spanish dress of the pastoral days of the Dons had become incongruous and the rich *mantas*, the gold embroidered vests and the ornamented breeches laid aside. The silver trappings for their horses had eaten up much of the money that was needed as times became bad. The money lenders were always on hand with quick credit or loans — sometimes at ten per cent a month.

Some glimpses of the changes of life on the ranchos, not related in time, have come down from the *Notes* made by Benjamin Hayes as he rode the trails as a circuit judge. He found that Couts had made Guajome Rancho into what he described as a paradise. "In summer especially, when all the country is dry, one feels that Guajome is like an 'oasis in the desert.' The twenty miles leading to it, from Temecula, present no cultivation at all . . . through the thirty-eight miles toward the town of San Diego, there are two small vineyards — Buena Vista and Encinitas — nothing more. All is to the eye 'a dreary waste' save where nature has sown the grass and wild oak and chance flower."

In Soledad Valley, formerly the town commons of the old pueblo, he stopped to water his mule, and the young widow of Don Bonifacio López who, as the owner of large numbers of horses had been known in Old Town as "The King," came out of her garden to greet him, her eyes smiling under a man's hat. Opposite her dwelling, he said, there was a narrow trail up the side of a steep hill ". . . up which Don Bonifacio used to gallop his horse, full speed, wheeling in an instant, down again at the same time . . . to the infinite admiration of his countrymen at the rodeo, themselves no inferior horsemen. He weighed near 300 pounds. If I lived there . . . it seems it might haunt me in my sleep."

Monserrate Rancho house in earliest days.

244

THE CARRIAGE ENTRANCE and enclosed patio of Spain kept the traditions of the Old World alive in the Cave J. Couts home up into modern times.

He rode to Rincón del Diablo Rancho, now the site of Escondido, to call upon Henry Clayton and his wife, the widow of Capt. Snook, whose father had been granted the ranch in 1843, and wrote, "it is bad to wake up some men out of the *siesta*; nevertheless, we had a pleasant chat . . . Nothing can surpass the uniform kindness of Mr. and Mrs. Clayton. One leaves them with regret." The Claytons sold their interest in the property to Oliver S. Witherby and he eventually came into sole possession.

At Monserrate, a rancho of more than 13,000 acres on the upper San Luis Rey River Hayes found the original owner, Don Ysidro María Alvarado: "I do not know why he has not prospered more. He lives almost in Indian style, on the banks of the river San Luis Rey; seems to have few cattle; nor has there been much ground in cultivation."

The Southerners who had come to California had exchanged cotton for cattle and Negroes for Indians, and resenting domination by the more heavily-populated North, hoped to bring about a secession of the "cow counties," including San Diego, and form the Territory of Colorado. A bill authorizing this legislation was submitted by Andrés Pico in 1859 and approved by the California Legislature by a two-thirds vote and sent to Washington for approval. It died in the confusion of events leading up to the Civil War.

In 1860 Abraham Lincoln, the candidate for the new Republican Party, was elected President. On December 20th of that year South Carolina seceded from the Union. By the summer of the next year, ten other Southern states had voted to follow the lead of South Carolina. The first battle of Bull Run was fought on July 21. San Diego was at the end of the most southerly trail, and though the battles were being waged a long distance away, there were relatives and friends on both sides, and the division in San Diego, as elsewhere, was sharp and bitter. The sympathy of the majority of its citizens, however, remained with the South throughout the war. The Bear Flag once raised for an independent California was flown again as the banner of State's Rights. The Butterfield Stage Line's southern service by way of Warner's, which had connected Southern California with the East, came to a halt on July 1, 1861, and Butterfield began running from St. Joseph, Mo., to Central California, by way of Salt Lake City.

California as a whole remained loyal and furnished more than 15,000 volunteers, most of them from the North, for Union service which consisted largely of duty within the state. Southern sympathizers, however, who included many of the leading state officials, organized the Knights of the Golden Circle, the Knights of the Columbia Star and the Committee of Thirty. They are believed to have numbered more than 30,000, in large part *Californios* who had been persuaded that a new government would speed up their land claims and that squatters and other lawless trespassers would be dispossessed. Arms were kept ready and ammunition stolen from Union depots in the expectation of guerrilla warfare. The loaded wagons from the gold fields disappeared. Cave Couts, the native of Tennessee and a graduate of West Point, respected but hot-tempered, became an acknowledged leader of Southern sympathizers, and it was indicated in correspondence that if he so chose he could have led a regiment from Southern California to join the Rebel cause. Many were willing to follow his leadership. Many Democrats voted Republican throughout the state, however, in the hope of averting disorder or any attempt to organize a new Pacific Republic.

Brig. Gen. George Wright, who succeeded to the command of Union forces in California, seized all boats and ferries on the Colorado River and gave orders that no one was to be permitted to cross the river without a special permit, and that all persons approaching the frontier were to be arrested for questioning.

Gen. Wright expressed the fear that a French fleet, acting in sympathy with the South, might seize the West Coast ports of Mexico, and he repeatedly urged that he be permitted to invade Sonora and capture the port of Guaymas, to keep open the Gulf of California for ferrying supplies up the Colorado. Two infantry companies were at Fort Yuma. His request went unheeded.

A request for two twenty-four-pounders, to control "as much as possible the harbor of San Diego," was made by Brev. Maj. L. A. Armistead, of the 6th Infantry stationed at New San Diego, and with a small force he went to "Oti" or Otay, near the border, to send warning to Indians not to take part in any troubles developing in Lower California. On June 18, 1861, Capt. G. A. Haller, another officer and fifty-two men of the 4th Infantry, arrived after a march of 387 miles in eighteen days from Fort Mojave, New Mexico, to relieve Armistead and his company.

In a letter, Whaley reported that secessionists were being arrested in San Diego "and there is no telling how soon there may be a row of some sort down here."

Continuing his efforts to halt the steady flight of Southern sympathizers into Confederate territory, Gen. Wright sent units of the new California Volunteers to reinforce Fort Yuma and established a military prison there. He also established a camp at Warner's on the route the secessionists were using through the mountains. This was on October 18, 1861, with Maj. Edwin A. Rigg in command. A month later it was moved about a dozen miles north to the Oak Grove area, and it was named Camp Wright.

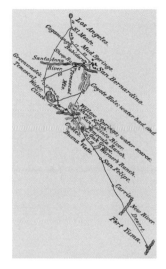

Army Map of Escape Route of Southern Sympathizers

Fleeing California at the same time was Daniel Showalter, an assemblyman of Mariposa County, who had just shot to death the assemblyman of San Bernardino, Charles W. Piercy, in a political duel fought with rifles. Showalter and seventeen well-armed and well-mounted men took the trail toward the Colorado, but when they reached Temecula, in order to avoid Camp Wright, they dropped down into San Luis Rey Valley and took a southeasterly course through the mountains toward San Jose Valley. Maj. Rigg intercepted two advance men and then, acting on reports received from Indians, encountered the rest of the party at the ranch of John Minter at Mesa Grande, about two and a half miles southwest of Lake Henshaw. They were taken to Camp Wright, and Maj. Rigg made the following report:

Army Map locating Showalter Party of Secessionists

They now regret that they did not resist. If they had they would have given us a hard fight. There is no doubt but every one of them is a rank secessionist, and are on their way to lend aid and comfort to the enemy.

While not denying Southern sympathies, and though incriminating letters on them indicated they were going into Mexico only to avoid seizure and questioning at Fort Yuma, they insisted they were on their way to Sonora to engage in mining, and all signed oaths of allegiance to the United States. However, they were ordered taken to the prison at Fort Yuma. After a few months they were released. Showalter became a lieutenant colonel and fought with the Confederates in a number of major engagements.

247

About the time of the capture of the Showalter party, John J. Warner, as a member of the Home Guard of Los Angeles, and in spite of all the unfriendly treatment he had received at the hands of the U.S. military, made a reconnaissance for the Union command, to check on reports of other bands of armed men, one of which was reported heading for Jacumba Pass, but he reported he found only prospectors carrying guns for protection against the Indians. The regular Army infantry was withdrawn from San Diego and replaced for the rest of the war by various units of the California Volunteers. As the winter was a cold one, and with a heavy rainfall of more than fifteen inches, the Volunteers tore down Davis' old warehouse at New Town and ripped wood from his wharf to be used as firewood. At one time the Volunteers at Camp Wright were in a state of mutiny, with twelve in the guard-house and others refusing to drill with packed knapsacks. The flight of Confederate sympathizers across the Colorado continued for the duration of the war.

The Bars and Stars were raised in late February of 1862 over Tucson by a Confederate force which succeeded in capturing an advance force of California Volunteers. When the main companies of Volunteers from Camp Drum at Wilmington and Camp Wright

THE CIVIL WAR wracked the whaling industry in the Pacific as well as elsewhere. Here is the "stone fleet," the whaling ships sunk to blockade East harbors.

in San Diego County moved across the Colorado River and advanced toward Tucson, and with the news of a Union victory in New Mexico, the Rebels left Arizona for El Paso.

Grand warnings were issued for the Confederates to keep their ships out of the Pacific, and a fleet of six small wooden vessels, with less than 100 guns and 1000 men, patrolled the coast from Alaska to Panama, to protect the whaling fleet centered in Hawaiian waters, and American ships engaged in trade off China and Japan. The sloops of war were the *Lancaster, Saranac, Wyoming, Narragansett, St. Mary's* and once more, the *Cyane.* One ship was replaced and two were added in 1863. A privateer being outfitted at San Francisco was seized and the crew arrested.

The war deepened the depression in San Diego. In a letter written to Whaley on March 5, 1861, A. S. Ensworth wrote:

The fact is, there is literally & truly no money in this country . . . The Mexicans have nearly all got rid of their cattle . . . Mannasse (Jo) during the last month, has been riding about the county collecting cattle for old debts, which he intends to start with up the country about the 1st of April. Hinton is now at work getting his cattle off of the mountain & bringing them down to Agua Hideunda. The Estudillos will start nearly all their cattle up the country this spring, & sell them to pay debts. As a specimen of the way these people are in debt (those who have any cattle left) I will observe, Antonito Serrano owes Jo. M. & Co. $2800 & Jesus Machado owes them about $1500. Neither of them could pay these debts with all their property. Bill Williams is flat, & is living in town. B. Lopez's estate will not pay the debts. Sylvester Marron owes Jo. M. & Co. more than he can pay. Soto is the only one that holds his own, & his wife was in here the other day asking for credit, & because I would not give it to her got into a great passion. The fact is, things down this way, have come to a head.

By the end of the year he was commenting that the *rancheros* so lacked money even for sacks of flour that "many is the time they have come after dark for it, for fear of being seen by some man whom they were owing . . ."

San Diego also was facing competition from San Pedro as a port for Southern California, and a report from a correspondent, "Selden" in a San Francisco newspaper, belittled the future prospects of San Diego and stated facts which Ensworth, in a letter to Whaley, charged were inaccurate:

They are thrown out for the purpose of retaining troops, Gov't transportation and depot, in the vicinity of that place, and to build that humbug town, San Pedro, about which more gass has been expended, & more ink wasted, than relative to any other point in the state . . . Vive Humbug!

The correspondent "Selden" was J. J. Warner, the former state senator from San Diego, who also was publishing a pro-Democrat, but anti-slavery newspaper in Los Angeles and earning the enmity of many of his former friends.

Cattle brands were recorded on pieces of hides. This is brand of Joseph Swycaffer.

Brand register of Joseph Mannasse

Brand register of Guadalupe Marrón

A divided and disturbed little town was lashed by a storm in January, 1862, that for a time threatened to wash away the adobe walls of the mansions which had stood for more than thirty years. A letter written by A. S. Ensworth and addressed to Thomas Whaley reads:

> It was not only a flood of waters falling from the Heavens, but such a South-Easter I have never known, the tide backing up the waters of the bay which was running in from the river to a hight (sic) never before witnessed by Americans . . . all the old walls around town, which were not well protected, have gone down to rise no more.

The waters washed away the walls of the corrals at the rear of the Bandini and Estudillo houses, and in back of the Franklin House, and damaged many of the business structures. All the rivers of the county ran full, from hill to hill, and Hayes said that a George P. Abbotts thought a good-sized vessel might have gone a mile or more up the San Luis Rey River. A coffin from the old Catholic burial ground was swept down the river and into the bay. Late in the month Capt. T. L. Roberts, in command of the California Volunteers stationed at San Diego, was ordered to march his company to Warner's but he reported it would be impossible to move wagons over any roads for at least two months. They were able to make the trip in February, however. Roads were washed out over all Southern California, and there are reports that perhaps several hundred persons were drowned and that at least 200,000 head of cattle were lost either by drowning or starvation.

The river was still running heavily in May when at noon on Tuesday the 26th an earthquake, which was described as the worst since the one of 1811 that destroyed the San Juan Capistrano Mission, rocked the town and caused the river to wash over its banks. The entire population, Benjamin Hayes wrote, rushed into the streets and the public square, in terror, and for many nights thereafter many did not sleep in their homes, and some experienced nauseating sensations. Adobe homes were cracked or otherwise damaged. In many sections of La Playa the steep bank of Point Loma fell in, and the waters of the bay were reported considerably agitated, the tide rising several feet above normal. Between noon and 8 o'clock that night there were six lighter shocks. On Thursday morning there was a shock as severe as the one of Tuesday. Other slight shocks occurred on Friday, Saturday and Sunday. The reports from Vallecito indicated the quake had been very severe in the desert.

The heavy rains of 1861-62 produced bountiful grazing which caused the cattle and sheep to grow fat and multiply. Droughts followed the rains and destroyed the ranges. Smallpox brought death and a fear greater than that caused by the earthquake. The countryside dried out in one of the worst disasters ever to sweep California. Only 3.87 inches of rain fell in San Diego in the winter of 1862-63, and only 5.14 inches in the following winter.

In November of 1862 Couts, in letters to Abel Stearns, wrote:

> Small pox is quite prevalent — six to eight per day are being buried in S. Juan Capistrano — Indians generally. One case in San Dieguito and two in San Mateo is (sic) the nearest to us. I vaccinated the whole *rancheria* at San Luis some six weeks since, & hope they may escape, thus saving our community of the terrible disease.

Hard times were upon them. Couts commented that "I am badly in want of money. I have some debts, taxes on hand, no goods in my shop & no money." Many of the settlers as well as the old *rancheros* were deserting California for newly-discovered gold fields in the Colorado River country of Arizona. The grass that appeared on the ranges in October was drying up by November. The nights were cold and frosty. By late November cattle were being sent into Lower California, Couts reporting that probably 10,000 head had been taken there and thousands more were to be put on the trail within a short time.

In January a police force was organized for San Diego City to be under the sheriff, and all "Indians and Cholos" were ordered to leave the town. A frame building at the San Diego Mission was converted into a receiving hospital for smallpox victims, and funds were requested from the state to hire nurses and attendants.

Sentinels were posted at the ranchos to keep anyone from approaching without notice. Henry Clayton returned to San Diego from Los Angeles at night by stage and no door was open to him. The Ysidro Alvarado family was stricken. Both he and his wife succumbed. Mexicans who were to have buried the body of Don Ysidro, had instead left it on the road, gotten drunk and one of them tried to break into Couts' ranch house. The victims of smallpox in the vicinity of Couts' rancho were being buried in the San Luis Rey Mission and he commented, a "grave cannot be dug without striking human bones . . . they were digging little holes, barely deep enough to cover the coffins . . ." He sent his brother, Blounts, to remonstrate against it, and he was attacked by a Sonoran with a knife, Blounts killed him.

One of those who died of the smallpox was Juan Antonio, the captain-general of the Cahuillas, who had ambushed the leaders of the Indians who had threatened to ravage the white settlements. A correspondent writing for the *Los Angeles Star,* reported on Feb. 28, 1863:

Abel Stearns

251

Old Juan Antonio and four other Indian chiefs have died of smallpox and I have been informed that the bodies have not been buried and that they are being mutilated by hogs and dogs. Of course it is a matter of much annoyance to the whites in the neighborhood.

The smallpox ran its course by late spring, but the ranchos were sick with the loss of cattle and beset by the frantic efforts of squatters to feed their own stock at any cost. John Forster, who had acquired possession of Santa Margarita Rancho from Pío and Andrés Pico, indicated in a letter that he had "been under arrest . . . until today, when I was released, arrested again, and am now at liberty *de nuevo*, the charges are killing and slaying fifteen squatters, tearing down fences and playing the dickens generally. In both cases the plaintiffs have not gotten farther than entering very lame complaints . . ."

The main house of Santa Margarita Rancho in 1913.

As far as possible all cattle were being driven into the mountains, and conditions generally, as reported in the *Los Angeles News*, were discussed as follows:

The cattle of Los Angeles County are dying so fast in so many places, for want of food, that the larger *rancheros* keep their men busily engaged in obtaining the hides. Thousands of carcasses strew the plains in all directions, from the city, and the sight is harrowing in the extreme . . .

The spring continued dry, and in the summer there came strong north winds. Grasshoppers appeared and finished stripping much of the remaining grass. Conditions in San Diego County were much of the same. Forster, in a civil suit years later, testified:

. . . The climate was bone dry . . . There was no moisture and our cattle died off in very great numbers. About that winter, almost the whole country from north to south became almost depopulated of cattle from the fact that the country had been entirely overstocked about that time. Before the year 1864 had passed away, there was a perfect devastation. Such a thing was never before known in California.

Old ranch house at Los Peñasquitos

In May of 1864, when the drought was at its height, a sudden storm beat down on the weakened cattle and Forster said he lost three hundred in one night at Santa Ysabel and that the next day the rest of the cattle had to be turned loose to move about and keep up their circulation. Despite taking the cattle into the mountains, Forster estimated his loss at about fifty per cent. Others fared worse. Of a herd of between 6000 to 8000 cattle owned by Don Juan Avila of San Juan Capistrano, only some 800 were left after the drought. Debts were paid with cattle or hides at $2.50.

County records indicate that at assessment time in 1863 there were 13,206 cattle, 1793 horses and 5784 sheep subject to taxation on San Diego County ranches. A year later, at the same time there were only 8364 cattle, 1384 horses and 2823 sheep. Cattle decreased again in the following year, though sheep were on the increase. Surprisingly, a demand for wool from California began to develop in the Union states, as the normal supply from the South had been cut off by the war. The decline in the number of horses to 499 indicated that hundreds had been slaughtered or driven over the brinks of canyons, or over ocean cliffs, to save the grass for the cattle and sheep. It was said that fences could be built with bones.

The election of September 5, 1863, saw the Democratic state ticket win a large majority in San Diego County, though in Old Town itself, where merchants and traders were in the majority, the first returns seemed to indicate a Republican victory. Ephraim Morse had shut his store and worked indefatigably to get Northern sympathizers to the polls. A party led by Robert Israel got out the anvils from the smithy and began exploding powder in celebration. The picture soon changed, as recorded in a letter from George Pendleton to Cave Couts:

> As the returns came in from the interior, however, they began to hang their heads. Now when you meet one of them you will find his hat pulled down for his eyes as if he had been guilty of some dirty trick of which he was ashamed. They feel mighty bad and I hope the result may physic them until they are purged thoroughly of their Black Republicanism . . . I have all those fellows here spotted who voted the Black Republican ticket and shall see that they are hereafter kept from . . . having any voice in our Democratic meetings.

Republican enthusiasm revived somewhat with arrival of the news of the fall of Fort Sumter, and guns were fired off throughout the town. As the unhappy year wore on the bitterness increased, and Pendleton wrote to Couts, on December 6, 1863:

> The soldiers at New Town gave a *fandango* and supper at their post last night and of course all the hungry bellies acceded and what they consumed and carried off, it is supposed, will be sufficient to satisfy their appetites until next Christmas. A few years ago, to go to a soldiers' *fandango* was not thought the right thing by many who attended last night, and to my mind they are evidently preparing themselves for that state of society which will exist should Old Abe succeed in his damnable designs . . .

The turn of the year brought little change in San Diego. Ensworth, in a letter to Whaley, wrote:

> No news down this way — dull-dull very dull — stock dying — absolutely starving to death for want of grass. It is a devil of a year, Never, before, have I seen the time but what at some out of the way place — in some secluded nook or corner, a little hay could be cut. But this year the earth, from valley to hill top, is naked.

A few days later he penned another letter in which he enclosed a draft for $165, but the stage driver refused to accept it, in fear highwaymen would kill him on the road.

United States currency was discounted with succeeding Confederate victories, and Charles Johnson sold many greenbacks to Cave Couts for sixty cents on the dollar. Rumors were circulated that privateers were being outfitted in ports of China to raid the California coast. Many Southern sympathizers and distressed *Californios* left the state for Mexico, which a French Army had invaded and where the Austrian Maximilian was to be installed as emperor. Official Union Army military reports contain references to the *Californios* as bitterly opposed to the Stars and Stripes and that they hoped to see the French flag also flying over California.

The tide of war slowly shifted, and in 1864, when President Lincoln came up for re-election, George B. McClellan, the Democrat, received 180 votes in San Diego County, though this did not include the Colorado River precinct, and Lincoln only 52. Old Town, however, voted in favor of Lincoln, 34 to 25. The vote at Fort Yuma, an Army post, was 63 for Lincoln and 18 for McClellan. Robert Israel had been sent to the Cuyamaca precinct with a supply of whiskey believed sufficient to swing a Republican majority there. The vote, however, was McClellan 30, Lincoln 1. José María Estudillo had assured Pendleton that although he was a Republican he would not attempt to influence any of his *paisanos*, but evidently he fell into the hands of Morse, drank too much and "was yelling all day for Lincoln."

The news that Lincoln had swept all but two states arrived in San Diego by stage and "a lot of the boys about town made night hideous with their infernal howling, throwing coyotes completely in the shade . . . I cannot believe this report. It is too bad a dose to swallow . . ."

Union military victories were celebrated with another Army *baile* and on the same night, Pendleton wrote, "we of the upper crust got off one at the Franklin House and had the elite of the town and the gals from the Punta . . . we kept it going until 4½ o'clock when the cocks warned us it was time to quit."

In another letter, Pendleton wrote:

Numbers of people are leaving the state for Mexico driven from their own country by oppression and taxation. Would that the burden of the taxes could fall on those who re-elected Lincoln, but these very persons, I suppose, are exempt from taxation and stealings . . .

The war was coming to an end but its aftermath left San Diego awash with troubles. Bands of mounted outlaws roamed the countryside around San Diego, raiding ranches of animals and supplies, and the alarmed residents were driven to appeal to the cavalry for protection. Starving Cahuilla Indians had left their mountain and desert homes to become idlers and thieves. A deputy sheriff of San Diego, F. L. Brill, was sent to attach 278 mares and colts and thirteen horses at Rancho de las Viejas, which was the property of Bill Williams, who had come down from Volcan Mountain, and the animals were turned over to another deputy named Andrew Kriss. That night most of the horses were run off by two *Californios* who were trailed into Lower California, where Kriss was shot to death. A William James who had been left in charge of a store Cyrus Kimble had built on the immigrant trail on Warner's Ranch, was found slain beside his bed, and with money, goods and three horses missing. It was generally believed in San Diego that Kimble, a Republican, had been the intended victim of secessionists who hated him, and that James was killed by mistake. That was on June 3, 1865. Two months later Kimble and George Williams, camping with their families at the Santa Ana River on their way to Los Angeles, were surprised by a gang of a half dozen men or more and shot to death. Kimble was believed to have been carrying $1000.

A man identified as A. B. Smith, presumably the Albert B. Smith who climbed the Plaza flagpole to shake out the American flag during the United States conquest of California, and later a county superintendent of schools, walked up to the town jail, poked a six-shooter through the bars, and started shooting at the manacled prisoners, killing one of them, and threatened to shoot a deputy sheriff, if he tried to interfere with his sport. Smith finally was subdued and placed under $1000 bail. The local correspondent of the *Alta California* reported sadly:

> For years this has been the quietest burg and county in the state, but right now it holds an envious and high position in the calendar of crime, even if it is in California.

The strife between the landholders and the squatters rose in intensity. In 1865 Cave Couts was indicted on a charge of murder, along with his brother, four Indians and a Negro workman. Details are missing from old records of the district court. Couts' attorney, who again was O. S. Witherby, was successful once more in having the indictment dismissed, this time on the grounds the district attorney had not posted his bond of office. The judge was Benjamin Hayes. Another indictment of Couts came in 1866. He was tried and acquitted on a charge of murdering one Juan Mendoza, and this time Benjamin Hayes appeared as his defense counsel. Mendoza had worked for Couts as his majordomo, after a reputed career as a badman in Sonora. Couts' defense was that he had discharged Mendoza, who then threatened to kill him

The Confederate raider
Shenandoah *which
sank whaling ships
in Pacific*

on sight. For months Couts stayed away from San Diego, with Mendoza, armed with a six-shooter and a knife, holding forth at various bars and sending challenges to Couts. In time Couts appeared in San Diego, reportedly on business, and checked into the Colorado House. In the tradition of the Old West, either by design or by chance, they walked toward each other in the area of the Plaza. Couts was carrying a shawl. He dropped it, to reveal a shotgun. Mendoza, according to witnesses, turned to flee and was struck with a blast from both barrels. He staggered into a heap of reeds and fell dead.

The Pacific became a war zone when the French fleet blockaded Mexican ports. Peru and Spain engaged in military clashes. In the Spring of 1865 the ship *Shenandoah* sailed from London and once at sea unfurled the Confederate flag. Operating as a privateer under the command of James I. Waddell, she destroyed a million dollars worth of whalers and merchant vessels, and evaded capture by the Pacific fleet. On August 1, 1865, the United States barque *Gen. Pike* arrived in the harbor with the crews of seven more vessels which had been burned by the pirates. The commander of the privateer professed to believe that the rebels had not surrendered, that the war was yet going on, and he intended to sail to Arctic waters where there were eighty American whalers reported.

The following year the fleet was increased to eleven, and then to seventeen, to protect an expanding Pacific commerce amid the French action against Mexico and Spanish attacks on Valparaiso and Callao.

CHAPTER FIFTEEN

"There was a beginning but you cannot see it.
There will be an end but you cannot see it."

LAST OF THE DONS

Three decades had passed since the missions had been secularized and the Indian lands confiscated. In that short time the Western expansion of the United States and the frequent rising and falling of the cattle market had witnessed the passing of most of the ranchos from the Dons to the new settlers, either through sales or mortgage foreclosures, on many occasions long before the final patents recognizing the original Spanish and Mexican grants were ever issued. The cattle that had roamed wild over the hills, and with no attempts to improve the stock, deteriorated with time. But it was the drought that finally broke the last of the Dons and turned friend against friend. The silver saddles of the pastoral years were sold to pay taxes and debts.

The ownership of Warner's Ranch continued to carry with it violence and death. A United States District Court had upset a Land Commission decision and granted the lower portion of the ranch, or 8800 acres including the ranch house and Buena Vista Valley, to Silvestre de la Portilla, one of the original grantees who had abandoned the valley because of troubles with the Indians.

The lands, however, after the departure of Warner, were occupied by the Carrillo family, and José Ramón Carrillo and his wife came into possession of Buena Vista Valley and they, in turn, lost it to a Los Angeles promoter, speculator and cattle baron by the name of John Rains, in settlement of an $1800 debt. Rains also

DONA JUANA MACHADO WRIGHTINGTON waits out the years with only the memories of the days when her home was a center of life and gaiety.

foreclosed on Warner and obtained the upper 18,000 acres. Now he claimed a virtual empire extending from Warner's all the way up into San Bernardino County. Ramón Carrillo became his majordomo.

In 1862 Rains was lassoed from his horse near Cucamonga, beaten, shot four times, and his body dragged off into the brush by the side of a road. The crime was never solved. Two years later Ramón Carrillo, while accompanying the widow of Rains, was murdered. Mrs. Rains herself had been threatened with lynching.

Warner served as a provost marshal and chief of the Los Angeles draft board during the Civil War, and afterward received a deed for a tract of land in Los Angeles. In later years he lost this too, and died blind and almost penniless in 1895 at the age of 88.

A knowledge of agriculture and business, which the old Dons did not possess and had little desire to learn, aided Cave Couts in weathering the economic storms. His ranch home at Guajome, built in the finest architectural tradition of the times, contained twenty rooms in four wings around a central patio 80 x 90. There was a central fountain, and in one of the many adjoining ranch buildings was a small chapel for worship. Couts also acquired the Buena Vista Ranch on his north and Los Vallecitos de San Marcos on his south.

The Osunas and their relatives, always in need of money, juggled their interests in trying to meet various loans on San Dieguito Rancho. Small loans carried interest rates of ten per cent a month. Shares of ownership were sold for as low as $315. The rancho was not finally patented to the heirs until 1871. When it came time to die, Doña Juliana Osuna instructed that for the wake her body was to be dressed in a black or blue wool dress and be stretched out on the hard earth instead of in bed or on a table.

John Forster, the Englishman, had surrendered possession of Rancho de la Nación, the lands of which embrace all of National City and Chula Vista, in 1856. He had been borrowing sums of from $15,000 to $25,000, at three per cent interest, for a number of years. The ranch passed into the possession of a French resident of San Francisco, F. A. L. Pioche, who also acquired San Felipe Rancho from Forster.

Eight years later, during the great drought, the Picos transferred possession of their vast Santa Margarita Rancho to Forster, who was their brother-in-law, for a sum of $14,000. Mortgage records show subsequent loans totalling nearly $60,000, at two per cent a month, from the agency through which the Frenchman, Pioche, had acquired Rancho de la Nación. But Forster managed to save the ranch. In later years, however, the Picos and Forster

260

engaged in a lengthy civil litigation over what had been agreed upon as to final possession and ownership. The Picos lost.

The widow of Santiago Arguello disposed of her rights to 3000 acres in the San Diego Mission lands, which contained altogether twelve square leagues, or a large part of present San Diego City, for $500. The son, José Antonio Arguello, mortgaged a share for $3000 at one and a half per cent per month. A patent for the land was issued to the Arguello heirs and assignees in 1876.

The Marróns began selling their interests in Agua Hedionda Rancho as early as 1859 and it was leased to Francis Hinton in 1860 for a loan of $6000, with José Marrón and José María Estudillo retaining the right to come and gather salt from the lagoons for their families. Soon after the ranch became the property of Robert Kelly.

The entire ranch of Las Encinitas was sold by Andrés Ybarra and his wife to Joseph Mannasse and Marcus Schiller for $3000 in 1860. Though Pío Pico once had bought Los Peñasquitos Rancho at a sheriff's sale, because of a $420 unpaid debt, he returned it to the Alvarado family, to whom he was related. By the time the patent was granted, ownership had passed to Capt. George A. Johnson, of the Colorado River Navigation Company, through a marriage to Tomasa Alvarado.

Robert Kelly

The peninsula of San Diego, which comprised Coronado and North Island, left the possession of Pedro Carrillo soon after it had been granted to him. He sold it to Capt. Bezer Simmons for $1000 because he couldn't find anybody who could pay more. Four years later it was sold to William A. Aspinwall, the builder of the Panama Railroad and a founder of the Pacific Mail Steamship Company, and his partners, for $10,000. The peninsula had been included within the boundaries of the pueblo as drawn by Capt. Fitch but despite that, the grant was recognized by the Land Commission.

Twenty-six years after their father's death, the Pedrorena children, a son and three daughters, won title to Rancho El Cajon. The Arguellos were never able to sustain their claim to La Punta, south of the bay and squatters moved onto the land and resisted all efforts to dislodge them.

A thousand acres of the common lands of Soledad Valley which had supplied grain and other foods for Old Town under both Spain and Mexico, and which had been coveted by many, in 1856 finally became the property of an Irishman, Andrew Cassidy, who had come to San Diego to operate a U.S. tidal and meteorological station, and who had married Rosa Serrano. She was the daughter of José Antonio Serrano, who built a home in Old Town sometime

Andrew Cassidy

after 1850. Cassidy found himself hard-pressed during the drought, and in a letter to Couts pleaded for payment of money owed to him, remarked that he also had come into possession of Serrano's Pauma Rancho, and would be willing to trade it, and that Louis Rose was offering only seven cents for hides and "I would not listen to him." The wool market was equally depressed. In another letter a month later he wrote of a debt of $1000 that had to be paid to Mannasse and Schiller within forty days and he had tried everything possible to raise money but had failed:

I have sent cattle with Serrano to La Paz (on the Colorado); he came home without a dollar. He gave the cattle away to Forster on three months' credit. In my opinion he might just as well (have) given them away.

The rancho passed into other hands and a number of years later a third of it was auctioned by the sheriff for $126.84 in back taxes.

Capt. George W. Hamley, who as master of the whaler *Stonington*, assisted in the American conquest, finally quit the sea for San Diego as had so many other sailors, and obtained possession of Rancho Guejito y Cañada de Paloma in the Bear Valley district north of Escondido. The ranch originally had been granted to José María Orozco, who had sided with the *Californios* and fired on Albert Smith while he was attempting to free a tangled American flag on the Plaza flagpole.

The smallest of the San Diego ranchos, La Cañada de los Coches, situated west of Flinn Springs and a little over twenty-eight acres in size, was patented to the Catholic Church as a result of a bequest by Doña Apolinaria Lorenzana. Long before that took place the ranch had become the home of Julian Ames, the former otter hunter, who erected a grist mill and also sold soap to the residents of Old Town. Ames became prosperous. Doña Apolinaria, who also had lost the 8800-acre Jamacha Rancho by means which she never understood, lived out her days, blind, and supported by friends and public aid, though remembered by the Indians she had befriended in the pastoral days at the missions.

The crumbling buildings on the low hill overlooking the San Diego River, which Fr. Junípero Serra had called the "Mother Mission" of California, again were under the protection of the Catholic Church. On May 23, 1862, President Lincoln had conveyed 22.21 acres, which contained the buildings and cemetery, to the Church. The Mission once held sway over more than 3000 square miles of the richest lands of San Diego County.

Many of the other figures of the exciting days of conquest, settlements and exploration, continued to serve their country with distinction. But the dead of San Pasqual lay in forgotten graves in Old Town. The names on the small wooden crosses had weathered away and were no longer remembered. Kit Carson, who had assured Gen. Kearny that the *Californios* would not fight, joined the Union Army in the Civil War, was named a brigadier general of Volunteers in campaigns against the Navajo Indians in Arizona, and became a legend of the West. Beale, the young Naval lieutenant who brought word of the San Pasqual disaster to San Diego and became an Indian agent as well as a trail-breaker, was named United States minister to Austria-Hungary by President Grant.

The adventurer who participated in the recapture of San Diego so many years before, John Bidwell, became a member of Congress and then Prohibition candidate for President.

Capt. Samuel du Pont, who took over the civil government of Mexican San Diego in the name of the United States, as a rear admiral commanded a fleet of ironclads and monitors in some of the most brilliant actions of the Civil War. Naval Lt. Stephen Rowan, who directed the raising of the American flag in Old Town, fired the first naval shots of the Civil War, became commander of the *New Ironsides* and eventually rose to the rank of vice admiral. Lt. William Maddox, who commanded the Marine squad at the flag raising, is the only man to have had three destroyers named after him. The *USS Cyane*, after thirty-four years of service to her country, was taken out of service and fifteen years later sold for scrap.

Stephen C. Rowan, as a vice admiral

Emory, the young topographical engineer who expected so much of San Diego, became a general in the Union Army, as did Capt. Nathaniel Lyon, who had opened a new route over the mountains. Lt. Col. Bankhead Magruder, who had caned Lewis Franklin in the Plaza, resigned his commission, and became a Confederate general. After the war, he fought for Maximilian in Mexico. Andrew B. Gray, the engineer with the U.S. Boundary Commission, and one of the original developers of New Town, also became a Confederate general.

Capt. Derby, the engineer who first turned the flow of the San Diego River, continued his humorous writings under the name of John Phoenix, built roads in the untamed Northwest, but began to go blind at the age of 34, and died in 1861. James Lassitor, known to passengers on both the Birch and Butterfield Lines, as operator of Lassitor's Place in Green Valley and as station master at Vallecito, was murdered and robbed in the desert in 1863, while he was returning from a successful prospecting trip to the new Arizona gold mines. Albert B. Smith took his own life.

The Hungarian count, Agoston Haraszthy, who was named the first sheriff in San Diego, became an assayer for the government mint in San Francisco, and was accused and cleared of embezzling more than $150,000 in gold. He subsequently was sent to Europe to gather cuttings to improve the grape culture of California, and as a result was credited with the growth of the state's wine industry. The last heard of Agoston Haraszthy was in 1871, when he disappeared from a plantation he owned in Nicaragua. It is believed he fell into a creek and was eaten by alligators.

A few San Diegans were still clawing away at the mountains that for so long had frustrated hopes for the future. Pete Larkins and Joe Stancliff, who had packed oats down the hay road in Oriflamme Canyon, from Cuyamaca Valley to Vallecito, for the Butterfield stages, built a little station at the foot of Mountain Springs, on the bitter but more direct trail that led from Ft. Yuma to San Diego, and with a long team of oxen were literally dragging occasional immigrant wagons and teams up the steep rocky hillsides.

The end of the war brought reports of mass desertions from the Union and Confederate Armies, and there were expectations of new waves of immigrants, particularly from the ravaged South where an old order had come to a violent close, and by November, 1865, the *Wilmington Journal* reported there were 300 wagons, mostly from Texas, between the Rio Grande and Fort Yuma. The *Journal* remarked "it is feared that the love of the Union is not very strong among this multitude."

The new wave would be a new generation and belong to a new era of law and order and progress. The hand of the past and the weight of isolation had left their marks on Old Town. The editor of the *Wilmington Journal*, A. A. Polhamus, visited San Diego in 1865, by steamer. He wrote:

Walking up the hill we passed through the deserted Presidio which is in ruins. The ground is covered with ice plant and the pretty flowers would seem to denote that where they grow some unknown hero's foot had trod, else their beauty is in vain. On returning to the town we found it as quiet as a village graveyard, and the appearance of many of the houses conveys the impression that they are sepulchers for the dead rather than for the living. San Diego was at one time much larger than it is now. Between three hundred and four hundred inhabitants, four stores, three hotels, one church, one school with fifty-three pupils. The county contains 13,000 square miles yet has but one town, San Diego, one church, one school, no newspaper.

The old ways and the old feelings died slowly. Mary C. Walker, of Manchester, N.Y., arrived from San Francisco in 1865 to teach school at Old Town, and was forced to resign after befriending a mulatto woman. The next year she married the widower Ephraim Morse. She recalled the following scene:

A Spanish circus visited San Diego soon after my arrival. It exhibited in the evening in a corral with high adobe walls, the company having no tents. The place was lighted by strips of cloth laid in cans of lard and then set on fire. The primitive lanterns were set on high posts and at best furnished a poor light. The spectators included nearly all of the population of the town who could pay the admittance fee of fifty cents. I think the Indians were admitted at half price. The Americans and Spanish occupied one side of the corral, and the Indians squatted on the ground on the other. The performances on the trapeze and the tightrope looked especially weird and fantastic in the smoky light of these primitive lanterns.

A promising wealth still glistened in the sun. A rich gold lead, assaying $160 a ton, was struck twenty miles north of San Diego in the direction of Escondido. Gold discoveries at Jamacha, however, proved worthless, since nobody could locate the source of the loose, rich quartz scattered about the ground.

But the hills were green once more and the cattle and the sheep were fat and multiplying, and the new tides of immigrants into California would need meat and wool. The mountains and the deserts would remain as brooding challenges and the eyes of pioneers would turn more and more to the harbor and the open sea as the gateway to the future. And here was a climate that despite occasional vagaries beckoned gently to American pioneers as it had to the Silver Dons.

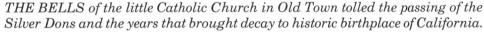

THE BELLS of the little Catholic Church in Old Town tolled the passing of the Silver Dons and the years that brought decay to historic birthplace of California.

265

1833	Secularization of the California Missions.
1835	San Diego is made a pueblo.
1836	Gov. Juan B. Alvarado's California independence is brief; turmoil follows.
1837	President Andrew Jackson leaves the White House.
1837	Indians kidnap Leiva's two daughters at Jamul.
1837	Juan Bandini leads rebellion; captures Los Angeles.
1838	Pueblo status is abolished; San Diego made subprefecture of Los Angeles.
1839	Indians plunder San Diego backcountry ranchos.
1841	John Bidwell leads first immigrant wagon train over the Sierra Nevada to San Joaquin Valley.
1841	First Catholic bishop finds fewer than 150 persons in San Diego; moves to Santa Barbara.
1842	Capt. William D. Phelps, of the *Alert*, spikes the guns of Ft. Guijarros.
1842	Manuel Micheltorena arrives at San Diego with his "Battalion of Cholos"; succeeds Gov. Alvarado.
1843	Gov. Micheltorena reinstates missions under the Franciscans.
1844	President James K. Polk announces his determination for U.S. possession of California.
1844	John C. Frémont's exploratory expedition reaches Ft. Sutter.
1845	Gov. Micheltorena faces revolt of the *Californios*.
1845	The United States annexes the Republic of Texas.
1845	New Gov. Pío Pico orders land confiscation and sale of the California missions.
1846	Juan María Osuna and José Antonio Estudillo are last San Diego *alcaldes* under Mexican rule.
1846	The United States declares state of war exists with Mexico.
1846	Commodore John D. Sloat, USN, captures Monterey; Capt. John B. Montgomery captures San Francisco.
1846	Capt. Samuel F. du Pont, USN, and *USS Cyane* take San Diego; first American flag raised in Plaza.
1846	Mexican Gov. Pío Pico issues farewell proclamation; flees California.
1846	Mexicans besiege San Diego.
1846	Commodore Robert F. Stockton, USN, and U.S. fleet secure San Diego.
1846	Battle of San Pasqual.
1846	Indian massacre at Pauma.
1847	American flag raised at Mexico City.
1847	Signing of Cahuenga Capitulation.
1847	Mormon Battalion arrives in San Diego.
1848	James Marshall discovers gold at Coloma.
1848	Mexico signs Treaty of Guadalupe Hidalgo.
1849	Gold Rush begins; cattle prices soar; southern rancheros drive cattle to San Francisco.
1849	U.S. Boundary Commission arrives at San Diego.
1849	Pacific Mail Steamship Co. begins service to San Diego.
1849	First Constitutional Convention meets at Monterey.
1850	San Diego first county created by the Legislature.
1850	William H. Davis begins New San Diego.
1850	City of San Diego is incorporated; holds first election; Joshua Bean elected mayor.
1850	California admitted to the Union.
1851	Federal Land Commission requires all landholders to prove valid title.
1851	San Diego Herald, first newspaper, begins publication.
1851	The Garra Indian uprising begins.
1852	Maj. Gen. Joshua Bean captures Garra; execution at San Diego.
1852	Phineas Banning and D. W. Alexander begin first San Diego-to-Los Angeles stage line.
1853	First meeting, San Diego County Board of Supervisors.
1853	Lt. George Derby, USA, arrives to divert San Diego River into False Bay.
1853	Federal government authorizes Pacific Railroad Surveys; final report condemns possible San Diego routes.
1853	Whaling industry begins to grow in San Diego.
1854	San Diego & Gila, Southern Pacific and Atlantic Railroad organized.
1855	Mormons strike coal at Point Loma.
1857	Mexicans massacre Gen. A. J. Crabb's fillibusters at Caborca.
1857	Dred Scott Decision brings the nation to the brink of Civil War.
1857	James Birch wins first transcontinental overland mail contract, San Diego to San Antonio; first mail arrives.
1857	Birch stages begin first scheduled transcontinental overland passenger service from San Diego.
1858	Butterfield Great Overland Stage Line begins regular scheduled mail and passenger service from Tipton, Mo., to San Francisco.
1859	John Brown raids Harper's Ferry.
1860	San Diego Herald publishes its last edition.
1860	Abraham Lincoln elected president.
1861	The Civil War begins.
1861	State-wide storm brings 30-inch rain to San Diego; destroys 25% of California's taxable property.
1861	Earthquakes and flood tides damage San Diego.

1861 All stage travel discontinued over Southern route because of Civil War.

1861 First Battle of Bull Run.

1861 First transcontinental telegraph reaches San Francisco.

1862 Congress passes the Pacific Railroad Bill.

1862 Two years of drought begin; cattle herds of the rancheros are decimated.

1862 Smallpox epidemic begins at San Juan Capistrano.

1863 Smallpox epidemic reaches San Diego.

1863 Locust plague destroys crops; squatter and ranchero troubles become serious.

1864 Drought reaches its worst in San Diego.

1865 Lee surrenders at Appomattox, ending the Civil War.

JUSTICES OF THE PEACE (ALCALDES)
AT SAN DIEGO 1841-1850

UNDER MEXICAN RULE

1841 Rosario Aguilar, juez de paz

1841 Jesús Moreno, suplente (substitute)

1842 José Antonio Congora, juez de paz

1842 José M. Alvarado, suplente

1843 Joaquín Ortega, juez de paz

1843 José Antonio Congora, juez de paz (succeeded Ortega in May)

1843 José María Orozco, suplente

1844 Juan María Marrón, juez de paz

1844 Thomas Wrightington, suplente

1845 Francisco M. Alvarado, juez de paz

1845 José Antonio Estudillo, juez de paz (temporary)

1845 José Ramon Arguello, suplente

1846 José Ramon Arguello, sub-prefect, appointed in April, until arrival of Americans

1846 José Antonio Estudillo, juez de paz

1846 Juan M. Osuna, juez de paz (at first declined office and possibly did not act)

1846 Miguel Pedrorena, juez de paz (served in Estudillo's absence)

UNDER AMERICAN RULE

1846 Joaquín Ortega, juez de paz (from August)

1846 Henry D. Fitch, suplente (from August)

1847 Henry D. Fitch, juez de paz

1847 Lt. Robert Clift, juez de paz (succeeded Fitch in June)

1847 Philip Crosthwaite, suplente (possibly was appointed with Fitch)

1847 Thomas Wrightington, suplente (believed to have served in Crosthwaite's place)

1848 Juan Bandini, juez de paz (March 29-Sept. 27)

1848 E. L. Brown, suplente (appointed April 15)

1848 Juan María Marrón, juez de paz (elected Oct. 3)

1849 Dennis Gahagan, alcalde

MAYORS AFTER INCORPORATION

1850 Joshua Bean

1851 David B. Kurtz

1852 George P. Tebbetts

NOTE: The city charter was revoked in 1852, after which the town was governed by a Board of Trustees until 1889.

GOVERNORS OF CALIFORNIA 1833-1867

MEXICAN RULE

1833-1835   José Figueroa

1835-1836   José Castro, ad interim to January, 1836.

1836   Nicolás Gutiérrez, ad interim, (January to May).

1836   Mariano Chico, May to August.

1836   Nicolás Gutiérrez, ad interim to November.

1836-1842   Juan B. Alvarado, ad interim 1836-1839.

1842-1845   Manuel Micheltorena

1845-1846   Pío Pico

AMERICAN RULE
Military

1846   Commodore John D. Sloat, July 7th

1846   Commodore Robert F. Stockton, July 29th

1847   General John C. Frémont, January 19th

1847   General Stephen W. Kearny, March 1st

1847-1849   Colonel Richard B. Mason, May 31st

1849   General Persifor F. Smith, February 28th

1849   General Bennett Riley, April 12th

Civilian

1849-1851   Peter H. Burnett, Democrat.

1851-1852   John McDougal, Democrat.

1852-1856   John Bigler, Democrat.

1856-1858   J. Neely Johnson, Know-nothing.

1858-1860   John B. Weller, Democrat.

1860   Milton S. Latham, Democrat.

1860-1862   John G. Downey, Democrat.

1862-1863   Leland Stanford, Republican.

1863-1867   Frederick F. Low, Union.

BALLAD CREDITS

1—Old Spanish-American Song; 2—Quoted by Horace Bell, Reminiscences of a Ranger (Filibusters); 3—Sam Foss; 4—John Steven McGroarty; 5—Mexican War Ballad; 6—Dr. E. D. French, Medical Corpsman, Battle of San Pasqual; 7—A Mormon Song, 1856; 8—Gold Mining Song; 9—Lt. George Derby; 10—Old World Ballad; 11—Cowboy Song of the Chisholm Trail; 12—Joaquin Miller. Permission of Juanita Miller. 13—Old Nantucket Song; 14—Song of the Immigrant Trail; 15—Robert Penn Warren.

ACKNOWLEDGEMENTS

For professional assistance, Dr. George P. Hammond, Director, and John Barr Tompkins, Head of Public Services, the Bancroft Library, University of California; Robert Dougan, Librarian, Herbert Schulz, Curator of Manuscripts, Edwin H. Carpenter, Western Americana Bibliographer, and Haydee Noya, Cataloguer in the Department of Manuscripts, Henry E. Huntington Library and Art Gallery; Carl S. Dentzel, Director, Southwest Museum, Los Angeles; Donald C. Biggs, Director, James de T. Abajian, Librarian, California Historical Society; Philip F. Purrington, Curator, Old Dartmouth Historical Society & Whaling Museum, New Bedford, Mass.; Bertram B. Moore, retired Assistant San Diego County engineer; Clyde L. Simpson, History Section, Security First National Bank, Los Angeles; Allan R. Ottley, California Section Librarian, California State Library, Sacramento; Buford Rowland, Acting Chief, Legislative Branch, National Archives, Washington D.C., Ruth I. Mahood, Chief Curator, Los Angeles County Museum; Richard H. Dillon, Librarian, Sutro Library, San Francisco; Harry D. Williams, Head of Library Photographic, James V. Mink, Assistant Head, Department of Special Collections, University of California Library; Dr. Abraham Nasatir, Professor of History, San Diego State College.

Aldrich, Lorenzo D.
A Journal of the Overland Route to California and the Gold Mines (Los Angeles, Dawson's Book Shop, 1950).

The Alta California
Various Articles, 1852 through 1865 (California State Library, Sacramento)

Ames, George Walcott, Jr., ed.
Diary of John S. Griffin, Asst. Surgeon with Kearny's Dragoons 1846-1849 in *California Historical Society Quarterly* Vol. 21 (1942).

Arguello, Santiago
Personal Correspondence (The Bancroft Library, University of California).

Atherton, Lucien C.
The Early History of the San Diego Presidial District, 1542-1782 (Master's thesis, Graduate Division, University of California).

Audubon, John W.
Audubon's Western Journal: 1849-1850 ed. by Frank Heywood Hodder (Cleveland, The Arthur H. Clark Co., 1906).
Illustrated Notes of an Expedition Through Mexico and California, New York, 1852.

Bancroft, Hubert Howe
History of California, Vols. I, II, III, IV, V, VI, VII (San Francisco, The History Company, 1890).
California Pastoral: 1769-1848, Vol. XXXIV (San Francisco, The History Company, 1888).

Bandini, Juan
History of Upper California, manuscript, and *Personal and Official Correspondence* (The Bancroft Library, University of California).

Banning, William and George Hugh
Six Horses (New York, London, The Century Company, 1930).

Bartlett, John Russell
Bartlett's Personal Narrative, Two volumes (New York, D. Appleton & Company, 1854).

Beattie, G. W., intr. by
Diary of a Ferryman and Trader at Fort Yuma, 1855-1857 in *Historical Society of Southern California Annual* Vol. XIV, Parts 1, 2, (1928 and 1929 respectively).

Belcher, Edward
Narrative of a Voyage Around the World, as Performed in Her Majesty's Ship Sulphur, During the Years 1836-1842 (London, Henry Colburn, 1843).

Bell, Horace
Reminiscences of a Ranger (Santa Barbara, Wallace Hebberd, 1927).

Bell, James G.
A Log of the Texas-California Cattle Trail, 1854 in *The Southwestern Historical Quarterly* Vol. XXXV No. 3 (Austin, The Texas State Historical Association, 1932).

Bidwell, John
California in 1841-1848, manuscript (The Bancroft Library, University of California).

Bieber, Ralph P., ed.
Southern Trails to California in 1849, The Southwest Historical Series Vol. V (Glendale, The Arthur H. Clark Company, 1937).

Bigler, Henry W.
Diary of a Mormon in California, 1848 (The Bancroft Library, University of California, 1872).

Black, Samuel F.
San Diego County, California (Chicago, The S. J. Clarke Publishing Company, 1913).

Bloom, Lansing B., ed.
From Lewisberg (Pa.) to California in 1849, Notes from the Diary of William H. Chamberlin in *New Mexico Historical Review* (Historical Society of New Mexico and University of New Mexico, 1945).

Bonsal, Stephen
Edward Fitzgerald Beale (New York and London, G. P. Putnam's Sons, 1912).

Boston Journal of Commerce
The First Whaling in Scammon's Lagoon, Scrapbook No. 17 by W. O. Ayres, at The Whaling Museum, New Bedford.

Brandes, Raymond S. trans. & annotated
Times Gone By in Alta California, Recollections of Juana Machado Wrightington in *Historical Society of Southern California Quarterly* Vol. XLI No. 3 (1959).

Brayet, Garnet M. and Herbert O.
American Cattle Trails 1540-1900 (Western Cattle Industry study in co-operation with American Pioneer Trails Association, Bayside, New York, 1952).

Browne, J. Ross
Explorations in Lower California, 1868 (Harper and Brothers, 1868, reprinted by Arizona Silhouettes, 1952).

Bryant, Edwin
What I Saw in California, (New York, D. Appleton & Company, 1848).

Camp, Charles L.
Kit Carson in California in *California Historical Society Quarterly* Vol. I (1922-1923).

Caughey, John W.
California (Englewood Cliffs, N. J., Prentice-Hall, Inc., 1953).

Chamberlin, Eugene Keith
Nicholas Trist and Baja California in *Pacific Historical Review* Vol. XXXII No. 1 (Pacific Coast Branch of the American Historical Association, Berkeley, University of California, 1963).

Chapman, Charles E.
A History of California—The Spanish Period (New York, The Macmillan Company, 1939).

Clarke, Dwight L.
Stephen Watts Kearny—Soldier of the West (University of Oklahoma Press, 1961).

Cleland, Robert Glass
California—The American Period (New York, The Macmillan Company, 1926).
California Pageant: The Story of Four Centuries (New York, Alfred A. Knopf, 1955).
Drought, Lawlessness and Smallpox in *The Historical Society of Southern California Quarterly* Vol. XXXV No. 1 (1953).
Transportation in California Before the Railroads with Special Reference to Los Angeles in *The Historical Society of Southern California Annual* Vol XI, Part 1 (1918).
From Wilderness to Empire (New York, Alfred A. Knopf, 1959).
Pathfinders (Los Angeles, Powell Publishing Company, 1929).
The Cattle on a Thousand Hills (San

Marino, The Huntington Library and Art Gallery, 1941).
This Reckless Breed of Men (New York, Alfred A. Knopf, 1952).

Clendenen, Clarence C.
Dan Showalter — California Secessionist in *California Historical Society Quarterly* Vol. XL No. 4 (1961).

Colton, Rev. Walter, USN
California Diary of Rev. Walter Colton, Foreword by Joseph A. Sullivan (Oakland, Biobooks, 1948).
Three Years in California (1850)

Cooke, Philip St. George
Journal of the March of the Mormon Battalion of Infantry Volunteers Under the Command of Lieut. Col. P. St. George Cooke, from Santa Fe, N. M. to San Diego, Calif. (Washington, D.C., *Senate Documents,* 30 Congress, special session, No. 2, 1849).
Report on the March of the Mormon Battalion, February 5, 1847. (Washington, D.C., *House Documents,* 30 Congress, 1st session, No. 41, 1848).

Corle, Edwin
The Gila — River of the Southwest (New York, Rinehart & Company, Inc., 1951).

Couts, Cave J.
Couts Papers and *Stearns Papers* (San Marino, California, Henry E. Huntington Library & Art Gallery).
The Journal of Cave Johnson Couts from Monterey, Nuevo Leon, Mexico to Los Angeles, California During the Years 1848-1849. (San Marino, California, Henry E. Huntington Library and Art Gallery).

Cowan, Robert Ernest
Bibliography of the History of California and the Pacific West, 1510-1930 3 vols. (San Francisco, The Book Club of America, 1914).

Cureton, Gilbert
The Cattle Trail to California 1840-1860 in *Historical Society of Southern California Quarterly* Vol. XXXV No. 2 (1953).

Daily Picayune
January 23 and March 30, 1850 (New Orleans).

Dakin, Susanna Bryant
The Lives of William Hartnell (Stanford University Press, 1946).

Dana, Richard Henry, Jr.
Two Years Before the Mast (New York, Dodd, Mead & Company, 1946).

Davis, Abel
Memoirs of Abel Davis, manuscript (John F. Forward, Sr. Memorial Library, San Diego)

Davis, Edwin Adams
The Story of Louisiana, Vol. 1 (New Orleans, J. F. Hyer Publishing Company, 1960).

Davis, William Heath
Seventy-five Years in California (San Francisco, John Howell, 1929).
Correspondence, 1850-1855. (San Diego Public Library)

DeFrate, Julia Flynn
This Was Yesterday, manuscript (John F. Forward, Sr. Memorial Library, San Diego)

Derby, George H.
Letters and Papers, 1849-1859 (The Bancroft Library, University of California).
Phoenixiana, by John Phoenix (1855)
Topographical Reports of Lt. George H. Derby, with introduction and notes by Francis P. Farquhar in *California Historical Society Quarterly* Vol. XI, Nos. 2, 3, 4 (1933)
Plans and Estimates for Turning San Diego River, (Bancroft Library, University of California)

Derby, George H. and
R. S. Williamson
Reports on Geology and Topography of California (Washington D.C., 31st Congress, 1st Session, Sen. Exec. Doc. 47, 1850).

DeVoto, Bernard
Course of Empire (Boston, Houghton Mifflin Company, 1952).
The Year of Decision 1846 (Boston, Little, Brown & Company, 1943).

Dobyns, Henry F., ed.
Hepah, California — The Journal of Cave J. Couts from Monterey, Nuevo Leon, Mexico to Los Angeles, California, During the Years 1848-1849 Arizona Pioneers' Historical Society, 1961).

Driese, Don
California's Lost Battalion in *San Diego Historical Society Quarterly* Vol. VII No. 2 (1961).

du Pont, S. F.
Extracts from the Private Journal — Letters of Capt. S. F. du Pont while in Command of the Cyane during the War with Mexico, 1846-1848 (Privately printed in Wilmington, Delaware, 1885).

Durivage, John E.
Correspondence of John E. Durivage. (New Orleans Daily Picayune, 1849).

Duvall, Robert Carson
Extracts from the Log of the USS Frigate Savannah in *California Historical Society Quarterly* Vol. III No. 2 (1924).

Edwards, E. I.
Lost Oases — Along the Carrizo (Los Angeles, The Westernlore Press, 1961).

Emory, William H.
Report of the United States — Mexican Boundary Survey, Vols. 1 and 2 (U.S. Department of Interior, 1857).
Notes of a Military Reconnoissance from Fort Leavenworth in Missouri to San Diego, California. (30th Cong., 1st sess., H. Exec. Doc. 41, Washington, D.C., 1848).

Engelhardt, Fr. Zephyrin, O.F.M.
Missions and Missionareis of California Vols I and II (Santa Barbara Mission, 1929 and 1930 respectively).
Vols III and IV (San Francisco, The James H. Barry Company, 1913 and 1915 respectively).
San Diego Mission (San Francisco, The James H. Barry Company, 1920).
San Luis Rey Mission (San Francisco, The James H. Barry Company, 1921).

Erskine, Michael
Journals and Other Memoranda — Diary of the Texas-California Cattle Trail 1854 (Archives of the University of Texas Library).

Fitch, Henry D.
Letters of a Merchant (Bancroft Library, University of California).

Fitch, Josefa C.
Narracion de la Sra. Viuda del Capitan Enrique D. Fitch, 1875 (The Bancroft Library, University of California).

Forbes, Alexander
California: A History of Upper and Lower California (London, Smith Elder & Company, 1839).

Forster, Juan
Forster vs Pico — Calif., County of San Diego, 18th Judicial District, February 24, 1873.
Pioneer Data (The Bancroft Library, University of California).

Frémont, John Charles
Memoirs of My Life (New York & Chicago, Belford, Clarke & Co., 1887).

Notes of Travel in California (New York, D. Appleton & Company, 1849).

Geiger, Maynard J., O.F.M.
The Life and Times of Fray Junipero Serra or The Man Who Never Turned Back, 1713-1784 2 vols. (Washington, D.C., Academy of American Franciscan History, 1959).

Gerhard, Peter and
Bulick, Howard E.
Lower California Guidebook (Glendale, The Arthur H. Clark Company, 1958).

Gilbert, Benjamin F.
California and the Civil War: A Bibliographical Essay in *California Historical Society Quarterly* Vol. XL No. 4 (1961).

Gillespie, Archibald H.
Correspondence of a Government Agent (University of California at Los Angeles).

Goetzmann, William H.
Army Exploration in the American West 1803-1863 (New Haven, Yale University Press, 1959).

Golder, Frank Alfred
The March of the Mormon Battalion from *Journal of Henry Standage* (New York, The Century Company, 1928).

Graebner, Norman A.
Empire on the Pacific (New York, The Ronald Press Company, 1955).

Griffin, John S.
Journal of John S. Griffin, 1846 (The Bancroft Library, University of California).

Grivas, Theodore
Military Governments in California 1846-1850 (Glendale, The Arthur H. Clark Company, 1963).

Guinn, J. M.
Yuma Indian Depredations and the Glanton War and *Depositions of William Carr and Jeremiah Hill* in *Historical Society of Southern California Annual* Vol. VI Part I (1903).
The Passing of the Cattle Barons of California in *Historical Society of Southern California Annual* Vol. VIII Part 1 and 2 (1909-1910).

Hager, Anna Marie and Everett
Gordon, Compilers
The Topical Index (Los Angeles, The Historical Society of Southern California, 1959).

Halleck, Henry W.
Halleck's Report—Executive Document No. 17 (Thirty-First Congress, House of Representatives, Washington, D.C., 1850).

Hammond, George Peter, ed.
The Larkin Papers (Berkeley, University of California Press, 1951).

Harris, Benjamin Butler
The Gila Trail—The Texas Argonauts and the California Gold Rush, Edited and Annotated by Richard H. Dillon (Norman, University of Oklahoma Press, 1960).

Hayes, Benjamin
Emigrant Notes and *Scrap Books 1850-1874; Hayes' Exceptions to the Survey of the Cuyamaca Front, 1873.* (The Bancroft Library, University of California).

Heilbron, Carl H.
History of San Diego County (San Diego Press Club, 1936).

Herring, Hubert
History of Latin America From the Beginnings to the Present (New York, Alfred A. Knopf, 1955).

Heuer, W. H.
Report of the Chief of Engineers 1870 (The Bancroft Library, University of California).

Hill, Joseph J.
History of Warner's Ranch and Its Environs (Los Angeles, Young & Mc-Callister, 1927).

Hittel, John S.
The Resources of California (San Francisco, A. Roman & Company, 1874).

Hittel, Theodore Henry
History of California Vols I and II (San Francisco, Pacific Press Publishing House and Occidental Publishing Company, 1885).

Hudson, Millard F.
A Pioneer Southwestern Newspaper and Its Editor in *Historical Society of Southern California Annual* Publication Vol VIII Part 1 and 2 (1909-1910).
The Pauma Massacre in *Historical Society of Southern California Quarterly* Vol VII, Part 1 (1906).

Hunt, Aurora
The Army of the Pacific (Glendale, The Arthur H. Clark Company, 1951).

Hunter, J. Marvin, comp. and ed.
The Trail Drivers of Texas (Nashville, Cokesbury Press, 1925).

Hunter, Milton R.
The Mormon Corridor in *Pacific Historical Review,* Vol. VIII (1939).

Jackson, Helen Hunt
Glimpses of California and the Missions (Boston, Little Brown & Company, 1907).

Jaeger, Edmund
North American Deserts (Stanford University Press, 1957).

James, Harry C.
The Cahuilla Indians (Los Angeles, Westernlore Press, 1960).

Janssens, Victor Eugene August
The Life and Adventures in California of Don Agustin Janssens, 1834-56, Edited by Wm. H. Ellison and Francis Price. (San Marino, California, Henry E. Huntington Library, 1953).

Jensen, James M.
Cattle Drives from the Ranchos to the Gold Fields of California in *Arizona and the West Quarterly* Vol. II (Tucson, University of Arizona Press, 1960).

Kearny, Stephen W.
Reports of San Pasqual (30th Congress, 1st Session, Senate Executive Doc. No. 5-13-16, Washington, D.C., 1848).

Kibby, Leo P.
California Soldiers in the Civil War in *California Historical Society Quarterly* Vol. XL No. 4 (1961).

Lancey, Thomas C.
Cruise of the Dale, scrapbook from *San Jose Pioneer* (The Bancroft Library, University of California).

Larkin, Thomas O.
Documents for the History of California, 1839-1856, 9 vols. *Official Correspondence as U.S Consul and Navy Agent, 1844-1849,* 2 vols. *Notes on the Personal Character of Californians, 1845* (The Bancroft Library, University of California).

Layne, J. Gregg
Western Wayfaring Routes of Exploration and Trade in the American Southwest (Los Angeles, Automobile Club of Southern California, 1954).

Lesley, Lewis Burt, ed.
Uncle Sam's Camels (Cambridge, Harvard University Press, 1929).

Lorenzana, Apolinaria
Memorias de la Beata (The Bancroft Library, University of California).

Los Angeles Times
The Sperm Whale is a Very Deep Fellow by Irving S. Bengelsdorf, Ph.D. (May 3, 1962).

Loveland, Cyrus C.
California Trail — The 1850 Missouri-to-California Journal of Cyrus C. Loveland, edited and annotated by Richard H. Dillon (Los Gatos, California, The Talisman Press, 1961).

Lyman, Chester S.
Personal Diary and Record of Around the Horn to the Sandwich Islands and California 1845-1850, edited by Frederick J. Teggart (Yale University Press, 1925).

MacMullen, Jerry
San Diego War Vessel Alerted! in *San Diego Historical Society Quarterly* Vol. VII No. 2 (1961).

Marrón, Felipa Osuna de
Recuerdos y Papeles Originales, 1878 (The Bancroft Library, University of California).

Martin, Douglas D.
Yuma Crossing (Albuquerque, University of New Mexico Press, 1954).

Martínez, Pablo L.
A History of Lower California trans. by Ethel Duffy Turner (Mexico D. F., Editorial Baja California, 1960).

McClellan, R. Guy
The Golden State — A History of the Region West of the Rocky Mountains; Embracing California (Philadelphia, William Flint & Company, 1872).

McCracken, Harold
Hunters of the Stormy Sea (New York, Doubleday & Company, 1957).

McGinty, Brian
The Carrillos of San Diego in *Historical Society of Southern California Quarterly* Vol. XXXIX No. 1, 2, 3, 4 (1957).

McPherson, William, ed.
From San Diego to the Colorado in 1849 — The Journal and Maps of Cave J. Couts (Los Angeles, Arthur M. Ellis, 1932).

Meyers, William H.
Journal of a Cruise to California and Southern Islands in the U.S. Sloop of War, Cyane, 1841-44. (The Bancroft Library, University of California, Berkeley.)

Mofras, Eugene Duflot de
Travels on the Pacific Coast ed. and trans. by Marguerite Eyer Wilbur (Santa Ana, California, 1937).

Moore, Bertram B.
History of San Diego Roads and Stages, manuscript (San Diego Historical Society)

Morison, Samuel Eliot
The Maritime History of Massachusetts (Boston, Houghton Mifflin Company, 1921, 1941).

Morrison, Lorrin L.
Warner — The Man and the Ranch (Los Angeles, published by the Author, 1962).

Morrow, William H.
Spanish and Mexican Private Land Grants (Los Angeles, Bancroft-Whitney Company, 1923).

Nasatir, Abraham P.
French Activities in California (Stanford University Press, 1945). *The French Consulate in California* in *California Historical Society Quarterly* Vol. XI (1932).

National Archives and Records Service
The War of the Rebellion: A Compilation of the Official Records of the Union and Confederate Armies, Series I, Vol. L, Part I (Washington D.C., General Services Administration).

Nordhoff, Charles
California: A Book for Travellers and Settlers (Harper & Brothers, 1872).

Northrop, Earl V.
The Authentic Location of the Butterfield Overland Stage Trail in *The Valley Imperial,* Imperial Valley Pioneers First Annual Historical Volume (1956)

Ogden, Adele
The California Sea Otter Trade 1784-1848 (University of California Press, 1941).

Parker, Horace
Anza-Borrego Desert Guide Book (Palm Desert, California, Desert Magazine Press, 1957).

Phelps, W. D.
Fore and Aft, Boston, 1871 (The Bancroft Library, University of California).

Pico, Pío
Documentos Para la Historia de California, two volumes, (The Bancroft Library, University of California). *Correspondence with the Mexican Government, 1846-1848,* Introduction by George Tays in *California Historical Society Quarterly* Vol. XIII No. 2.

Correspondencia (The Bancroft Library, University of California).

Pomfret, John E., ed.
California Gold Rush Voyages 1848-1849 (San Marino, Henry E. Huntington Library & Art Gallery, 1954).

Porter, Valentine Mott
General Stephen W. Kearny and the Conquest of California 1846-1847 in *Historical Society of Southern California Annual* Vol. VIII, Parts 1 and 2, (1909-1910).

Pourade, Richard F.
The Explorers and *Time of the Bells —* The History of San Diego, Commissioned by James S. Copley (San Diego, The Union-Tribune Publishing Company, 1960 and 1961 respectively).

Powell, H. M. T.
Santa Fe Trail to California 1849-1852, ed. by Douglas S. Watson (San Francisco, The Book Club of California, 1931).

Ramsdell, Charles
San Antonio — A Historical and Pictorial Guide (Austin, University of Texas Press, 1951).

Rensch, Eugene
Lassator's In Green Valley in *San Diego Historical Society Quarterly.* Vol. III No. 2 (1957)

Rensch, Eugene and Ethel Grace
Historic Spots in California: The Southern Counties (Stanford University Press, 1932).

Roberts, Elizabeth J.
Indian Stories of the Southwest (San Francisco, Harr Wagner Publishing Company, 1917).

Robinson, Alfred
Life in California (New York, Wiley & Putnam, 1846).

Rolle, Andrew F.
An American in California: The Biography of William Heath Davis (San Marino, Henry E. Huntington Library and Art Gallery, 1956).

Romer, Margaret
From Boulder to the Gulf (Part V) in *Historical Society of Southern California Quarterly* Vol. XXXV No. 1, (1953).

Ruhlen, George
San Diego in the Civil War in *San Diego Historical Society Quarterly* Vol. VII No. 2 (1961).

Rush, Philip S.
Early California Postal Service in *The*

California Rancher (August, 1957)
The Jackass Mail Line in *The California Rancher* (July, 1957)
History of the Californias (San Diego, Philip S. Rush, 1958).

The Sacramento Union
Various Articles, 1857 through 1860 (California State Library, Sacramento)

San Diego County
Board of Supervisors
Minutes, 1853 through 1865 (Records Division, San Diego County Board of Supervisors)

San Diego Herald
Issues from 1855 to 1859 (San Diego Public Library).

Sandwich Island Gazette
December 2, 1837 (Public Archives, Honolulu, Hawaii).

The San Francisco Herald
Various Articles, 1858 (California State Library, Sacramento)

Scammon, Charles M.
The Marine Mammals of the North-Western Coast of North America (San Francisco, John H. Carmany & Company, 1874).

Smith, Walter Gifford
The Story of San Diego (San Diego, City Printing Company, 1892).

Smythe, William E.
History of San Diego 1542-1908 (San Diego, The History Company, 1908).

Stackpole, Edouard A.
The Sea-Hunters (Philadelphia, J. B. Lippincott Company, 1953).

Stearns, Abel
Correspondence of a Merchant (The Bancroft Library, University of California).

Stephens, B. A.
A Biographical Sketch of L. J. F. Iaeger in *Historical Society of Southern California Annual* Vol. I Part 4 (1888-1889).

Stephenson, Terry E.
Forster vs Pico—A Forgotten California Cause Celebre in *Historical Society of Southern California Quarterly* Vol. XVII No. 4 (1935), Vol. XVIII, No. 1 and No. 2 (1936).

Stockton, Robert F.
Despatches (29th Cong., 2nd Sess., H. Exec. Doc. 41).
Military and Naval Operations (30th Cong., 2nd Sess., Sen. Exec. Doc. 31).

Stone, Irving
Men to Match my Mountains, edited by Lewis Gannett (Garden City, N. Y., Doubleday & Company, Inc., 1956).

Stratton, James S.
Report of Spanish or Mexican Grants in California. Appendix to the *Journals of the Senate and Assembly,* California Legislature, 24th Session, Vol. I. (Sacramento, State Office: J. D. Young, Supt. State Printing, 1881).

Sweeny, Thomas William
The Diary of Thomas William Sweeny in *Journal of the Military Service Institution of the United States* (1909)
Correspondence and Manuscripts of Thomas William Sweeny (Henry E. Huntington Library and Art Gallery, San Marino, California)
Journal of Lt. Thomas W. Sweeny 1849-1853 ed. by Arthur Woodward (Los Angeles, Westernlore Press, 1956)

Taylor, Bayard
Eldorado or Adventures in the Path of Empire (New York, Geo. B. Putnam, 1850).

Tays, George
Revolutionary California — Doctoral Dissertation, 1932 (The Bancroft Library, University of California).

United States Government
War of the Rebellion—Official Records of the Union and Confederate Armies Washington D.C., 1880-1901).

Vallejo, Mariano G.
History of California, manuscript (The Bancroft Library, University of California).

Veeder, Charles H.
Yuma Indian Depredations on the Colorado in 1850 in *Historical Society of Southern California Annual* Vol. VII, Part 1 and 2 (1907-1908).

Virden, Bill
The Affair at Minter's Ranch in *San Diego Historical Society Quarterly* Vol. VII No. 2 (1961).

Walters, Helen B.
Confederates in Southern California in *Historical Society of Southern California Quarterly* Vol. XXXV No. 1 (1953).

Warner, Colonel J. J.
Reminiscences of Early California 1831-1846 in *Historical Society of Southern California Annual* Vol. VII, Part 1 and 2 (1907-1908).
California and Oregon in *Colonial*

Magazine, v.229 (The Bancroft Library, University of California).

Waters, Frank
The Colorado—(New York, Rinehart & Company, Inc., 1946).

Webb, Edith Buckland
Indian Life at the Old Missions (Los Angeles, Warren F. Lewis, 1952).

Whaley, Thomas
The Whaley Papers (San Diego, The Whaley House).

Whipple, A. W.
The Whipple Report—Introduction, notes and bibliography by E. I. Edwards (Los Angeles, Westernlore Press, 1961).

Wilkes, Charles
Narrative of the United States Exploring Expedition, During the Years 1838, 1839, 1840, 1841, 1842, Vol. V (Philadelphia, Lea & Blanchard, 1845).

Wilson, Benjamin Davis
Observations of Early Days in California and New Mexico (The Bancroft Library, University of California, 1877).

Winther, Oscar Osburn
Express & Stagecoach Days in California from the Gold Rush to the Civil War (Stanford University Press, 1936).
Via Western Express & Stagecoach (Stanford University Press, 1947).

Woods, Isaiah C.
Report to the Postmaster General, 1857 and 1858 (Post Office Department, Washington, D.C.)

Woodward, Arthur
Feud on the Colorado (Los Angeles, Westernlore Press, 1955).
Lances at San Pascual (San Francisco, California Historical Society, 1948).

Woodward, Arthur, ed.
Journal of Lt. Thomas W. Sweeny 1849-1853 (Los Angeles, Westernlore Press, 1956).

Wright, George
War of the Rebellion—Official Records of the Union and Confederate Armies Reports of Brig. Gen. George Wright . . . concerning the pursuit and capture of the Showalter party . . . (Washington, D.C., 1881-1901).

Young, Otis E.
The West of Philip St. George Cooke 1809-1895 (Glendale, The Arthur H. Clark Company, 1955).

ARTWORK SOURCES

The Bancroft Library, University of California, Berkeley. Map of San Dieguito Rancho. Map of San Diego Bay, 1839, by Capt. John Hall, Sketches of Lima, Peru, San Blas, Hide Houses, Sailor on a Horse, *USS Cyane,* Pacific Naval Squadron, Consular Ball at Mazatlán, San Pedro by William H. Meyers. Engravings of Gila River Country, Acapulco, Mazatlán, Tucson, Fort Yuma from John Russell Bartlett's *Personal Narrative.* Engraving of Military Plaza at San Antonio by Arthur Schote and drawing of El Paso by A. deVanducourt from *Report on the United States and Mexican Boundary Survey* by William H. Emory. Painting of the Battle of San Pasqual by Walter Francis. Survey of San Diego River in 1853 by George H. Derby. Painting of Gen. José Castro. Photographs of Juan Bautista Alvarado and Joaquín Carrillo from *La Reina, Los Angeles in Three Centuries* by Hill. Overland Mail poster from *The Almanac for 1860* of stage coach lines. Diseños of San Diego County ranchos.

California State Library, Sacramento. José Narvaez's map of Upper California, 1830. Sketch of Tubac from *The Apache Country,* 1869, by John Ross Browne. Photographs of Kit Carson, Stephen W. Kearny, John Drake Sloat, William Walker, Robert F. Stockton, Gov. Micheltorena, and Peter Burnett. California Bear Flag. Battle of San Gabriel from *Gleason's Pictorial Drawing Room Companion.*

John Howell Books, San Francisco. Drawings of San Francisco in 1849, California Wedding Party, San Francisco Before the Gold Discovery, from William Heath Davis' *Seventy-five Years in California.*

Henry E. Huntington Library and Art Gallery, San Marino, California. Drawings of Los Angeles, San Luis Rey Mission in 1848, Mormon Camp in 1852, Night Camp, Monterey by William Rich Hutton. Illustration of Colorado Desert and Signal Mountain, Woodcuts of Pass Between San Felipe and Vallecito, Valley of San Pasqual, Well in the Desert—Alamo Mocho, and Mission San Diego from *Pacific Railroad Reports,* Vol. V, Washington, D.C., 1856. Sketch of Rabbit-Hole Springs by J. Goldsborough Bruff. Color map of Texas, Oregon and California in 1849 by Samuel Augustine Mitchell. View of San Diego by H. M. T. Powell. Drawings of *A Recogida* and *Jornada del Muerto* by W. H. Hilton. Painting of Rodeo about 1880 from the Pierce Collection. Engraving of Abel Stearns. Daguerreotype of William Rich Hutton.

Los Angeles County Museum. Paintings of a Fiesta, Doña Mariana Coronel Grinding Corn, and Dancing on Veranda by Alexander F. Harmer. Photographs of Gen. Andrés Pico, Pío Pico's linen jacket, side saddle, ranchero's saddle, linsey-woolsey dress, anvil, Don Pico, candle lantern, leather shield, señorita's dress of 1820.

J. S. Copley, La Jolla, California. Map of an exploring expedition . . . in the year 1842 by Capt. J. C. Frémont. Drawing of John Frémont's Indian Guard and Volunteers from *Fremont's Life, Exploration and Public Services, 1856.*

Automobile Club of Southern California, Los Angeles. Painting of Capitulation of Cahuenga by Carl Oscar Borg. Maps for location of early roads and routes.

Robert B. Honeyman, San Juan Capistrano. Color lithograph of San Diego, 1850.

Utah State Historical Society, Salt Lake City. Painting of Mormon Battalion Reaching a Stream on Its March Across the Arizona Desert by George M. Ottinger.

Drawings of Whaling Station, Hunting the Whale, Whaling in California Lagoon, Gray Whales in Ice from *The Marine Mammals of the North Western Coast of North America* by Charles M. Scammon.

Marjorie Reed Creese, Cecilville, California. Paintings of Butterfield Stages.

The Whaling Museum, New Bedford, Massachusetts. Whaling Fleet Sunk, gravure in Providence Sunday Journal. Illustrated log, whaling ship.

Confederate Museum, Richmond, Virginia. Shenandoah Attacking the Whalers in Ice of Bering Sea.

N. H. Rose Collection owned by Ed Bartholomew. Going to Town by Gentilz. Photographs of Tiburcio Vásquez, Col. Giddings.

Southern California Rancher, March, 1949. Photograph of Juan Forster.

Marine Corps Museum, Quantico, Virginia. Photograph of William Maddox.

California Historical Society, San Francisco. Paintings of A California Patrón and Roping the Bear by James Walker, gift of Mr. and Mrs. Reginald Walker.

Official Mystic Seaport, Connecticut. Painting of Whaleship *Charles W. Morgan* by C. W. Ashley. Photograph by Louis S. Martel.

National Archives and Records, General Services Administration, Washington, D. C. Photographs of Brig. Gens. Philip St. George Cooke, William H. Emory and Thomas W. Sweeny, U.S. Signal Corps, Brady Collection. Sketches of San Pasqual Battlefield and Gen. Kearny's Route to San Diego by W. H. Emory. Sketches of U.S. Warship *Dale* and Fleet at La Paz by Gunner Meyers, from the Franklin D. Roosevelt Naval Prints Collection. Photograph of Embarkation of Camels for Southwest Desert. Army Map locating Showalter Party of Secessionists and Army Map of Escape Route of Southern Sympathizers. Painting of *USS Savannah.*

Security First National Bank, Historical Collection, Los Angeles. Sketch of San Diego in 1846 by William Emory.

Sketch of Indian Village at Temecula by Vischer. Painting of Old Catholic Church in Old Town by Miss Hunt. Photograph of Estudillo's adobe baking oven.

Union Title Company, Historical Collection, San Diego. Chart of San Diego County Ranchos. Sketch of San Diego in 1850. Sketch of Old Town and La Playa by Lt. R. S. Williamson. Photographs of Doña Juana Machado de Wrightington, Judge O. S. Witherby, E. W. Morse, C. P. Noell, Robert Kelly, Thomas Whaley, Andrew Cassidy, J. S. Mannasse, Marcus Schiller, James E. Birch, Santa Ysabel, Casa de Estudillo, Joseph Snook's Casa, Col. Cave J. Couts (from Mrs. John Jerome Brennan, Sr.), John Charles Frémont, José Guadalupe Estudillo, José Serrano, Lt. Edward F. Beale, Jonathan T. Warner, Philip Crosthwaite, Cmdr. Samuel Francis du Pont, Robert Decatur Israel, Louis Rose, John B. Magruder, William Heath Davis, Don Miguel de Pedrorena, Agustín Zamorano, Judge Benjamin Hayes, John Judson Ames, Lt. George H. Derby.

San Diego Junior League. Sketch of Casa de Bandini by Carol Ford. Sketch of Casa de Pío Pico by Carol Lindinmulder.

Office of the Chief of Naval Operations, Naval History Division. Photograph of Stephen Rowan.

Southwest Museum, Los Angeles. Sketches of Guajome Rancho, Upper house of Peñasquitos Rancho, Monserrate Rancho in San Luis Rey Valley, Santa Margarita Rancho, Buena Vista Rancho by E. S. Fenyes. Sketch of huts in San Felipe Valley by John Audubon.

Historical Shrine Foundation, San Diego. Painting of San Diego in 1853 by A. Sauerwein.

Junípero Serra Museum, San Diego, Cattle brand registers.

Union-Tribune Publishing Co. San Pasqual carreta road, Mule Hill, Santa Margarita Rancho Chapel at Camp Pendleton, Estudillo House Chapel; Maps locating and designating Old Town, La Playa and New Town buildings.

Image, an Art Division of Frye & Smith, Ltd. Paintings, The Jackass Mail Arrives and Kidnapping of the Leiva Girls; sketches, Fort Stockton and chapter pages by Masami Daijogo. Painting, Raising of the American Flag by D. Wayne Millsap.

PERMISSION CREDITS

California Historical Society. Excerpts from *Extracts from the Log of the USS Frigate Savannah.*

Bancroft Library, University of California. Quotations from J. J. Warner by Capt. Portilla and Gen. Castro; Excerpts from Judge Benjamin Hayes diaries from *Emigrant Notes* and *Scrap Books;* Excerpts from Santiago Arguello's *Letters of the Commandant and Prefect* and *Personal Correspondence;* Excerpts from Juan Bandini's *Personal and Official Correspondence;* Excerpts from John Bidwell's *California in 1841-48;* Excerpts from Henry W. Bigler's *Diary of a Mormon in California, 1848;* Excerpts from John S. Griffin's *Journal of 1846;* Excerpts from George H. Derby's *Letters and Papers, 1849-1859;* Excerpts from Henry D. Fitch's *Letters of a Merchant;* Excerpts from Josefa C. Fitch's *Narración de la Sra. Viuda del Capitán Enrique D. Fitch, 1875;* Excerpts from George Hammond's *The Larkin Papers;* Excerpts from Thomas O. Larkin's *Documents for the History of California, 1839-1856; Official Correspondence as U.S. Consul and Navy Agent, 1844-1849; Notes on the Personal Character of Californians, 1845;* Excerpts from Apolinaria Lorenzana's *Memorias de la Beata;* Excerpts from Felipà Osuna de Marrón's *Recuerdos y Papeles Originales;* Excerpts from Pío Pico's *Documentos Para la Historia de California; Correspondence with the Mexican Government; Correspondencia;*

Excerpts from Abel Stearn's *Correspondence of a Merchant;* Excerpts from Mariano G. Vallejo's *History of California.*

New Orleans Public Library. Excerpts from *Letters and Journal of John E. Durivage; New Orleans Daily Picayune.*

Department of Special Collections, the University Library, University of California at Los Angeles. Excerpts from Archibald H. Gillespie's letter to R. F. Stockton.

John Howell-Books. Excerpts from William Heath Davis' *Seventy-five Years in California.*

Henry E. Huntington Library and Art Gallery, San Marino, California. Excerpts from *Correspondence and Manuscript of Thomas William Sweeny;* Excerpts from *Journal of Benjamin Butler Harris' Experiences on the Gila Trail;* Excerpts from *Journal of Cave J. Couts;* R. F. Stockton's Letter to H. S. Turner; Letters from *Stearns* and *Couts Papers.*

Book Club of California. Excerpts from the *Diary of H. M. T. Powell.*

Historical Society of Southern California. Excerpts from *Recollection of Señora Doña Juana Machado Alipas de Ridington (Wrightington).*

INDEX

283

Rocha, Juan José, commissioner, 16, 89
Rocha, Manuel, 89
Rocha, Victoria, 89
Rocky Mountains, 58, 78, 148
Rodeos, 211, 212
Romero, Vicente, 31
Rosalind, English ship, 53
Rose Canyon, 104, 170, 172
Rose, Louis, 166, 170, 207, 262
Rose's Hotel, 170
Rose's Store, 170
Rose's Tannery, 170, 207
Rose's Wharf, 170
Roseville, 170
Rowan, Lt. Stephen C. USN, 79, 80, 81, 263
Ruiz, Estacio: Pauma Massacre, 116
Ruiz, Capt. Francisco María, 11, 12, 46, 62
Runing, Charles F., 224
Russell, Thomas, 47, 48, 49, 87
Russia, xi, 67
Russian Cannon (Sutter gun), 94
Russian Post, 94

Sackett's Wells, 187
Sacramento, 72, 174, 191
Sacramento River, 58, 121
Sacramento Valley, 78, 86
Saddles: description of, 68, silver, 158
Sag Harbor, xi, 233
Sailor Bill (Bill Williams), 102
St. Joseph, Missouri, 246
St. Louis Hotel, 145
Salazar, Ens. Alférez, 56
Salem, xii
Salt Lake City, 246
San Antonio, 143, 145, 146, 217, 218, 219, 220, 222, 224, 229
San Antonio Abad Rancho, 67
San Bernardino, 183, 205, 207, 212, 243, 247
San Bernardino County, 159, 184, 260
San Bernardo Rancho, 64, 104, 196
San Blas, 47, 49, 53, 54, 64, 142
San Buenaventura, battle of, 38
San Carlos Pass, 5
Sánchez, Father Francisco, 54
Sánchez, Tomás, 104
San Clemente, 65
San Diegans: flight of, 254; march on Santa Barbara, 38
San Diego, abandoned, 86; after Civil War, 254; agriculture (1846), 81; Americanization of, 233; army withdraws, 248; arrival of Bishop, 53-54; as frontier town, 157; battle of, 91; bypassed by stage lines, 225, 230; capture of, 80; Civil War, 246-256; conditions in 1852, 186; custom house established, 38; decline of, 243; decline of 1839, 40; defenses, lack of (1838-1839), 40; depression in, 249; description of in 1829, 12; description of in 1845, 69; description of in 1850, 157; description of in 1852, 186, 193; description of in 1853, 201;

description of by Captain du Pont, 81-82; description of by Frémont, 81; description of by Lieutenant Sweeny, 142; earthquake, 1863, description of, 250; end of boom, 206; first election, 14; Indians plan to attack (1837), 34; International Boundary Line, 136; Mormon census, 132; Old Town, fortification of, 1838, 40; Overland Mail terminus, 219; population, 14; protection of, 181; pueblo boundaries, 14, 15; pueblo formally organized, 14; pueblo status ends, 38; railroad surveys, 204, 205; raising of American Flag, 79; ransacked, 86; recapture by Americans, 87; *regidores* (councilmen), 14; revival of, 46; siege of, 88-89; social life, 193, 196; social life in 1829, 12; social life, military occupation, 94; storm of 1862, 250; storms of 1838, 40; sub-prefecture of Los Angeles, 38; threatened by Indians, 29; threat of attack, 179; town abandoned (1837), 28; troops withdrawn, 178; Vigilantes Committee, 187
San Diego *alcaldes,* 268
San Diego Bay, 15, 47, 65, 70, 73, 120, 136, 234; description, 120; description in 1850, 151; description of by Captain du Pont, 79; maps (Spanish), 151; silting of, 199; whales in, 233
San Diego City: first election, 162; incorporation of, 162
San Diego County, 5, 6; Bigler's description of, 127; creation of, 159; sheriff, 177
San Diego Filibusterers, 209
San Diego & Gila, Southern Pacific & Atlantic Railroad Co., 204
San Diego Guards, formation of, 207
San Diego Harbor, 87, 169, 247
San Diego *Herald,* 229; founding of, 167; closing of, 243
San Diego mayors, 268
San Diego Mission, 4, 44, 45, 46, 57, 63-64, 67, 133, 151, 158, 177, 188; as hospital, 251; conveyed to church, 262; description of, 47, 127; description of by Audubon, 149; description of by Captain du Pont, 82; end as military post, 213; sale of, 73
San Diego Mission *Asistencia,* 64
San Diego Mission Lands, sale of, 261
San Diego River, 64, 88, 120, 162, 199, 205, 262; changes channel, 46; flooding, 157; survey of, 199
San Diego & San Antonio Mail Line, 218
San Diego Volunteers (1837), 38
San Dieguito, 251; Indian executions, 37
San Dieguito Rancho, 65, 196, 214
San Dieguito River, 64, 67, 108
San Dieguito Valley, 44
Sandwich Island Gazette, 34

Sandwich Islands, 127
San Felipe, 8, 181, 224
San Felipe Pass, 100, 141, 142, 169, 205
San Felipe Rancho, 73, 260
San Felipe Valley, 73, 126, 152, 164, 174, 220, 225
San Fernando, 36, 39, 122, 136
San Fernando Hills, gold, 139
San Fernando Mission, 55, 94
San Francisco Chronicle, 224
San Francisco Harbor, 87, 121
San Francisco Herald, 224
San Gabriel, 28, 162, 185
San Gabriel Mission, 44, 45, 46, 56, 73, 191, 209
San Gabriel River, 122
San Gorgonio Pass, 8, 84, 139, 142, 204, 209
San Joaquín City, 192
San Joaquín Valley, 56, 178, 191
San José del Cabo, 134, 135
San José Valley, 64, 92, 181, 247
San Juan Capistrano, 172, 251, 252; sale of, 73
San Juan Capistrano Mission, 43, 45, 46, 122, 209
San Luis Obispo, 52, 70, 172
San Luis Rey, 35, 39, 146
San Luis Rey Mission, 44, 45, 57, 66, 74, 84, 86, 92, 99, 121, 178, 181, 191, 251; sale of, 73
San Luis Rey River, 66, 101, 204, 245, 250; valley, 127
San Luis Rey Valley, 4, 64, 94, 247
San Marcos, 66
San Miguel Mountain, 172
San Onofre Rancho, 65
San Pasqual, 101, 125, 134, 166, 224, 262, 263; battle, 101, 121; Carreta Road, 104; results of battle, 119; Stockton's report, 102
San Pasqual Hill, 104, 206
San Pasqual Road, 104
San Pasqual Valley, 67, 103, 104, 112
San Pedro, 80, 83, 85, 87, 88, 249
Santa Ana River, 255
Santa Anna, General, 23, 54, 166; defeated, 25
Santa Barbara, 36, 47, 52, 54, 123, 144, 172; troops join Alvarado, 38; troops to San Diego, 39
Santa Catalina Island, 67
Santa Clara, 191
Santa Clara River Valley, 204
Santa Cruz Island, 67
Santa Fe, New Mexico, 6, 86, 87
Santa Fe Rancho, 196
Santa Fe Trail, 6, 74; extended to Pacific Coast, 6
Santa Margarita Rancho, 65, 84, 86, 90, 94, 121, 252, 260
Santa María Valley, 102, 104, 151
Santa María Valley Rancho, 64
Santa Mónica, 104
Santa Rita, 35
Santa Ysabel (Isabel), 22, 63, 94, 101, 102, 115, 151, 164, 178, 181, 182, 206, 220, 224, 252; *asistencia,* 102; earthquake, 207; punitive

285

This third volume of the History of San Diego was designed by René Sheret, Art Director for Image, the Art Division of Frye & Smith, Ltd. Lithography by Frye & Smith, Ltd., on Hamilton Louvain 80 pound text. Typography by Linotron, the Typesetting Division of Frye & Smith, Ltd., using Mergenthaler Linotype's Linofilm system. The type face used in this book is Century Schoolbook. Binding is by Cardoza Bookbinding Co.